Margaret Frances Sullivan

Ireland of today

the causes and aims of Irish agitation

Margaret Frances Sullivan

Ireland of today
the causes and aims of Irish agitation

ISBN/EAN: 9783744736589

Printed in Europe, USA, Canada, Australia, Japan

Cover: Foto ©ninafisch / pixelio.de

More available books at **www.hansebooks.com**

IRELAND OF TO-DAY

THE CAUSES AND AIMS OF IRISH AGITATION

BY

M. F. SULLIVAN

WITH AN INTRODUCTION

BY

THOMAS POWER O'CONNOR, M. P.

I have thought, if I could be in all other things the same, but by birth an Irishman, there is not a town in this island I would not visit for the purpose of discussing the great Irish question, and of rousing my countrymen to some great and united action.—JOHN BRIGHT, Dublin, Nov. 2, 1866.

J. C. McCURDY & CO.,
PHILADELPHIA, PA.; CINCINNATI, O.; CHICAGO, ILL.
ST. LOUIS, MO.

PUBLISHERS' NOTE.

THE purpose of this book is to present a popular, convenient and correct account of the causes and aims of Irish agitation. The intimate relations which exist between the United States and England on the one hand, and between the United States and Ireland on the other, make a concise, impartial and complete manual a necessity for all who desire to inform themselves on the issue which is being so vigorously fought at the present time between the English government and the masses of the Irish people.

Without going too remotely into the history of the country—its mythical and fabulous period not being touched at all—the reader will find in these pages ample information concerning the land laws and customs, evictions, "boycotting," agrarian crime, manufactures, revolutionary movements, coercion laws, penal laws, parliamentary history, education, etc., in Ireland; while especial attention is paid to the immediate causes leading to the organization of the Land League, its growth, operations and principles, with authentic biographies of its leaders, up to the time of its attempted suppression by the English government and the arrest and imprisonment of its foremost advocates. All the facts stated and statistics quoted are from standard authorities.

The portion which treats of the establishment of peasant proprietary in other European countries will be found particularly curious and valuable; while the description of the home-life of the Irish cottier-farmer, who held his little farm from day to day at the will of his landlord, from whom he had no lease and who could raise his rent a dozen times a day if he so chose, will be found a social picture without a parallel in any other part of the globe.

The advantages of the Land Acts of 1870 and 1881 are fairly and fully presented. The illustrations include portraits of the principal leaders of the agitation, with scenes and places prominently identified with it.

INTRODUCTION.

By THOMAS POWER O'CONNOR, M. P.

FOR good or ill, the Irish question is evidently destined to occupy for some time to come a prominent place in public attention. All indications point to the probability of the present generation seeing the close in some form or other of the struggle between England and Ireland, which has been fought with such varying fortunes and in so many different forms for so many centuries. At all events, the Irish people have reached the point when they are convinced that they are going to win back their national rights. Under such circumstances, the Irish problem will be forced upon the notice of all men; and it becomes a matter of necessity to know something of the questions which underlie that problem. An American can least of all men avoid the discussion of the subject. A considerable portion of his fellow-citizens are Irish by birth; a still more considerable portion are Irish by descent; and, of recent years, the battle of the Irish people at home has been fought with resources largely drawn from the Irish settled on the American continent.

Under such circumstances, it is more than ever opportune that the public should be placed in possession of the real issues at stake in this great struggle. Unfortunately, much as has been written, and as is written daily, on Irish subjects, the acquisition of the real merits of the case is far from easy. It is one of the disadvantages of the Irish people in this struggle that the history is told to the world by their enemies, for the English newspaper or journal or history is the authority which the mass of mankind accepts, and is obliged to accept. London publishes some of the greatest newspapers of the world;

the *Times* has an international as well as a national circulation, while the Irish newspapers are rarely heard of out of Ireland, and are not known even by name by the majority of the English-speaking people. Thus, by a singular fatality, the press—in which, as a rule, all causes find hearing, if not advocacy—is closed to everything on the side of the Irish people, and—worse than this—closed while it seems to be open.

Nor is ignorance of the real history of Ireland confined to those who are not Irish. It is an essential part of the English system of rule in Ireland to suppress all study of Irish history in Irish educational institutions. No discussion of the events of Irish history from the Irish point of view is contained in any of the governmental school-books; not a word is allowed to be spoken on Irish history from the Irish point of view in the queen's colleges, which are supported by governmental endowment; and thus the strange state of things is brought about that, even among educated Irishmen, an intimate acquaintance with the smallest details of English history often exists side by side with almost absolute ignorance, even of the leading events in the history of Ireland. The knowledge of Irish history which an Irishman attains he gains outside his school and without the assistance of his schoolmaster.

And when the Irishman does set himself to the study of the history of Ireland, he finds immense difficulties in his way. There have been innumerable works on Ireland—many of them very able—but the history of Ireland has yet to be written. What is required in the Irish history of the future is that the story should be told in unexaggerated and calm language. The facts require no coloring, and the conclusions no forcing: the former can be allowed to stand in their simplicity, and the latter are inevitable to any rational mind.

I have read the work to which these few words are a preface, and I find a clear and honest setting-forth of the past and present of the Irish question. The writer puts the case in a simple, straightforward and practical way, and any intelligent person who reads these pages will have an accurate idea of the struggle of the hour. Many of the most popular fallacies with regard to Ireland herself and the acts and objects of her present advocates are met by undisputed facts and figures; the series of historic events are traced which have led to the long-delayed but inevitable reckoning between the Irish landlord and the Irish tenant which the world sees to-day; and the demands of the Irish people on the questions of education and self-government are treated lucidly and with moderation.

The work is indeed a storehouse of facts and argument, and will, I believe, do much toward making the Irish question better understood, and the motives and objects of the Irish people more justly appreciated.

CONTENTS.

	PAGE
PUBLISHERS' NOTE	17
PREFACE. BY THOMAS POWER O'CONNOR	19
WHAT IS THIS IRISH QUESTION?	27

CHAPTER I.
IRELAND PRIOR TO THE LAND WAR 33

CHAPTER II.
HOW THE PEOPLE LOST THE LAND 40

CHAPTER III.
THE REASON IRELAND HAS NO MANUFACTURES 58

CHAPTER IV.
HOW THE PEOPLE LOST THEIR PARLIAMENT 79

CHAPTER V.
A LETTERED NATION REDUCED BY FORCE AND LAW TO ILLITERACY 110

CHAPTER VI.
THE IRISH TENANT TO-DAY 136

CONTENTS.

CHAPTER VII.
The Peasant-Farmer in Other Countries 153

CHAPTER VIII.
Peculiar Features of Irish Landlordism 183

CHAPTER IX.
The Landlords sow the Seed of the Land League . . . 237

CHAPTER X.
The Men who Gathered the Crop 304

CHAPTER XI.
A Peaceful and Constitutional Movement 362

CHAPTER XII.
A Landlord's Agent goes into the Dictionary 389

CHAPTER XIII.
Driven from Home by Famine and Law 395

CHAPTER XIV.
Liberty and Crime in Ireland 403

CHAPTER XV.
The Land Laws 411

CHAPTER XVI.
What is the End to be? 441

Index 453

WHAT IS THIS IRISH QUESTION?

THIS: England and Ireland are members of the British empire. They are supposed to enjoy alike the benefits of the British constitution; those benefits are administered to both by the same personal government. But England is the richest, Ireland the poorest, country in the empire. England's population has continually increased; Ireland's has continually diminished. Englishmen prefer to live in their native country: emigration has been only a trivial incident in their national history; Irishmen prefer to live in their native country, yet there are four times as many of them in foreign countries as in their own: with them emigration has been a chronic national necessity. England hums with manifold industries; Ireland's vast water-power, capable of turning the machinery of the world, is silent. England's wharves are forests of masts; Ireland's beautiful harbors are empty except when the English ship carries away the products of her soil. In England famine is unknown, although she has to import food; in Ireland famine is frequent, although she exports food enough to feed her entire population.

In England the proportion of voters to the male population is one in four; in Ireland it is one in twenty-four. England, the richest, is the most lightly-taxed, portion of the empire; Ireland, the poorest, is the most heavily taxed. In England there is liberty of conscience and education; in Ireland a charter has been refused to the only university in which four-fifths of her students can conscientiously seek degrees. England permits Scotchmen to shape imperial legislation for Scotland and appoints only Scotchmen to office in Scotland; the representatives of Ireland in the imperial Parliament are never consulted about legislation for that country, and the government offices there are filled with Englishmen and Scotchmen. England governs Scotland by her sons and in kindness; England governs Ireland by her enemies and in hatred.

In proportion to population, there is much more crime of all kinds committed in Scotland and England than in Ireland; yet the suspension of habeas corpus is not attempted in those countries. In eighty years fifty-nine savage coercion bills, by which personal liberty has been extinguished, have been inflicted on Ireland. England gives to all her other dependencies geographically separated from her the right to make their domestic laws on their own soil—home rule; England destroyed the Parliament of Ireland and denies her home rule.

Why?

To answer these questions this book was written.

IRELAND OF TO-DAY.

CHAPTER I.

IRELAND PRIOR TO THE LAND WAR.

IRELAND has an area of twenty million acres. It is about three-fifths the size of Illinois or Iowa, a little more than one-third the size of Oregon, not one-third the size of Colorado. It would not cover one-fifth of California. Its population is five millions. The country being almost entirely devoid of manufactures, the population must live by the land. They have not, however, twenty million acres to live upon: six million acres are waste-land. Five million people must live, therefore, on and by fourteen million acres of land. The land must feed them, clothe them, house them, educate them.

But they do not own the land. They are simply a nation of tenants engaged in farming; and the nature of their tenantry for centuries has been such that the land could not feed, clothe, house or educate them. The land is owned largely by persons whose title, however perfect legally while the country is forcibly ruled by the vast power of the British empire, originated in confiscation or in fraud; and these persons do not, as a rule, reside upon their estates. They live in England or on the Continent the greater part of every year. They draw enormous rents from the estates and invest or spend the money abroad. None of it returns to Ireland.

For centuries it was the privilege of the Irish landlords to regulate the rent of land in Ireland as they pleased; they could increase it as often as they pleased, and could, whenever they pleased, expel the tenant from the farm he tilled, whether he paid his rent or not. As there was no other occupation for him to engage in, and as the rent he had been required to pay was so excessive that he could not save any money to procure another farm, he and his family were commonly compelled to seek the poorhouse or to die of want on the highways.

Americans should understand at the outset this extraordinary difference between the relations of landlord and tenant in Ireland and the relations of landlord and tenant in the United States. Here a lease binds alike the man who owns and the man who rents; in Ireland the landlord would give no lease. Here rent cannot be increased during the period covered by the lease; there the rent could be increased whenever the landlord chose to increase it. Here the tenant's right is good during the period covered by the lease if he complies in good faith with its conditions; there the tenant could be ejected at the caprice of the landlord, and what are known in Ireland as "evictions" were of constant occurrence, generally under heartrending circumstances. Here the law respects and protects equally the rights of the landlord and the rights of the tenant; there the law respected only the landlord: the tenant had no rights.

It is obvious, without further illustration, that the landlord-and-tenant system which has prevailed in Ireland would not be tolerated for a day in the United States or in any other free country on the face of the globe. It was a system established by military force and maintained by laws deliberately contrived, and the army and the navy of Great Britain have been employed to compel the people to submit to these laws. To prevent armed insurrection, which has been threatened from time to time, the British government has kept in Ireland a standing army varying from one hundred and twenty thousand men a hundred years ago to fifty thousand at the present time—thirty-five thousand regulars and fifteen thousand military constabulary; and, in addition to paying exorbitant rents to the landlords, the Irish people have had to pay taxes to support this armed occupancy. Thus has it come to pass that the Irish people are poor, that they have been without education, that they have no manufactures or commerce, and that they hate the British government.

The English invaded Ireland in the twelfth century. Prior to that period the country was known throughout the civilized world for the excellence and number of its institutions of learning, to which students flocked from England and the Continent, and which sent all over Europe men eminent alike for virtue and for scholarship. There was a native Parliament, in which the popular voice found copious expression; the native law, known as the Brehon Code, was fair and just, and contained many admirable provisions for the protection of life, the security of property and the advancement of civilization.

The ravages of the Danes and other marauders and the quarrels of native soldiers, who fought with one another when there was no foreign foe at hand, had weakened the country, and the English invaders did not meet with successful resistance. But they encountered gigantic difficulties in subjugating the people, who, now under this leader, now under that, rose with such strength as they possessed and periodically strove to expel the intruders.

The right of the English to occupy the soil of Ireland was never acquiesced in by the people of Ireland. The English did nothing to win the goodwill of the people, and the annals of century after century are only repetitions of the same tragic story of rebellion and massacre. The power of England constantly waxed and the strength of Ireland constantly waned.

The ingenuity of the statesmen of England was called into requisition to complete the victories of her soldiers. Laws were passed during each successive reign for the perpetuation of the conquest so severely accomplished by arms. These laws were directed at

The land;
The manufactures;
The schools;
The Parliament;
The religion;
The idea of nationality.

All these laws had only one aim—the reduction of the country into a market for the English manufacturers.

The lands were confiscated on various pretences, as we shall hereafter see; but the purpose of the confiscation was to place the revenue arising from the soil in the hands of Englishmen, who would spend it in England and not turn it into capital for Irish manufactures.

Every industry which appeared in the country was suppressed by the English Parliament as soon as its suppression was asked by English manufacturers, who would not tolerate competition in Ireland.

The native schools were suppressed by law because they made the people too intelligent to submit to the intolerable burdens of foreign hostile legislation. The native tongue was by law prohibited. The native Parliament was abolished.

As religion, sincerely cherished, is dearer to the human heart than all other possessions, material or ideal, the invading power assailed the faith of the Irish people with a barbarity which even its most stubborn enemies have never failed to denounce, and which will for ever shock the sensibilities of mankind.

Unfortunately for the victims, the vast majority of the people of Ireland were Catholics and the majority of the English sovereigns were Protestants. There is nothing in the personal history of the English Crown to justify the belief that had all the monarchs been of one faith, and that the faith of all the Irish people, Ireland would have fared better at the hands of her invaders. The makers of laws against religion were hypocrites. They avowed themselves the police of a creed claiming to be superior to the religion preferred by the Irish people; they were, in truth, only land-stealers. The penal laws concerning religion in Ireland were mere land-grabbing statutes. The Protestant English Crown said to the land-owning Irish Catholic, "You are worshipping at a false altar. If you do not come to mine, I will punish you by confiscating your land." It was not to save his soul the Crown was anxious, but to get his land; and, to get his land, the Crown overthrew his altar. Nine times in ten he clung to the altar and lost his land. If the Crown had been of another creed and the Irish landowner had been a Protestant, the result would have been the same, the method different. The possession of the land was the ultimate object, and it was seized on every excuse and on none.

The extraordinary fertility of the soil made its ownership of supreme importance in the scheme of conquest. The methods by which it was gradually wrested from its natural owners, the laws passed for the suppression of education, of religion, of manufactures, of commerce, of the Irish Parliament, and, what was transcendently superior to all these, for the extinction of the idea of Irish nationality, may now be considered in detail.

CHAPTER II.

HOW THE PEOPLE LOST THE LAND.

UNDER various pretences the English invaders, while affecting to govern Ireland for Ireland's good, practically confiscated all the cultivable lands of the country. At the close of the seventeenth century the lands under cultivation covered an area of less than twelve million acres. The confiscations for refusal to adopt the creed of the State-Church, for attempted insurrection, and for any other fault which could be imputed to the people, were as follows:

	Acres.
During the reign of James I.	2,836,837
At the Restoration	7,800,000
During 1688	1,060,792
Total	11,697,629

In a word, the whole island, with the exception of the estates of a few English families, was boldly taken away from its natural and rightful owners, and not a shilling was granted them in payment for it.

The land thus confiscated was disposed of by the English Crown by three methods: It was given in large estates to favorites of the reigning monarch; it was sold to English or Scotch colonists and the proceeds went into the royal purse; and it was offered gratuitously to other colonists from foreign countries upon two conditions—that they should do everything in their power to drive out the native Irish, and that they should not suffer any of the natural owners to recover any portion of it as remuneration for service, in return for labor or by the payment of money.

In the confiscations and the bestowal of the lands afterward according to royal caprice was laid the foundation of the system of landlordism which exists to this day. Many of the persons upon whom estates were conferred would not reside in Ireland, and were not expected to do so. They were in many instances English soldiers whose arms were needed in foreign wars; in other cases they were convivial companions of the monarch, and could not be spared from his revels; and in still others they were persons yet lower in social character. These newly-created landlords appointed agents to manage their estates for them; then was laid the foundation of the system of absentee landlords and ever-present bailiffs. The bailiff's duty was to get the highest rent he could for every acre, and the landlord's privilege was to spend the income thus acquired. Of course he spent none of it in Ireland; even the bailiff's wages he was often required to extort after the rent had been collected.

The Scotch and English colonists were called "undertakers;" and as an historical curiosity, as well as to illustrate perfectly the manner in which the natural owners of the land were to be prevented from recovering it, the following royal order is reproduced:

"*Articles concerning the English and Scotch undertakers, who are to plant their portions with English and inland Scottish tenants.*

" 1. His Majesty is pleased to grant estates in fee farm to them and their heirs.

" 2. They shall yearly yield unto His Majesty, for every proportion of one thousand acres, five pounds six shillings and eight pence English, and so ratably for the greater proportions; which is after the rate of six shillings and eight pence for every threescore English acres. But none of the said undertakers shall pay any rent until the expiration of the first two years, except the natives of Ireland, who are not subject to the charge of transportation.

" 3. Every undertaker of so much land as shall amount to the greatest proportion of two thousand acres, or thereabouts, shall hold the same by knight service *in capite;* and every undertaker of so much land as shall amount to the middle proportion of fifteen hundred acres, or thereabouts, shall hold the same by knight service as of the castle of Dublin; and every undertaker of so much land as shall amount to the least proportion of a thousand acres, or thereabouts, shall hold the same in common socage; and there shall be no wardships upon the two first descents of that land.

"4. Every undertaker of the greatest proportion of two thousand acres shall within two years after the date of his letters patent build thereupon a castle with a strong court or bawn about it; and every undertaker of the second or middle proportion of fifteen hundred acres shall within the same time build a stone or brick house thereupon with a strong court or bawn about it; and every undertaker of the least proportion of a thousand acres shall within the same time make thereupon a strong court or bawn at least; and all the said undertakers shall desire their tenants to build houses for themselves and their families near the principal castle, house or bawn for their mutual defence or strength. . . .

"5. The said undertakers, their heirs and assigns, shall have ready in their houses at all times a convenient store of arms, wherewith they may furnish a competent number of able men for their defence, which may be viewed and mustered every half-year, according to the manner of England.

"6. Every of the said undertakers, English or Scotch, before the ensealing of his letters patent, shall take the oath of supremacy, . . . and shall also conform themselves in religion according to His Majesty's laws.

"7. The said undertakers, their heirs and assigns, shall not alien or demise their portions, or any part thereof, to the *meer Irish*, or to such persons as will not take the oath; and to that end a proviso shall be inserted in their letters patent."

The oath was that of acceptance of the creed of the State-Church, which was Protestant. As nine-tenths of the Irish people were Catholics, they could not take it; that for ever excluded them from recovering possession of their land, even as purchasers or as heirs.

The natural owners of the land did not tamely submit to its confiscation, and the English Crown was compelled to employ troops to drive them off. The manner in which the troops complied with the orders of the Crown can be most appropriately described in the reports of commanding officers and in the words of English historians.

Malby, an officer of Queen Elizabeth, wrote to her: " At Christmas, I marched into their territory [Shan Burke's], and, finding courteous dealing with them had like to have cut my throat, I thought good to take another course; and so, with determination *to consume them with fire and sword, sparing neither old nor young*, I entered their mountains. I burnt all their corn and houses and committed to the sword all that could be found, where were slain at that time above sixty of their best men, and among them the best leaders they had. This was Shan Burke's country. Then I burnt Ulick Burke's county. In like manner I assaulted a castle where the garrison surrendered. I put them to the misericordia of my soldiers: they were all slain. Thence I went on, sparing none which came in my way; which cruelty did so amaze their followers that they could not tell where to bestow themselves. Shan Burke made means to me to pardon him and forbear killing of his people. I would not hearken, but went on my way. The gentlemen of Clanrickard came to me. I found it was but dallying to win time; so I left Ulick as little corn and as few houses standing as I left his brother, and what people was found had as little favor as the other had. *It was all done in rain and frost and storm*, journeys in such weather bringing them the sooner to submission. They are humble enough now, and will yield to any terms we like to offer them."

Similar reports were made by others.

Hollinshed describes the progress of the army: "As they went they drove the whole country before them into the Ventrie, and by that means they preyed and took all the cattle in the country, to the number of eight thousand kine, besides horses, garrons, sheep and goats, and all such people as they met they did without mercy put to the sword. By these means the whole country having no cattle nor kine left, they were driven to such extremities that for want of victuals they were either to die and perish for famine or to die under the sword."

It was lawful to kill "the meer Irish," provided the persons slain had not become loyal to the English Crown. Sir John Davies, one of the officers of James I. in Ireland, thus reports: "The real Irish were not only accounted aliens, but enemies, and altogether out of the protection of the law, so as it was no capital offence to kill them; and this is manifest by many records."

An Englishman committed the blunder of killing an Irishman who had become "loyal." He pleaded in defence, when on trial, the law that his victim was a "meer Irishman," and therefore that it was not a crime to kill him. But it was proved that the Irishman was "loyal," and the slayer "was recommitted to jail until he shall find pledges to pay five marks to our lord the king for the value of said Irishman."

If the Irish did not become loyal after being driven off their lands, they could be lawfully killed; if they became loyal, they became in effect slaves to the Crown, and whoso killed them then had to pay the king for the destruction of his property.

Thousands, after being driven off their own lands, were forced on shipboard, carried to Virginia and the West Indies and sold as slaves. Six thousand were compelled to go to Sweden and fight for Gustavus Adolphus.

The lord deputy, who was directing the expulsion of the people from their lands in Ulster in the beginning of the seventeenth century, thus reported: "I have often said and written it is *famine that must consume the Irish*, as our *swords* and other endeavors worked not that speedy effect which is expected; *hunger* would be a better, because a speedier, weapon to employ against them than the sword. . . . I burned all along the lough (Neagh) within four miles of Dungannon, and killed one hundred people, sparing none, of what quality, age or sex soever, besides *many burned to death*. We killed man, *woman and child*, horse, beast and whatsoever we could find."

Sir George Carew reports that "harassing the country" the English "killed all mankind that were found therein. . . . Wee came into Arleaghe woods, where wee did the like, not leaving behind us man or beast, corn or cattle, except such as had been conveyed into the castles."

The English historian Moryson writes: "No spectacle was more frequent in the ditches of the towns, and especially in wasted countries, than to see multitudes of these poor people, the Irish, dead, with their mouths all colored green by eating nettles, docks, and all things they could reach above ground."

Cromwell's savage way of driving the people off their lands was not surpassed by the methods of any of his predecessors. When the garrison at Drogheda surrendered he explicitly promised them that their lives would be spared. After the surrender not only were the soldiers butchered in cold blood, but Cromwell put to the sword "every man that related to the garrison and all the citizens who were Irish, man, woman and child," says the English historian Clarendon. Cromwell himself wrote to the English Parliament: "I wish that all honest hearts may give the glory of this to God alone, to whom, indeed, the praise of this mercy belongs."

Lingard, the English historian, says: "No distinction was made between the defenceless inhabitant and the armed soldier; nor could the shrieks and prayers of three hundred females who had gathered round the great cross preserve them from the swords of these ruthless barbarians."

Cromwell had gone to Ireland the avowed exponent of liberty of conscience. "I believe in freedom of conscience," he cried; "but if by that you understand leave to go to mass, by the horns of Beelezebub, you shall repent your error!"

Cromwell had at least the virtue of killing his victims promptly. He may have been scandalized by reading how an English officer, annoyed by the presumption of an Irishman who clung to his land and his life, tied the man to a Maypole and put out his eyes with his thumbs, and he was probably aware that children had been kept alive longer than English interests demanded when the English soldiers threw the infants of Irish land-owners up in the air and caught them on the points of their bayonets. Francis Crosby, an English officer, used to hang men, women and children on a tree before his door and watch with amusement the infants clinging to the long hair of their mothers.

Cromwell understood the value of famine as one of the resources of war. He took with him into Ireland scythes and sickles to cut down the harvests and starve those who escaped his sword. He also understood the use of fire on occasion. Some of the

CARRICKFERGUS CASTLE.

women in Drogheda took refuge in a church-steeple; he put the torch to it. For those who escaped sword, famine and fire he had still another resource: it was slavery in a distant clime. "I do not think thirty escaped with their lives," he wrote from Drogheda; "those that did are in safe custody for the Barbadoes."

When Cromwell had done his worst, with all his resources, some of the natural owners of the Irish land still occupied it. Then the English Parliament selected one province in the country—the one most barren and desolate, Connaught—and to it consigned, on penalty of death if they left it, all the people who had survived the war of extermination. Some of those who were compelled to submit to this order had themselves been engaged in driving off the land its rightful owners; they were descendants of the English to whom the lands had been given previously by the English Crown, and they were now compelled to submit to the miseries they had helped to inflict on the people to whom the land belonged. They petitioned the Parliament in vain. Among them was a grandson of the poet Spenser; he pleaded the great name he bore, but his entreaties were derided. Some of the people who refused to leave their land were promptly hanged; hundreds were shipped to the West Indies as slaves; some went mad; some committed suicide.

At that time was established, and in this "legal" manner, the title by which many of the present race of Irish landlords obtained their claims to the estates they now hold. An eminent Protestant lawyer of Ireland has said that he supposed no man at the bar of that country ever traced an Irish title back to its origin without discovering that it was born in confiscation.

The ferocity of the English troops in Ireland did not abate with time, nor did the English soldier of a hundred years later think any less lightly of "killing a meer Irishman." In the Cornwallis correspondence will be found an episode as frightful as any that occurred during the confiscations of the lands. A squad of English soldiers forced their way into a humble cottage, where they found a young Irishman with his aged mother. While her arms encircled the boy and her piteous cries resounded in their ears, they shot him dead. The officer in command of the squad was tried by court-martial and acquitted, the defence being that he *suspected* the young man of being a rebel!

English legislation, as well as troops, was employed to prevent the rightful owners of the land in Ireland from recovering any part of it. This legislation is comprised in what are commonly called the "penal laws." They were ostensibly enacted in behalf of the Protestant religion and for the purpose of suppressing the Catholic faith in Ireland. Their real purpose was to prevent the natural owners of the lands from recovering them and from engaging in any pursuit of profit or of honor. The vast majority of the people were Catholics: every penalty that ingenuity could devise was laid on that faith. An examination of the statutes reveals only one always-present object—to prevent the people from recovering or acquiring land or other property. They were to be reduced to a condition of unlettered serfage.

The penal laws are thus described by the Protestant historian Lecky. In reading his summary of them truth requires that "Englishman" should be substituted for "Protestant," and "Irishman" for "Catholic :"

"It required, indeed, four or five reigns to elaborate a system so ingeniously contrived to demoralize, to degrade and impoverish the people of Ireland. By this code the Roman Catholics were absolutely excluded from the Parliament, from the magistracy, from the corporations, from the bench and from the bar. They could not vote at parliamentary elections or at vestries. They could not act as constables or sheriffs or jurymen, or serve in the army or navy, or become solicitors, or even hold the position of gamekeeper or watchman. Schools were established to bring up their children as Protestants; and if they refused to avail themselves of these, they were deliberately consigned to hopeless ignorance, being excluded from the university and debarred, under crushing penalties, from acting as schoolmasters, as ushers or as private tutors, or from sending their children abroad to obtain the instruction they were refused at home. They could not marry Protestants; and if such a marriage were celebrated; the priest who officiated might be hung. They could not buy land, nor inherit it, nor receive it as a gift, from Protestants, nor hold life-annuities, or leases for more than thirty-one years, or any lease on such terms that the profits of the land exceeded one-third of the rent. If any Catholic householder by his industry so increased his profits that they exceeded this proportion, and did not immediately make a corresponding increase in his payments, any Protestant who gave the information could enter into possession of his farm. If any Catholic had secretly purchased either his old forfeited estate or any other land, any Protestant who informed against him might become the proprietor. The few Catholic land-holders who remained were deprived of the right which all other classes possessed—of bequeathing their land as they pleased. If their sons continued Catholics, it was divided equally among them. If, however, the eldest son consented to apostatize, the estate was settled upon him; the father from that hour became only a life-tenant, and lost all power of selling, mortgaging or otherwise disposing of it. If the wife of a Catholic abandoned the religion of her husband, she was immediately free from his control, and the chancellor was empowered to assign to her a certain portion of her husband's property. If any child, however young, professed itself a Protestant, it was at once taken from its father's care, and the chancellor could oblige the father to declare upon oath the value of his property, both real and personal, and could assign for the present maintenance and future portion of the converted child such proportion of that property as the court might decree. No Catholic could be guardian either to his own children or to those of another person, and therefore a Catholic who died while his children were minors had the bitterness of reflecting upon his deathbed that they must pass into the care of Protestants. An annuity of from twenty to forty pounds was provided as a bribe for every priest who would become a Protestant. To convert a Protestant to Catholicism was a capital offence. In every walk of life the Catholic was pursued by persecution or restriction. Except in the linen trade, he could not have more than two apprentices. He could not possess a horse of the value of more than five pounds, and any Protestant, on giving him five pounds, could take his horse. He was compelled to pay double to the militia. He was forbidden, except under particular conditions, to live in Galway or Limerick. In case of war with a Catholic prince, the Catholics were obliged to reimburse the damage done by the enemy's privateers. . . . To facilitate the discovery of offences against the code, two justices of the peace might at any time compel any Catholic of eighteen years of age to declare when and where he last heard mass, what persons were present and who officiated; and if he refused to give evidence, they might imprison him for twelve months or until he had paid a fine of twenty pounds. . . . A graduated scale of rewards was offered for the discovery of Catholic bishops, priests and schoolmasters, and a resolution of the [Irish] House of Commons pronounced 'the prosecuting and informing against papists' 'an honorable service to the government.' . . . Such were the principal articles of this famous code. . . . It was framed by a small minority of the nation for the oppression of the majority who remained faithful to the religion of their fathers. . . . It was framed and enforced, although by the treaty of Limerick the Catholics had been guaranteed such privileges in the exercise of their religion as they enjoyed in the reign of Charles II.; although the sovereign at the same time promised, as soon as his affairs would permit, to summon a Parliament in this kingdom and endeavor to procure the said Roman Catholics such further security in that particular as may preserve them from any disturbance on account of their religion; although not a single act of treason was proved against them; and although they remained passive spectators to two rebellions which menaced the very existence of the Protestant dynasty in England."

The first of these laws was passed in 1691. The volunteers of '82 abolished some of them; they were not finally repealed until the country was about to rise in insurrection, in 1829.

The confiscations deprived the people of Ireland of all the land.

The penal laws deprived them of the right of

recovering, even by peaceful means, what had been taken from them by force.

The penal laws also deprived them of personal property.

The penal laws deprived them of education.

Such were the advantages the Irish people obtained from the English invaders for six hundred years after the invasion.

CHAPTER III.

THE REASON IRELAND HAS NO MANUFACTURES.

IT is frequently remarked by observing Americans that we get no skilled labor from Ireland. An examination of the industrial statistics of that country exposes a remarkable fact—that it is a country without manufactures. The fact is remarkable because Nature is not responsible for it; and the universal development of the vast system of modern exchanges makes it more conspicuous. Economists have stated again and again that in Ireland there is enough water-power to run the machinery of the world. That she has no extensive coal-beds does not account for the absence of factories, because coals can be delivered in Dublin cheaper than in Manchester or London; and France, with her immense diversity of manufactures, has to import coal. On the other hand, the soil of Ireland is capable of producing at a minimum of outlay raw material which could profitably be manufactured for the home and foreign markets; and, instead of devoting her energy in this direction, we find that her one article of trade, in which she is relatively insignificant—the linen—is produced largely from imported flax, her own soil not being adapted to the cultivation of the best flaxseed. Excepting a few linen-factories, with a small number of minor productions scarcely worthy classification, she is a country without manufactures. She has nothing to sell except the food produced by her land; she has to send abroad, chiefly to England, for everything she buys. A country thus situated cannot be a prosperous country. A country thus situated cannot furnish skilled labor to the new and active world in which so many of her sons have sought homes.

A country in which there is but one means of living, and that one means dependent on inexorable physical laws, must have periods of suffering. The more diversified the forms of remunerative activity in which a people are engaged, the more protection have they against financial panics; the more constant their prosperity, the more enterprising their capital. A country with only one activity, and that farming, must be a poor country, doomed to periodical misery and to constant poverty. If the almost total lack of manufactures in Ireland be her own fault, she is not entitled to the sympathy of mankind. If, on the contrary, her want of manufactures is a want created and maintained by foreign legislation enforced in her territory, the economist will discover in her anomalous condition an extraordinary phenomenon, and the lover of justice, honesty and fair play in commerce a striking example of the helplessness to which a more powerful country may reduce the victim of prohibitory laws.

Ireland was not always without manufactures. In the United States, in Canada, in Australia, where the Irish people are free to choose the forms of industry which they will follow, we find them in all the industries. As a rule, they are not capitalists, for obvious reasons; for the same reasons they are not skilled in any of the mechanical trades when they immigrate; but the young Irish enter into all the trades, become skilled in them, and, as soon as they are able, follow the example of all other nationalities: they become manufacturers as soon as they get money enough. The charge of idleness made against them in Ireland has been emphatically denied by John Bright, who has borne willing testimony to their zeal and energy in England and in the countries of the Western continent. He says, "They are the hardest-working people in the world." They lack, manifestly, neither the natural aptitude nor the desire to engage in mechanical and other manufacturing occupations.

It must, therefore, be opportunity they lack in Ireland. It will be seen that they have been deprived of opportunity by laws enacted with the greatest deliberation by the government which still claims the right to rule them; and it is reasonable to declare that the interests of the English manufacturers require that Ireland shall continue to be a country without manufactures. The legislation of

England for Ireland has uniformly been in the interest of the English manufacturers. It is perfectly natural that it should be.

If the United States Congress should attempt to make a discriminating tariff for the purpose of giving one group of States commercial advantages over another group, the integrity of the National Union would reasonably be considered in danger. If, to foster the development of a certain industry in Ohio, prohibitory duties were laid on the exportation of all articles of that nature from Pennsylvania and New York, it is extremely probable that the doctrine of secession would take on an almost benign aspect in New York and Pennsylvania. The fact is unquestioned and unquestionable that the British government destroyed and effectually prohibited manufactures in Ireland—an integral part of the British empire—for the benefit of the English manufacturers; yet there are careful and reflecting Americans who wonder why Ireland has no manufactures, and why the Irish people talk about their right to a legislature of their own to enact laws for the regulation of their domestic affairs!

Let us examine the record.

The exchanges which Ireland had with other countries before the suppression of her trade were the exportation of cattle, living and cured; the exportation of hides; the exportation of wool, raw and manufactured; the exportation of glass, tallow, and many other articles of less value in the aggregate. The countries to which these exports were carried in Irish ships were England, the American colonies and the countries of the East between which and the West of Europe commerce had sprung up. The cattle trade gave Ireland a large revenue; the woollen industry became a source of increasing wealth with the gradual enlargement of the foreign markets, especially the convenient market of the rapidly-growing American colonies. Had this trade not been meddled with, it would have enriched Ireland with capital to invest in the many new articles of commerce which the growth of the arts, the demands of extending civilization and the application of the physical sciences to industry were, and are, still creating or multiplying. But English law was invoked by the English manufacturers to suppress Irish trade for their benefit; and, following that suppression, capital, having nothing to do in Ireland, went out of the country and did not return. Without capital, production is impossible; without production, there can be no skilled labor. Without the exchanges which capital and skilled labor jointly produce, a country is necessarily poor.

The principle which was always present in English economical legislation for Ireland was that Ireland should be the private and exclusive market of the English manufacturer. Nothing should be produced in Ireland which could be sent from England into Ireland; nothing should be sent from Ireland into England which could be produced in England;

Ireland should not be suffered to sell anything in any foreign market which the English could sell there; Ireland should not buy from any one but England. These resolves reduced the economical relations of Ireland with mankind to a very simple basis. They were faithfully carried out by the English Parliament. The exportation of cattle was forbidden. Next the exportation of cured meats was forbidden. Gradually all exports were forbidden except what the English manufacturers wanted: they were quite willing that the linen trade should be encouraged in Ireland, because it was inconvenient for them and too expensive, as the flaxseed would have to be imported. And when the American war broke out the trade of Ireland was utterly annihilated; she was not permitted to send anything to the colonies, and she could receive nothing from them except what was passed through English ports, although the ships from the colonies to England had to sail by her own doors. How vast the commerce of Ireland, unchecked, might have become may be imagined when we recall that of her thirty-two counties nineteen are maritime and the rest are washed by copious rivers that empty into the sea.

The money that had formerly been carried back from foreign ports by Irish ships ceased to come; and Swift says that the currency of Ireland, before the suppression of her trade, included the coins of every sovereign in Europe. The shrinkage in the circulation soon affected the home market: as the people were not permitted to sell, they had little to buy with; and it was not long after the closing of the foreign markets to Ireland by her foreign government that her home market became stagnant. This is the picture a capable writer of that period (Hely Hutchinson, a Protestant, and provost of Trinity College) gave of the condition of Ireland just a hundred years ago: "The present state of Ireland teems with every circumstance of national poverty. Whatever the land produces is greatly reduced in value; wool is fallen one-half in its usual price, wheat one-third, black cattle of all kinds in the same proportion, and hides in a much greater; buyers are not had without difficulty at those low rates, and from the principal fairs men commonly return with the commodities they brought there; rents are everywhere reduced, and in many places it is impossible to collect them; the farmers are all distressed, and many of them have failed; when leases expire tenants are not easily found; the landlord is often obliged to take his lands into his own hands for want of bidders at reasonable rents, and finds his estate fallen one-fourth of its value. The merchant justly complains that all business is at a stand, that he cannot discount his bills, and that neither money nor paper circulates. In this and the last year above twenty thousand manufacturers in this metropolis were reduced to beggary for want of employment. They were for a considerable length of time supported by alms; a part of the contribution came from England, and this assistance was much wanting, from the general distress of all ranks of the people in this country. Public and private credit is annihilated. . . . This kingdom has long been declining. The annual deficiency of its revenues for the payment of the public expenses has been for many years supplied by borrowing; the American rebellion, which considerably diminished the demand for our linen, an embargo on provisions for three years and highly injurious to our victualling trade, the increasing drain of remittances to England for rents, salaries, profits of offices and the payment of forces abroad, have made the decline more rapid."

It will not escape the observation of Americans that, while England continued to destroy the trade and commerce of Ireland—as if she were an enemy at war, while, in fact, she was profoundly at peace—England continued to tax Ireland like the most loyal and most abject of subjects, and even required her to pay part of the expense of the American Revolution, with whose avowed objects the four-fifths of the Irish people openly sympathized, their sympathy being expressed in public meetings and in messages transmitted to this country, in which Irish valor was so enthusiastically enlisted in the patriot cause. So deeply was Irish sympathy valued, and so anxious were the Americans to retain the good-will of the Irish people, that the Continental Congress sent to the Irish people an address, in which it declared: "You have been friendly to the rights of mankind;

and we acknowledge with pleasure and gratitude that the Irish nation has produced patriots who have highly distinguished themselves in the cause of humanity and America. On the other hand, we are not ignorant that the labors and manufacture of Ireland, like those of the silkworm, were of little moment to herself, but served only to give luxury to those who neither toil nor spin," alluding to the constant over-taxation of the country for the support of a foreign government on its own soil, and for pensions for favorites of the Crown, some of whom were infamous persons of both sexes and most of whom had never even set foot on Irish soil to bless or curse it. "We know that you are not without your grievances," the address continues. "We sympathize with you in your distress, and are pleased to find that the design of subjugating us persuaded the administration to dispense to Ireland some vagrant rays of ministerial sunshine. The tender mercies of the government have long been cruel toward you. We hope the patient abiding of the meek may not always be forgotten, and God grant that the iniquitous system of extirpating liberty may soon be defeated!"

"Vagrant rays of ministerial sunshine" was a very apt description of the few concessions which the English government reluctantly granted to Ireland while under the pressure of war with the colonies and threatened invasion by France. A few of the heavy duties on some minor articles for which the war created a higher demand in England were mod-

THE GREEN LINEN MARKET, BELFAST.

ified or removed, but a still larger boon was yet to be conceded.

The Irish Parliament sat in College Green, in the building which is now the Bank of Ireland, before which, as he was driven past it last summer, Charles Stewart Parnell reverently uncovered his head while his countrymen filled the air with their cheers; and, although English law had deprived eight-tenths of the Irish people of the right to sit in it as members or to vote for members, it contained a patriot minority, led by Grattan and his followers, who took advantage of the crisis in the affairs of Great Britain to insist on legislative independence for their country. It is needless to recount here the successive laws by which the mass of the people were shut out of Parliament; enough that a hundred years ago only members of the Church of England could sit in it or vote for those who were candidates. The Catholics in Ireland were seven-tenths of the population; the Presbyterians and other dissenters were another tenth: all were excluded. The patriot Protestant party had stoutly resisted the attempts of the government to send troops to America; and Grattan, in a famous debate, spoke of this country as the "only hope of Ireland, and the only refuge of the liberties of mankind." The troops were nevertheless ordered to cross the sea, and then a new condition existed in Ireland.

For the first time since the conquest, in the twelfth century, she was practically rid of English soldiers.

She needed none for the preservation of internal peace; but there were loud threats of French invasion, and volunteers were called for. Under the laws the Catholics could not bear arms; but after the Presbyterians and the Protestants began enrolling, a few Catholics were admitted to the ranks. In a short time sixty thousand men were enrolled; they accepted arms and ammunition from the government, but declined commissions and elected their own officers. The volunteers, having no foreign French foe to fight, turned their attention to politics, and they made, in convention, these specific demands: The abolition of all restrictions on Irish trade; the restoration of the independence of the Irish Parliament, which had been taken away by an act passed in 1495 forbidding the Irish Parliament to assemble for any purpose except to pass the measures proposed by the English Crown—measures for the ruin of Ireland; and the enlargement of the constitutional privileges of the country to include all classes of the people. The Crown had no means of resisting these demands while the American war lasted. The volunteers drew up before the Parliament building, where the agents of the English government sat as the ministers of the Irish Parliament and people. On the gaping mouths of their cannon were suspended placards bearing the suggestive words, "Free Trade or This;" and thus they awaited the surrender of the Crown. "Free trade" did not mean what is now popularly understood by that term: it meant simply the abolition of the restrictions which had been laid upon all Irish commerce, domestic and foreign. Powerless, the agents of the Crown yielded; the trade restrictions were abolished. Then the volunteers demanded that the Irish Parliament be given the right to make all the laws for Ireland. Again they were victorious; and for eighteen years the Parliament that sat in College Green, although composed of members of only one Church, and that the Church by law established, made laws for Ireland, and made them, in the main, wisely. The third demand of the volunteers was not granted —the political emancipation of their Roman Catholic brethren. Had Washington not caught Cornwallis at Yorktown, that right too could have been obtained: unfortunately for Ireland, the American war terminated too soon. The government trifled with the volunteers until after peace was declared; then, the troops returning from America to Ireland, the volunteers were disbanded, and four-fifths of the Irish people remained until 1829 deprived of civil and religious liberty, while paying enormous taxes to the government that thus kept them in serfage.

For eighteen years the Parliament of Ireland was independent of the English Crown in its right to initiate laws for the domestic government of Ireland; and during that period "it was, on the whole," writes the historian Lecky,[1] "a vigilant and intelligent guardian of the interest of the country." It

[1] Author of *Rationalism in Europe, History of England in the Eighteenth Century*, etc.

devoted itself with assiduity to the revival of the industries of Ireland and encouraged those which were best calculated to thrive under the then existing commercial conditions. It expended taxation judiciously for public works and improved the inland navigation. In ten years, from 1782 to 1792, the exports more than doubled. Sixteen years later Lord Clare wrote that there "is not a nation in the habitable globe which has advanced in cultivation and commerce, in agriculture and manufactures, with the same rapidity in the same period." Could any stronger argument be made for the expediency of permitting Ireland to try once more the experiment of making her own domestic laws on her own soil?

But it was intolerable to the English manufacturers that a rival should again be found in the country whose manufactures they had once succeeded in destroying, and they determined to destroy them again. A different method was required. The creation of capital in Ireland which would be invested in Irish factories was most to be feared. If the Irish Parliament continued independent, it would comply with the wishes of the majority of the Protestants and Presbyterians and emancipate the Catholics. Their admission into Parliament would make that body thoroughly national, since all classes of the people would then be represented in it. A thoroughly national Parliament would speedily reform all the laws by which Ireland had been reduced to the condition of a private market for the English manufacturer. There would be a reform of the land laws. The record by which the land of the Irish people had been boldly stolen from them would be examined—with what results, it was too easy to foresee. If the land were restored to the natural and legal owners, the money received for the fruits of the earth would belong to the people residing in Ireland, instead of being drawn out of the country by a foreign government and absentee landlords, to be spent in England or on the Continent. Peasant proprietary meant home capital in Ireland for the creation of manufactures which would interfere with the prosperity of the English manufacturers. The creation of capital in Ireland to be invested in productive industry was to be prevented at any cost and by resort to any expedient. The only certain expedient was the abolition of the Irish Parliament.

The bill by which the Parliament was abolished was called the "Act of Legislative Union with Great Britain," and it was passed in 1800. Since then there has been no Parliament in Ireland.

As an equivalent, Ireland has one hundred and five seats in the imperial House of Commons, which is composed of six hundred and fifty-two members. Less than a fifth of that body, how can the Irish members, even if acting as a unit in aims and methods, accomplish anything for the benefit of the trade of Ireland?

Had the woollen trade not been destroyed in 1699,

its remarkable development and the favoring natural conditions of the country must speedily have laid the solid foundations for many other industries in addition to those which existed with it. The Irish then had ships, and the harbors of the island were crowded with masts; the Irish flag was met on the highways of the ocean until forbidden to be seen there; the natural capital of the country was being utilized at home, and must have expanded its activity into new fields of occupation had it been left free. Had the woollen trade not been annihilated, it is entirely reasonable to say that Ireland would to-day fill a place in history very different from that to which her long series of industrial and political misfortunes have consigned her. Instead of being a country without manufactures, tall chimneys would smoke in her cities; the incalculable water-power that courses through her valleys would be turning myriad wheels; her cabins would be cheerful with thrift and her children's cheeks red with plenty; her farmers would have innumerable exchanges at home for which they would sell the fruits of the earth. There would be no famines, for money enough would circulate in the country to buy food for all in a land that can feed many times its own population. Instead of "profound indigence and chronic anarchy," we should behold there peace, prosperity and all the blessings, domestic and political, which only peace and prosperity can insure.

It is not enough to say that if England destroyed

the woollen trade, she encouraged the linen trade. For reasons too obvious for assertion, it was the woollen, and not the linen, trade that would have developed parallel industries in Ireland and built the edifice of diversified productiveness. Venice and the other Italian states carried on the manufacture of wool until the countries producing the raw material manufactured it; then the Italian manufacture dwindled into insignificance. The Flemings undersold the Italians, being nearer the wool-growing countries; then England undersold the Flemings for the same reason. The linen trade has never expired, but it has been of comparatively little significance in promoting other industries. So long as money has to be sent out of the country for the best flaxseed, it is impossible that it should be effectual in national development.

When Ireland was robbed of her manufactures, her trade, in the words of Swift, was "glorious and flourishing." She has never recovered from the shock, nor has it ever been possible that she should. The only source of profit left was the land; that was not owned by the people. The owners have done nothing to promote the establishment of manufactures. The landlord class are exclusively a consuming class.

From official returns it appears that there are only 67,744 persons, out of a population of 5,000,000, employed in textile industries in Ireland, and of these 60,000 are in 149 flax-factories. There are

8 cotton-factories, 60 woollen-factories, 1 worsted-factory, 4 hemp-factories, 11 jute-factories, 2 silk-factories; in all, 235 factories for textile products. Even in the linen trade Ireland has not of late years kept her lead. In 1868 the number of flax-factories in England and Wales was 128; in Scotland, 134; and in Ireland, 143. In 1875 the number in England and Wales was 141, in Scotland 159, against 149 in Ireland. In 1868 there were 13 cotton-factories in Ireland; in 1875, only 8. The poplin trade has not declined, but it has not grown. There has been an inconsiderable increase in silk. There has been an increase in the jute-manufacture; 11 factories are reported in 1875, against 2 in 1868, and the persons employed have risen from 20 to 2000. There is also a slight increase in hemp. And what of all the other manufactured articles that enter into the daily life of even the common people? Ireland has to buy them all from England—millinery, silk, gloves, hats, cloths, cottons, muslins, ribbons, soap, candles, iron, hardware, glass, furniture.

No more eloquent presentation of Ireland's poverty, arising from her want of exchanges, can be constructed than that which is found in the total of her exports and imports. The total value of her exports in the latest available official figures is £238,452; the total of her imports, £7,901,899. Had she home manufactures, a large proportion of this immense money balance on the wrong side would be kept at home and used for the prosperity of the country. So long as a foreign legislature, in which she is without effectual representation, continues to neglect, or, when not neglecting, to "coerce," her, there can be no adjustment of this wrong balance.

It was to be expected that the Land League, especially after the passage of the bill which promised but did not afford the only true solution of the Irish question—peasant proprietary—should undertake an effort to revive manufactures in Ireland. A home-manufacture association was formed, with branches throughout Ireland; and at the great national convention held in Dublin, over which Charles Stewart Parnell presided, and which was composed of delegates chosen by the Land League, he said that if Ireland had her own Parliament, she could foster and protect her industries as the United States protected theirs, but under the rule of a foreign legislature Ireland could do nothing by law either to create or to promote manufactures. "But," he continued, "we can protect our home manufactures and encourage new ones by our unwritten law, by the public and organized opinion of the great majority of the Irish people, in accordance with whose opinions all laws governing Ireland ought to be made. There are indirect methods of protection. Let us buy nothing abroad which we can get at home; what we must buy abroad let us buy in America; and let us buy nothing in England." A resolution embodying this declaration was unanimously adopted, and its spirit was instantly felt throughout the country. Advertisements appeared in the leading journals announcing Irish manufactures; the shop-windows were filled with goods made at home; the various corporations and unions advertising for supplies required that where the articles called for could be made in Ireland, only the Irish-made should be received; and several companies were formed for manufactures in the cities. Shopkeepers who imported what they could get at home were quietly "boycotted," and, short as was the interval between the meeting of the national convention and the suppression of the League by the government, it had succeeded in awaking in the minds of the people another incentive to struggle determinedly to the end for the recovery of their inalienable right to make their own domestic laws on their own soil.

CHAPTER IV.

HOW THE PEOPLE LOST THEIR PARLIAMENT.

AS the next agitation in Ireland will be for the restoration of the national Parliament, it is desirable that the manner in which that Parliament was abolished, in 1800, should be clearly understood.

Ireland is the only British dependency in which there is not a legislature for making domestic laws. The Home-Rule demand in Ireland is that that country be placed in the same relation to the British Crown as are all its other dependencies—in the same relation which each State of the American federation holds to the national government. Each American State has its own legislature for the enactment of laws which affect only the State, while the Congress at Washington makes the laws which affect all the States. The Home-Rule demand in Ireland is that she be given her own home legislature to make those laws which affect her only, while the imperial Parliament should continue to make the laws for the general government of the empire. If the functions now discharged by each State legislature were usurped by Congress, Americans would quickly realize the reasonableness of the demand for Home Rule in Ireland. The Home-Rule agitators there have asked nothing except that Ireland make on her own soil, in a legislature elected by all of her own people, the laws which regulate her domestic affairs. Ireland, in making this demand, simply asks the privilege of attending to her own housekeeping instead of having it ordered and disordered by the head of the house across the street. As to the affairs of the street itself the heads of both houses should consult.

England can keep her own house on the one side of the Channel; Ireland wants to keep her house on the opposite side of the Channel. In matters outside their respective houses they should be required to consult for the common good.

In their present connection England is simply a tax-assessor and tax-collector in Ireland, and charges so exorbitant a commission that the employer would like to dispense with her services and substitute some of the family to attend to the business for considerably less pay.

History is wanting in evidence that one country ever assessed, collected and expended taxes in another country economically, wisely or honestly.

The abolition of the Irish Parliament was accomplished by corruption and misrepresentation. English statesmen have affirmed this so often, and the official records of the government so boldly confess it, that it is useless to repeat it by way of argument for the reparation of the gigantic wrong then inflicted. But, as Lord Cornwallis—of whose achievements in this country we have heard something—was the chief officer of the Crown in Ireland when the Parliament was abolished, it will be interesting to American readers to hear the story of that event as it were from his own lips.

It is not true that the Irish Parliament ever was a national Parliament as we now understand that term, because the entire people of Ireland were not represented in it. But it began to show a national spirit when Sir Edward Poynings was the chief officer of the English Crown in that country, and to extinguish it he procured the passage by the English Parliament of what is known as Poynings's law. It was, in substance, that the Irish Parliament should meet only when the king of England desired it to meet, that it should meet only at his pleasure, and that when it had done his business in Ireland the members should go home. That law was passed in England in 1495; of course it had to be accepted in Ireland. A Parliament thus fettered was indeed no Parliament, but in course of time astute men in it found ways to do slight favors for the country without the previous permission of the Crown; and when the religious fanaticism of the subsequent period introduced new elements of distress into Irish life, it was deemed prudent to expel the Catholics from their seats and to deprive them of the right to vote for Protestants who were candidates. Yet the Catholics were seven-tenths of the population, according to Lord Cornwallis. A Parliament which contains no representatives of that proportion of the people of a country can scarcely be designated a national Parliament.

But there were factors in its composition which rendered it less than representative of the minority who were eligible. Two hundred and sixteen members represented only manors. Manor-proprietors who sent into the Commons men acceptable to the government were rewarded with peerages, and thus the Upper and Lower Houses were simultaneously degraded and corrupted. Still further to withdraw the Parliament from public opinion, should any be developed by events, the Lower House, unless dissolved by the Crown, continued for an entire reign. The Irish Parliament of George III. continued for thirty-three years.

Nevertheless, in the middle of the eighteenth century the Irish Parliament began to feel the faint throbs of a national pulse. Supine under their yoke, the Catholics, having no share in the government, devoted themselves as best they could to those forms of production which were possible in a country in which manufactures might easily be promoted with capital. The Presbyterians, suffering like the Catholics on account of their religious views, engaged largely in manufacture, especially in the North; and, although the land had been confiscated and Catholics could not even buy it at any price, the English who had settled on the estates taken from the native owners became interested in the material growth of a country which they intended to make their home. Enough money was in circulation to keep a healthy feeling between the agricultural and the manufacturing classes, and some of the manufactures attained such proportions as to arouse the jealousy of the English producers, who immediately appealed to the king and the Parliament of England to suppress in Ireland every manufacture which would rival any in England, and to tolerate in Ireland only such industries as would help the English market. In principle, the Irish should be permitted to make only such articles as the English could not sell to them. Law after law was passed in England for the destruction of Irish manufactures; the finishing blow was given in the beginning of the eighteenth century by the prohibition of the last that remained, the woollen trade. Irish ships, which had been met on every ocean highway, were excluded from the sea, and the country sank into abject poverty, whose depths reached the famine-pits at frequent intervals.

The vitality of the Irish must have astonished their foreign government. Commerce by water was practically abolished except with England, but the domestic trade revived slightly from time to time, and as a little capital came to the despondent manufacturers they began to appeal to the Irish Parliament to help them by endeavoring to obtain a modification of the laws by which Irish industry had been destroyed. These manufacturers were chiefly Protestants, and they received countenance—in some degree at least—from the English land-owners in Ireland who had money to spare; while the Presbyterians, who were so busy in Ulster, were strengthened by accessions from Scotland, Irish land and water-power being so cheap that many availed themselves of the chance to better their condition by emigrating from the neighboring country, bringing at least some money into Ireland. It was the Protestant and Presbyterian manufacturers who first imbued the Irish Parliament with national sympathy and aspiration.

It is proper to say "Protestant *and* Presbyterian," because in those days Presbyterians were not Protestants: that designation belonged exclusively to members of the Church by law established. It is worthy of mention, for justice' sake, that it was the Protestants, and not the Presbyterians, who founded Orangeism in Ireland: neither Catholics nor Presbyterians were eligible for admission to the original Orange lodges. The object of Orangeism was one toward which the Presbyterians had shown decided animosity—the perpetuation of English rule in Ireland; on the contrary, the Presbyterians were accused, and justly, of downright democratic tendencies.

The temper of the Irish Parliament in the second half of the eighteenth century was one to give the English Crown some solicitude. Lords were sent over as viceroys, and they selected as their representatives in the two Houses the ablest men who could

THE FOUR COURTS, DUBLIN.

be induced to accept official posts, with the understanding that their duty was to the king of England, and not to the people of Ireland. Gradually an opposition had grown bold, energetic and sagacious; while a literature outside Parliament, of which Swift and Molyneux were the parents, helped to organize public opinion, which reacted upon Parliament. When the American war broke out there was undisguised joy among the masses of the Irish people; the courage of the opposition in Parliament received substantial access of resolution, although the prevailing hypocrisy in public affairs required that formal sympathy should be expressed with the Crown in its reverses; but the victories of the rebels were sincerely celebrated with prudent decorum by the patriots in and out of Parliament.

The king's necessities in America precipitated an altogether unprecedented state of affairs in Ireland. All the troops that could be sent to the colonies were urgently needed there, and the regulars in Ireland were demanded, although, with invasion threatened by France, their withdrawal was a confessed menace to the safety of the Crown in Ireland. Nevertheless, they were withdrawn after a debate which no student of great oratory can have missed—that in which Flood appeared as the advocate of the Crown and Grattan as the exponent of the sympathy of the Irish people with the American rebels. Flood had enjoyed the confidence of all classes of the people until he entered the Irish Cabinet; from that moment he was looked upon with suspicion; and when he described the troops to be sent out from Ireland to America as "armed negotiators," Grattan poured out upon him a withering invective from whose effects he never recovered, characterizing him as standing " with a metaphor in his mouth and a bribe in his pocket, a champion against the rights of America, the only hope of Ireland, the refuge of the liberties of mankind." The regulars having been sent, Ireland was actually without defence, and the formation of volunteers began with the consent of the government. "The cry to arms," writes Lecky, "passed through the land and was speedily responded to by all parties and all creeds. Beginning among the Protestants of the North, the movement soon spread, though in a less degree, to other parts of the island, and the war of religions and castes that had so long divided the people vanished as a dream."

The character of the volunteers was unique. Furnished with arms by the government, they paid their own expenses, refused commissions from the Crown, elected their own officers, and became speedily a threat instead of a defence. Having no battles to fight with France, they devoted their moral force to coercing the English government; and with their formidable numbers, estimated to have been from sixty thousand to a hundred thousand, armed, equipped and drilled, with not a battalion in either island to confront them, they became the masters of Parliament and compelled it to assume a virtue which it had not: they compelled it to nationalize itself. Poynings's law was still in force; they demanded its repeal. All the prohibitory laws which had strangled industry and trade in Ireland were still in force; they demanded their repeal. The penal laws by which seven-tenths of their countrymen were excluded from participation in the government of their country were still in force; they demanded their repeal.

It has always been characteristic of English dealings with Ireland never to grant her any concession except under compulsion of force, and then to grant less than is demanded. It was only as a preventive of insurrection, the duke of Wellington told the stubborn dullard who wore the crown in 1829, that Catholic emancipation was conceded; but coupled with it was a suffrage law which disfranchised many of those who had become voters while the Irish Parliament was independent, as we shall soon see it. The movement to effect repeal of the Act of Union would probably have succeeded had O'Connell not been too old and feeble to maintain the vigor of the people. The present first minister of Great Britain is authority for the confession, openly made, that the abolition of the Irish Church Establishment, the hoary relic of penal law, was made necessary by Fenianism, which set out on a different errand. When the secret records of these disturbed days shall be uncovered by another generation, or when their story is told by a candid politician, the world will read that the Land Act of 1881 was wrung from the Crown by ministerial assurance that if some relief were not allowed the Irish tenants insurrection would inevitably ensue.

To resist the demands of the volunteers in 1782 was impossible; to grant them all the Crown would not consent. But Poynings's law was repealed; the Irish Parliament was conceded the exclusive right to legislate for Ireland; the trade restrictions were all removed. But the third demand—political equality for all classes of the people—was withheld; and before the volunteers could coerce it the government disbanded them.

We have reached the Irish Parliament as Cornwallis found it. It had enjoyed independence for sixteen years. His mission was to abolish it because its independence had unfettered the manufacturers of Ireland, to the anger and injury of the English manufacturers; because there was every reason to believe that, as it had allowed the Catholics the right to vote for members, it would soon allow them the right to be members and to enter the race of life on the same terms as those possessed by the non-Catholic minority; and because there was danger that when all the people united in the government of their country in a native congress, they would dispense with the services of a foreign Crown. It was necessary, therefore, to abolish the independent Irish Parliament in order to consolidate the British empire.

All representative bodies fluctuate in the relative merit of their *personnel*. No country has always been able to command at all times the services of its ablest and most virtuous sons. When the Irish Parliament, with eighty thousand volunteers at its back, in 1782 declared itself independent, removed the restrictions which a foreign Parliament had placed upon Irish manufactures and commerce, and wisely fostered every form of industry, it contained a very large proportion of able and determined men, although the vast majority of the people had no voice in its halls; in 1798, when Cornwallis proceeded on his mission to abolish it, many of the ablest members of the former period were absent. Neither Grattan nor Curran was there—the one the most effective wit, the other the most eminent patriot and the most powerful orator, of the time. In 1782 the government councillors were weak and commonplace, while the patriots had the genius, the eloquence, the courage, of the country on their side; in 1798 the government had Castlereagh for chief secretary, and a host of mercenary men whose faculties had been sharpened by necessity and who were as keen as they were unscrupulous. In 1782 the Parliament was literally on fire with patriotic ardor, and men were ready and anxious to make sacrifices, if necessary, of personal interests for the general good of the whole people; in 1798 a spasm of selfish office-seeking was in progress, and place and promotion were the chief objects of a large number in Parliament and of their friends, who hoped to obtain one or the other through their influence.

Let it not be forgotten that the Parliament in 1798 contained no representatives of the majority of the Irish people, and that the minority represented was composed in considerable part of manor-proprietors and their placemen, of Englishmen, Scotchmen and other aliens who had no permanent interest in Ireland. It ought also be recalled that the Upper House in Ireland never contained a dozen men of mark. The Protestant lords saw in the Protestant Crown exclusive privileges for themselves which they could not hope for after the Catholics of Ireland obtained their political rights; a few Catholic lords were vacillating and nerveless, incapable of serving their country and willing to sell out her independence for their own profit.

The task of Cornwallis was not so difficult, therefore, as it would have been a few years earlier. The English agents, who had been acquainted with the designs of the Crown, had ample time to pack the Lower House as fully as possible with persons expressly selected for the object in view. The borough system quite as truly as gold corrupted and extinguished the Irish Parliament. It was declared on the floor of the Lower House that less than ninety individuals returned a majority of that body. Yet so tenacious was the little flicker of national spirit which still burned there that as soon as the intentions of the lord-lieutenant became publicly known the people arose, and by their determined resistance kept the imperial corruptionists at bay for more than a year.

Cornwallis's description of the men who were at that time foremost under English protection in ruining Ireland is the best possible explanation of his final victory in buying them up and destroying the legislative body which was cursed by their presence. On July 8, 1798, he writes to the duke of Portland as follows, the letter being marked "private and confidential" (his allusion to the rebels needs no comment): "The principal persons in this country and the members of both Houses of Parliament are in general averse to all acts of clemency, and although they do not express, and are perhaps too much heated to see, the ultimate effect which their violence must produce, would pursue measures that could only terminate in the extirpation of the greater number of the inhabitants and in the utter destruction of the country. The words 'papists' and 'priests' are for ever in their mouths, and by their unaccountable policy they would drive four-fifths of the community into irreconcilable rebellion. . . . I should be very ungrateful if I did not acknowledge the obligations I owe to Lord Castlereagh, whose abilities, temper and judgment have been of the greatest use to me, and who has on every occasion shown his sincere and unprejudiced attachment to the general interests of the British empire." At other times the noble lord wrote of Castlereagh, "He is so cold that nothing can warm him;" but when he wished to give him a persuasive recommendation to the favor of the imperial government he pleaded that he knew no favors were for the

Irish, but that an exception should be made in the case of Castlereagh: "he is so very unlike an Irishman." When the news of the arch-traitor's suicide was spread it was another English lord (Byron) who wrote:

> "So he has cut his throat at last! He? who?
> The man who cut his country's long ago."

In a letter to Pitt dated July 20, Cornwallis makes the first avowal of his chief business in Ireland. He informs the minister that he does not see at that moment the most distant encouragement for the project. A few days later he tells Ross that there is no law in the country except martial law, and that numberless murders are committed by his people without any process or examination. His yeomanry, he adds, "are in the style of the loyalists of America, only more numerous and powerful and a thousand times more ferocious." Many letters are full of the loathsome details of betrayals of the rebels, of the sums paid informers, the artifices resorted to to obtain the secrets of suspects, and the rewards held out to the base and the infamous. In August, Cornwallis issued general orders appealing to the regimental officers to assist in putting a stop to the licentious conduct of the troops; in September his thoughts revert to the Parliament. The Catholics who have kept out of it by the determination of His Majesty must be conciliated. Some advantages must be held out to them in the proposed union of the two countries—"the union of the shark with its prey," as Lord Byron termed it. The lord-lieutenant has been talking with some of his official friends, and is beginning to think that they would not be averse to the union, provided it were a Protestant union; but they would not hear of the Catholics sitting in the imperial Parliament. This bigotry does not please him, nor does he see in it the promise of success. He writes Ross that he is convinced that until the Catholics are admitted into a general participation of rights there will be no peace or safety in Ireland. A private and somewhat alarming letter is despatched to the duke of Portland by hand. The progress of rebellion, the disaffection of the Catholics and the apparent resolution of the discontented to effect a general insurrection convince Cornwallis that if the union be not speedily accomplished it will sóon be too late to attempt it. In October, Cornwallis writes Pitt: "It has always appeared to me a desperate measure for the British government to make an irrevocable alliance with a small party in Ireland (which party has derived all its consequence from, and is in fact entirely dependent upon, the British government) to wage eternal war against the papists and Presbyterians of this kingdom, which two sects, from the fairest calculations, compose about nine-tenths of the community." In the same letter he prophesies that if Catholic emancipation is not granted then, it will be extorted at a later time—a prophecy literally fulfilled and acknowledged by the duke of Wellington thirty years afterward.

All the transactions in progress at this time are either unknown to Cornwallis, or he leaves the mention of some of them to others, or his editor—careful of his reputation—omits them. In November the lord-lieutenant writes to Ross: "Things have gone too far to admit of a change, and the principal persons in this country have received assurances from the English ministers which cannot be retracted." No information of the nature of these assurances appears previously in the correspondence, but the evidence is accessible elsewhere. Pitt writes from Downing street to Cornwallis that the Speaker of the Irish House of Commons (John Foster) had been in London, and had conversed with him on the proposed union. Pitt believed he would not obstruct the measure, and if it could be made personally palatable to him he might give it fair support. The premier suggests that the prospect of an English peerage be held out to him, with some ostensible situation. Time proved the minister did the Speaker gross injustice; Foster had been cautious in talking with the minister, and the latter was so accustomed to thinking that every man had his price that he misconstrued Foster's wariness into the solicitation of a bribe.

A week or two later Cornwallis, in a letter to Ross, expresses his frank opinion of the men in Ireland who were acting for the English government in carrying on the project of the union: "They are detested by everybody but their immediate followers, and have no influence but what is founded on the grossest corruption."

Yet the enterprise moved slowly and painfully. Castlereagh admits to a friend that "there is no predisposition in its favor," but, while the bar is almost a unit against it, the Orangemen are for it, believing that the Catholics will oppose it; he hopes that the arrangement proposed for the Catholic clergy will secure their support. No arrangement, in fact, was ever made for them, but a few favored the measure; among these was the archbishop of Dublin. Castlereagh closes this letter with an important statement: "The principal provincial newspapers have been secured, and every attention will be paid to the press generally." November 27, Cornwallis writes a secret letter to the duke of Portland, describing minutely the steps he had felt it his "duty to make in consequence of Your Grace's despatch enclosing heads of a union between the two kingdoms;" and the steps must have been humiliating enough to a man of Cornwallis's professed disgust for such atrocious business. He summarizes the results of his approaching "the most leading characters" on the subject: Lord Shannon is favorable, but will not declare himself openly until he sees that his doing so "can answer some purpose;" "Lord Ely (relying on the Crown in a matter personal to himself) is prepared to give it his utmost support;" Lord Yelverton had no hesitation about it: he was made Viscount Avonmore; Lord Perry would not pledge himself against it: he had a government pension of three thousand pounds a year.

In December, Cornwallis writes to the duke of Portland that Speaker Foster and Sir John Parnell, chancellor of the exchequer—the great-grandfather of Charles Stewart Parnell—are still in London, and that he hopes they will not have left it before Castlereagh shall arrive there: "Some of the king's Irish servants appear to be the most impracticable in their opinions, and I feel confident that Your Grace will leave no means untried to impress these gentlemen more favorably before their return to this kingdom." The plain hint was not lost—with what result, the final record will show. Lord Castlereagh bore a letter to Pitt in which Cornwallis declared: "That every man in this most corrupt country should consider the important question before us in no other point of view than as it may be likely to promote his private objects of ambition or avarice will not surprise you"—an allegation true as to Pitt, who proceeded solely on that assumption, for he was not silly enough to believe that any man of sound sense in Ireland would be moved by other motives than avarice or ambition in betraying the right of his country to make her own laws under a British constitution guaranteeing her that right. But it was a careless exaggeration on the part of Cornwallis: he approached men whom he could not corrupt. A great meeting of the bar held that month revealed the fact that only thirty-two were in favor of the measure, while five times as many opposed it; and of those thirty-two, five only were left without government appointment. It is not unlikely that the five had been won by what Barrington calls "simple metallic corruption." Intimidation was tried with more or less success on those who were exceptionally dangerous; in the beginning of the year 1799 it was even proposed to disgown Saurin, one of the ablest Protestant lawyers. The threat was not carried out; and after the union had been consummated he accepted the office of attorney-general for Ireland, and prosecuted Sheil energetically for speeches not half so "treasonable" in behalf of Catholic emancipation as his own had been against the union. Plunkett, another of the patriots of the bar of 1799, accepted the office of solicitor-general soon after the passage of the act: it was he who prosecuted Robert Emmet.

That "simple metallic corruption" was being carried boldly on there was no attempt to conceal in government circles. January 10, Castlereagh acknowledges the receipt of five thousand pounds from the English secret-service fund, and adds: "Arrangements with a view to further communications of the same nature will be highly advantageous, and the duke of Portland may depend on their being carefully applied." Cornwallis was busy trying to make converts among those then holding positions under the government. He writes to the duke of Portland that, finding Sir John Parnell determined not to support the union, "I have notified to him his dismission from the office of chancellor of the exchequer, and I shall pursue the same line of conduct without favor or partiality whenever I may think it will tend to promote the success of the measure."

Cornwallis may have had occasion to deeply regret his failure to corrupt Parnell; for after the first test vote in the Commons—which was a great surprise to the government—the lord-lieutenant writes to the duke of Portland: "I have now only to express my sincere regret to Your Grace that the prejudices prevailing amongst the members of the Commons, countenanced and encouraged as they have been by the Speaker and Sir John Parnell, are infinitely too strong to afford me any prospect of bringing this measure, with any chance of success, into discussion in the course of the present session."

The test vote should not have so deeply discouraged Cornwallis. It is thus analyzed by Barrington: The House was composed of three hundred, of whom eighty-four were absent. Of the two hundred and sixteen who voted, one hundred and eleven were against the government; and of the one hundred and five who voted with it, sixty-nine were holding government offices, nineteen were rewarded with office, one was openly bought during debate, and thirteen were created peers or their wives were made peeresses for their votes. Three were supposed to be uninfluenced. The absentees were presumably against the union; were they for it, the government could have required their attendance. Castlereagh addressed himself assiduously to corrupting them during the recess; and when the question came up again in the following year, forty-three of the eighty-four voted for the union.

It is difficult to determine who were the more astonished at the result of the test vote, the government or the people; but the joy of the latter exceeded the dismay of the former. The weak *personnel* of the Parliament, the unblushing effrontery with which bribery had been carried on in and out of its halls, the pertinacity with which Castlereagh was known to continue his efforts in any given direction, and the vast power of the British empire—which was understood to be at the service of the corrupters—had naturally driven the masses of the people into the conviction that the scheme must succeed. Its failure inspired the drooping country with wild enthusiasm, which vented itself in all forms of popular demonstration. Grattan was unquestionably accurate when he said "that the whole unbribed intellect of Ireland" was opposed to the union. But the government agents returned to their work resolved to accomplish after the recess what they had not won before it. They first secured the absentees; they then elaborated a gigantic fraud on the Catholics by circulating the information that although, for obviously politic reasons, no pledge would be publicly made to the clergy, the imperial government, after the passage of the act, would provide for the payment of the Catholic priesthood on the same terms as those enjoyed by the clergy of the Established Church, and a like lure was cast about the dissenters. There is not the least doubt that Cornwallis honestly desired that this assurance should be in good faith, and there is ample testimony that he was authorized by Pitt and his associates to make it. But after the union was an accomplished fact the pledge was broken; the king positively affirmed that he had never been spoken to on the subject, and would never have consented to it had he been; and, in consequence of what Pitt affected to consider for a moment dishonor at the king's hands, he resigned, only to again accept office soon afterward.

It is certain that Cornwallis was adroit enough to secure the support of a very large number of Catholics and the silence of the rest, and that the enterprise was thus substantially forwarded. But he did not rely on promises from those who had no votes: he continued to buy those who had. A bill was audaciously introduced by Castlereagh providing what he euphemistically termed "compensation" for those who would lose their seats by the Act of Union. His terms were generous enough: every aristocrat who returned members was to receive in cash fifteen thousand pounds for each member, every member who had purchased a seat should have his money refunded from the Irish treasury, and every member who was in any manner a loser by the union should

ROYAL EXCHANGE AND ENTRANCE TO CASTLE, DUBLIN.

be amply repaid. The amount drawn from the people of Ireland in taxes for this shameless proceeding was fixed by the secretary at seven million five hundred thousand dollars. Thus did the English agent actually make the Irish people pay out of their own pockets the bribes by which their servants were induced to betray them to their enemies! A parallel for this deed will be sought in vain in ancient or in modern history.

The passage of the bill showed that the government had actually secured a majority, although a small one, and the patriots became disheartened. In their distress they appealed to the absent Grattan to return to the House and once again lift up the mighty voice which eighteen years before had won the independence of the now-degenerate body. The reappearance of the venerable statesman on the floor of the House at the most critical juncture which had occurred since his withdrawal from politics furnishes an illustration of the manner in which "history" is made.

First we have the intimation from Cornwallis (the date is January 15, 1800): "Grattan, I hear, is to be introduced after twelve to-night, until which period the debate is to be prolonged. I pity from my soul Lord Castlereagh, but he shall have something more than helpless pity from me. . . . Grattan has, you know, the confidence of forty thousand pikemen." The next day Cornwallis wrote to Portland that Grattan took his seat at seven in the morning, having been elected for Wicklow at midnight: "He appeared weak in health, but had sufficient strength to deliver a very inflammatory speech of an hour and a half sitting." The biographer of the lord-lieutenant thus describes the scene: "The election had been timed by Mr. Grattan's friends so as to prevent his taking his seat until the unusual hour mentioned above, when he was supported in to the House apparently in a fainting state. . . . The scene was well gotten up, but the trick was too palpable and produced little effect." The truth was that Cornwallis and Castlereagh, profoundly dreading the influence of Grattan, had resorted to all possible devices to prevent his election, and the writ was withheld until the last moment the law allowed; it was only by waking up the proper officer after midnight that the return was gotten to Parliament at seven in the morning. The allegation that Grattan's entrance at that time was a bit of theatricalism invented by him or by his friends is therefore a mere falsehood. Instead of appearing a "palpable trick," his arrival is pronounced by Barrington, who was present, "electric." Grattan, he says, was reduced almost to the appearance of a spectre. "As he feebly tottered into the House to his seat every member simultaneously rose from his seat." Would they, corrupt and incorrupt, have so risen in homage to a "palpable trick"? "He moved slowly to the table; his languid countenance seemed to revive as he took those oaths that restored him to his pre-eminent station; the smile of inward satisfaction obviously illuminated his features, and reanimation and energy seemed to kindle by the labor of his mind." Almost breathless, amid the deep silence Grattan attempted to rise, but could not keep his feet. He was given permission to remain in his chair. "Then," says Lecky, "was witnessed that spectacle—among the grandest in the whole range of mental phenomena—of mind asserting its supremacy over matter. . . . As the fire of oratory kindled, as the angel of enthusiasm touched those pallid lips with the living coal, as the old scenes crowded on the speaker's mind and the old plaudits broke upon his ear, it seemed as though the force of disease was neutralized and the buoyancy of youth restored. His voice gained a deeper power, his action a more commanding energy, his eloquence an ever-increasing brilliancy. For more than two hours he poured forth a stream of epigram, of argument, of appeal. He traversed almost the whole of that complex question; he grappled with the various arguments of expediency the ministers had urged; but he placed the issue on the highest grounds: 'The thing he proposes to buy is what cannot be sold—liberty.'" "Never," adds Barrington, "did a speech make a more affecting impression; but it came too late."

It was too late. Bribery had accomplished its undertaking; and, lest the people should rise up on the purchased traitors and rend them, Cornwallis had prudently increased the military in the country to one hundred and twenty thousand men. So convinced was he that the people might attempt to save by force what they had lost by fraud that in extremity he resolved to accept even Russian and Dutch soldiers if no others could be had. On the test vote, February 6, 1800, the government had a majority of forty-three; and thus the Parliament of Ireland was doomed, while the tramp of soldiery resounded through the streets of Dublin to warn the indignant that their cause was lost and to admonish the reckless that their courage would not avail. It was thus that Cornwallis consolidated the British empire.

"In the case of Ireland," writes the historian of Rationalism, "as truly as in the case of Poland, a national constitution was destroyed by a foreign power contrary to the wishes of the people. In the one case the deed was a crime of violence; in the other it was a crime of treachery and corruption. In both cases a legacy of enduring bitterness was the result."

The remaining letters of Cornwallis touching on Irish affairs are appeals to the British ministers to fulfil his promises made to the traitors, to pay the price for which they had sold the constitutional liberty of their country; and scattered at intervals between his dignified and often piteous entreaties are coarse demands from his subalterns for money to reimburse themselves or to deliver to the commoner creatures who preferred cash. Reviewing the obstinate refusal of the king to consent to religious equality in Ireland, which he had promised, and the unfaithfulness of the ministers in dishonoring his pledges, he writes: "Ireland is again to become a millstone about the neck of Britain, and to be plunged into all its former horrors and miseries."

CHAPTER V.

A LETTERED NATION REDUCED BY FORCE AND LAW TO ILLITERACY.

THE Irish immigrants in the United States are taunted by thoughtless Americans with the crime or the misfortune of ignorance. Why is Ireland ignorant? Was she an unlettered country when invaded by England? and has she been constantly resisting the efforts of the English government to educate her?

The authentic history of Ireland begins, by the common consent of historians, in the fifth century.[1] There is no dispute about the character, the mission or the principal acts of St. Patrick. It is conceded that before the close of that century a bishop's see

---

[1] "Whether the Irish had an alphabet or a literature of their own before the arrival of St. Patrick, in the fifth century, was for a long time a contested question. It is now, however, generally admitted that there is every reason to believe they had both. Dr. Todd, a writer exceedingly cautious in making any assertions or advancing any opinions without being prepared to corroborate them by sufficient proof, has endorsed this view in very explicit terms. . . . Dr. Todd also states that there is every reason to believe that . . . this ancient alphabet was superseded by the present Roman characters, introduced by (the saint)."—*Dublin Review* (1871); article, "The Brehon Law of Ireland."

existed at Clogher, that Armagh was the seat of a metropolitan, and that public schools and seminaries flourished. Irish learning and civilization have here their authentic beginning. The cathedral-school at Armagh rose rapidly in importance, and became the first university of Ireland. The number of students, both native and foreign, so increased that the university, as we may justly call it, was divided into three parts, one of which was devoted entirely to students of the Anglo-Saxon race. We need not stop to determine how many other establishments similar to those of Armagh were really founded in the lifetime of St. Patrick. The rapid extension of the monastic institute in Ireland, and the extraordinary ardor with which the Irish cenobites applied themselves to the cultivation of letters, remain undisputed facts.

"Within a century after the death of St. Patrick," says Bishop Nicholson, "the Irish seminaries had so increased that most parts of Europe sent their children to be educated here, and drew thence their bishops and teachers."[1] In the eighth century grants were made by the kings for the extension of education; in the ninth there were seven thousand students at the university of Armagh, "and the schools of Cashel, Dindaleathglass and Lismore vied with it in renown."[2]

[1] *Christian Schools and Scholars*, pp. 62, 63. Mosheim's *Ecclesiastical History*, p. 279: "Irishmen . . . cultivated and amassed learning beyond the other nations of Europe in those dark times."
[2] *Christian Schools and Scholars*, vol. i., p. 63.

Montalembert says that Ireland was one of the principal centres of Christianity from the fifth to the eighth century,[1] "and not only of Christian holiness and virtue, but also of knowledge, literature and that intellectual civilization with which the new faith was about to endow Europe, then delivered from heathenism and the Roman empire."[2] "While the Gothic tempest[3] was trampling down the classic civilization, Ireland providentially became the nursery of saints and the refuge of science. Her two most ardent passions then were to learn and to teach. In Iceland, the Orkneys, Scotland, Britain, Gaul, Germany, even in Italy, her missionaries were everywhere transplanting in the loosened soil the pagan tree of knowledge and the Christian tree of life. As the Goths conquered Rome, the Celts conquered the Goths." "There were also trained an entire population [in a monastic city] of philosophers, of writers, of architects, of carvers, of painters, of calligraphers, of musicians, poets and historians, but, above all, of missionaries and preachers destined to spread the light of the gospel and of Christian education not only in all the Celtic countries of which Ireland was the nursing-mother, but throughout Europe, among all the Teutonic races, among the Franks and Burgun-

[1] "From the sixth century the fame of the Irish schools stood high in Europe."—*Dublin Review* (vol. xvi., 1871), "The Brehon Law of Ireland."

[2] *Monks of the West*, vol. iii., p. 84.

[3] *Attempts to Establish the Protestant Reformation in Ireland*, Thomas D'Arcy McGee, p. 22.

dians, who were already masters of Gaul, as well as amid the dwellers of the Rhine and the Danube, and up to the frontiers of Italy." "This preponderance of the monastic element in the Irish Church . . . maintained itself not only during all the flourishing period of the Church's history, but even as long as the nation continued independent;"[1] and the Church preserved learning until learning and the Church and independence passed away together.[2] "They survived internal feuds and the fierce inroads of the Danes; the schools flourished even in the presence of famine, and one of the general rules was that students who came from abroad should be fed and lodged free. From Ireland as from a fountain-head contemporaneous nations 'drew those streams of learning which afterward so copiously overspread the Western world. . . . It was thence that many foreign churches received their greatest ornaments. It was there our own Alfred received his education;[3] and at what time soever the Irish gained the knowledge of letters, that period must have been an early one, and is justly set down as such by the writers of that country.'"

Over to the court of Charlemagne went Clement

---

[1] *Monks of the West*, vol. iii., p. 87. [2] *Ibid.*, p. 53.
[3] "In the latter end of the seventh century, Alfred, an Anglo-Saxon prince, son of Oswy, king of Northumbria, and who was himself afterward king of Northumbria, having been exiled from England, retired to Ireland, where he studied for many years in its seminaries."—*Annals of the Four Masters*, p. 441, note. "Alfred the Great also received his education there."—*Ibid.*, p. 101, note.

and Dungal;[1] in the court of Charles the Bald, John Scotus Erigena[2] taught science and philosophy; the life of the great saint of Iona, written by Adamnan in the seventh century, was carried to the principal churches of the Continent by many a saint and scholar who had seen the Book of Kells;[3] and the monks of St. Gall sang the psalms to music which they had learned from Irish choir-masters. The seed that Columba had planted in Scotland had ripened into many harvests, and Ireland supplied teachers to the Hebrides as well as to the Continent,[4] and on the rocks of Iona as well as on the

[1] "Tiraboschi quotes an edict of the emperor Lothaire, published in 823, for the re-establishment of public schools in nine of the chief cities of Italy, from which it appears that Dungal was at the time still presiding over the school of Pavia. He seems to be the same who in 811 addressed a long letter to Charlemagne on the subject of two solar eclipses which were expected to take place in the following year, and may be yet further identified with the 'Dungalus Scotorum præcipuus' who is noticed in the catalogue of the library of Bobbio, where he at last retired, bringing with him a great store of books which he presented to the monastery. Among them were four books of Virgil, two of Ovid, one of Lucretius, and a considerable number of the Greek and Latin fathers."—*Christian Schools and Scholars*, vol. i., p. 196.

[2] Hallam says, "But two extraordinary men, Scotus Erigena and Gerbert, stand out from the crowd in literature and philosophy."—*Literature of Europe*, vol. i., p. 32.

Interesting notes on this subject will be found in Very Rev. Bede Vaughan's *Life of St. Thomas of Aquin*.

[3] Written by St. Columba in the sixth century, and deposited in the church of Kells. It is now in Trinity College, Dublin.

[4] "We again repeat what it required all the learning of Usher, White, Colgan and Ward to prove—namely, that the holy and learn-

Scottish Highlands lingered for ages the hymns of the disciples of Columbkille. Wherever an Irish college was founded, on whatever soil it flourished, religion and learning were hand in hand, and to the labors of the student were joined those of the scribe and the artisan. Europe was enriched by manuscripts made by Irish hands, "and the researches of modern bibliopolists are continually disinterring from German or Italian libraries a Horace or an

ed Scotia of the ancients was Ireland. The name of Scotia became the exclusive possession of the Scotch—that is to say, of the Irish colonists in Caledonia—only in the eleventh or twelfth century, in the time of Giraldus Cambrensis, at the moment when the power of the true Scots declined in Scotland under the influence of the Anglo-Norman conquest."—Montalembert, *Monks of the West*, vol. iii., p. 162, note.

"Joannes Duns Scotus, a native of Down, and hence surnamed Dunnensis, signifying 'of Donn,' was born near Downpatrick in the latter end of the thirteenth century. . . . Being educated for some time in the schools of Ireland, he went to England and entered Merton College in Oxford; he became a Franciscan friar, and was a lecturer at Oxford and afterward at Paris on theology, philosophy, etc., and from his great abilities and acuteness of intellect he was denominated *The Subtle Doctor*. In theology, metaphysics and philosophy he was scarcely equalled by any man in Europe, and his great rival as a theologian, St. Thomas Aquinas, divided the literary and religious world into two great sects, the followers of the one being denominated *Thomists*, and of the other *Scotists*. . . . And it may also be observed that Joannes Scotus Erigena, an Irishman and one of the most learned and celebrated men in Europe in the ninth century, and Marianus Scotus, as well as Duns Scotus, have been all absolutely claimed by . . . Scotch writers as natives of Scotland, for which they had no grounds but the surname Scotus; but the Irish in ancient times . . . were called Scotii or Scots, and Ireland was named Scotia."—*Annals of the Four Masters*, p. 583, note.

Ovid or a sacred codex whose Irish gloss betrays the hand which traced its delicate letters."[1]

Music, poetry and art were assiduously cultivated in Ireland until the Danish invaders, by the sacking of Armagh, the destruction of nearly every monument of art which fell in their way and the prohibition by them of letters, broke up the schools in the portions of the island they overran; but with the victorious ascendency of Brian Boru[2] the schools were rebuilt and the arts again resumed their sway. So profoundly peaceful did Brian's kingdom become after his chastisement of the Danes that the poets, to illustrate the tranquillity, good order and chivalry of the time, devised the legend of a beautiful lady "in the richest attire, and with a quantity of gold and jewels about her, travelling over the kingdom without damage either to her honor or to her property."[3] Wherever the Irish bards went they carried their love for the national instrument, the harp, and their poetry was rhymed.[4] The historians of art

[1] *Christian Schools and Scholars*, vol. i., p. 75.

[2] "Besides repairing the schools burned by the Danes, and everywhere giving orders for students to be sought out to fill them with, he likewise erected many new seminaries of education for the increase of science and useful knowledge in his country."—*Winne*, vol. i., p. 163.

A chronological poem on the Christian kings of Ireland, written by the abbot Giolla Moduda in the twelfth century, is among the preserved Irish manuscripts.

[3] The origin of Moore's "Rich and rare were the gems she wore."

[4] "Rhyme, if not invented in Ireland, was at least adopted by her versifiers so generally and at so early a period as sometimes to be

declare that the Irish introduced Celtic art, which was a formidable competitor against that of Byzantium, and Irish illuminations furnished the schools of Europe with models.

Was this civilization all gone when Strongbow landed?[1] Absurd supposition! "Whatever exaggeration may have been committed by the national annalists when they speak of the foreign students who resorted to the Irish schools,[2] it is impossible to doubt that they were eagerly sought by natives of the most distant lands, who, in an age when the rest of Europe was sunk in illiterate barbarism, found in the cloisters of Armagh, Lismore, Clonard and Clonmacnois masters of philosophy and science whose learning had passed into a proverb. Camden remarks how common a thing it is to read in the *Lives* of our English saints that they were sent to

---

designated 'the art of the Irish.'"—*Christian Schools and Scholars*, vol. i., p. 76.

[1] "But, as the ravages of the Danes seldom penetrated farther than the seacoast, many copies [of the Brehon Laws] were still preserved, especially such as were in the custody of the Brehons themselves. That office was hereditary in certain families, and with the office were transmitted from father to son the manuscript copies of the laws. . . . One of the fragments in the Trinity College manuscripts (H. 3, 18) is undoubtedly upward of five hundred years old."—*Dublin Review* (1871); article, "The Brehon Law of Ireland," p. 399. Mr. Gladstone in his Mansion-House speech, during his recent visit to Ireland, had the candor properly to acknowledge the debt of Europe to the Irish schools.

[2] The Irish professors went over to Oxford to teach after the invasion.

study in Ireland, and the same expression occurs quite as frequently in the Gallican histories. Even in the eleventh century, Solgenus, bishop of St. David's, spent ten years studying in the Irish schools, *which were then as famous as ever.*"[1] As the early architecture of their native island is of itself an imperishable monument of the civilization which confronted the Saxon invader only to be overthrown by him, so the churches and monasteries of mediæval Europe, the seminaries and the universities refute the false assertion, industriously propagated and so commonly believed in our own day, that letters and civilization were carried over the Channel "on the long lances and mailed steeds"[2] of the soldiers of Henry II.[3] For two hundred years after the invasion the history of Ireland is the story of battles, pursuits and retreats, of which the sanguinary details contain the names of the monasteries assaulted and robbed—and every monastery was a seminary— of churches pillaged; and nearly every church was the centre of a group of schools. The *Annals of the Four Masters* are studded during the twelfth, thirteenth, fourteenth and fifteenth centuries with a brilliant chronology of doctors, poets and philosophers, as with saints and martyrs, whose works,

[1] *Christian Schools and Scholars*, vol. i., p. 79.
[2] Abbé Perraud, p. iii.
[3] Hallam (*Literature of Europe*) grudgingly admits that "as early as the sixth century" there was learning in the Irish monasteries, and that Ireland "both drew students from the Continent and sent forth men of comparative eminence into its schools and churches."

being in their native tongue, are now popularly unknown. Instead of the Saxon invaders carrying letters and civilization to Ireland, they went to destroy both.[1]

Mr. George Sigerson, the distinguished essayist, says in his interesting *Modern Ireland*:[2] "Those who delight in expatiating on the irreconcilable race-antipathies supposed to exist between the Anglo-Saxon and the Celt in these islands appear incapable of imagining a time when such feelings were unknown." But that time was prior to the invasion of Ireland for conquest and land-confiscation. "And yet it happens that when the people of England and Ireland were

[1] "With this antique guide in our hands (*Senchus Mor*, or Code of Brehon Laws) we cross the borders of the English Pale, with its belt of watch-towers garrisoned by wardens, who day and night scrutinize the woods spread before them, ready to flash a warning of the approach of the Irish enemy. Into the woods we enter as it were, and pass from them into the clearings where the dwellings of the chiefs are placed. And as we journey along, in place of the savage neglect we expected to find we observe a certain order and regularity. The roads and pathways are kept clean and free from brambles and brushwood, the streams are spanned with rustic bridges, and here and there the sound of a mill is heard. The land, too, is tilled, and where the countless cattle are browsing we hear the sound of bells tinkling from the necks of the foremost leaders of the herds and observe that the fields are irrigated. . . . Now, this is no ideal sketch. There is not a single feature of the landscape we have thus brought before us for which law and authority cannot be quoted from the *Senchus Mor*. . . . And the orchard and its beehives are all mentioned in its pages. Not only so, but distinct provisions are laid down for their protection and recovery of their estimated value." —*Dublin Review* (1871); article, "The Brehon Law of Ireland."

[2] London: Longmans.

more purely composed of these races than they are at present, no such antipathy was exhibited. This fact is apparent on a first glance at the relations which existed between these two nations in the matter of education. Venerable Bede says it was customary among the English, from the highest to the lowest, to retire to Ireland for study and devotion, and further adds that they were all hospitably received and supplied gratuitously with food, books and instruction." How marvellous the after-return! They whom the Irish freely lodged, fed and taught robbed the Irish of house, land and education! "Adhelm, his contemporary, in a passage in which he shows his desire to exalt some of his own countrymen, corroborates this statement. Why should Ireland, he asks, whither troops of students are daily transported, boast of such unspeakable excellence, as if, in the rich soil of England, Greek and Roman masters were not to be found to unlock the treasures of divine knowledge? 'Though Ireland, rich and blooming in scholars, is adorned, like the poles of the world, with innumerable bright stars, Britain has her radiant sun, her great pontiff Theodore.' Yet Adhelm himself admits that he received the greater part of his education at the hands of the Irish founder of that monastery of Malmsbury of which he was abbot. Camden also affirms that the migration of Anglo-Saxon students to Irish schools was the rule. 'Our Anglo-Saxons,' he says, 'flocked in early times to Ireland as if to purchase goods. Hence it is fre-

THE UPPER CASTLE YARD, DUBLIN.

quently read in our historians on holy men, "He has been sent to Ireland to school."' It cannot be doubted that the prosperity of the Irish schools of learning was great, and that it was chiefly due to the high value set upon learning by the Irish people generally —an idea they have cherished under the most adverse circumstances of later times. . . . The system of education which preceded the more modern university system in Ireland took in the study of law, history, philosophy in a restricted sense, poetry, music and languages. . . . The successive waves of invasion which burst upon the Irish shore laid waste all the land they touched. Men could not be expected to devote themselves to questions of abstract importance, when they were annually called upon to defend their lives or protect their property from fierce irruptions. The Danish marauders, as they plundered and burned church, monastery and the habitations of chief and noble, appear to have taken a perverse pleasure in destroying every manuscript on which they could lay hands. And when the Danes had been conquered, the Anglo-Norman invasion came to engage the inhabitants once more in a protracted struggle for life, land and native institutions. Thus Ireland lost her prominent position in the ranks of learning at a time when it was most important for her future to retain and develop it."

But learning and taste survived even the successful invasion. The small part of the island which the seekers for rich land succeeded in reducing by arms did not contain all the scholars or all the schools of Ireland. It remained for the makers of penal laws to crush all learning out of the country, and an examination of the articles against education in that code will not only at once disclose the cruel and bitter methods employed to reduce a lettered nation to illiteracy, but will also make apparent how complete the destruction of education then became, and how sturdily even the poorest of the native population struggled for the smallest fragments of a once-glorious heritage. As the penal laws were directed against the Catholics of Ireland, it was judicious to take from a Protestant a description of their effects. It is needless to remind the reader that almost the whole Irish population was Catholic, as it yet is.

Says Sigerson: " Over the heads of the bard, the schoolmaster and the priest hung the sharp sword of the penal laws. Religion forbade its ministers to abandon the land to its fate, and the old thirst for learning produced schoolmasters who might impart, against the law, some classical knowledge to those who desired to fill up the broken ranks of the ministry. Thus there were schools held in caves " (it was a crime for a Catholic to teach or to learn, as will be seen by a perusal of Lecky's summary of the penal laws, given in another chapter), " in mountain-glens, behind hedges—whence the name 'hedge-school'— where forbidden knowledge was imparted by an outlaw master to illegal pupils, with a youthful sentry posted on some neighboring eminence to give warning of the approach of the officers of the law." Thus did England endeavor to educate Ireland! "But if it was penal to look for education at home, it was doubly penal to seek for it abroad, even in those colleges which Irish officers serving in France and Spain had built out of their pay, and which they endowed with certain burses that might be obtained and held by any of their kinsfolk or of their native country." In the history of what other people will be found a parallel for this? These soldiers were brave men who had been defeated in the field by superior English force, and who, rather than suffer the degradation which the conquerors inflicted, preferred exile and foreign military service. Realizing the depth of ignorance into which the penal laws against education in Ireland would consign the masses of their wretched countrymen, they devoted to the foundation of these free colleges for Irish students the compensation allowed them in the armies in which they enlisted. But the English penal laws pursued them even into exile. It was a criminal offence for a Catholic father to send his child out of Ireland to school, and there were no schools left for him in Ireland. A few Catholic families who, for some exceptional reason, had money enough to allow the son the advantages to be obtained in these foreign colleges, and who were able to risk the consequences of defying the law, sent their sons abroad; and down to O'Connell's days it was still the practice: he studied at Douay.

There is to-day one institution of learning in Ireland, Trinity College, Dublin. It is a Protestant institution, and up to recent times Catholics were not admitted into it. It has a curious history. Says Sigerson: "The monastery of All-Hallows was dissolved—it enclosed a Catholic seminary—and its confiscated grounds given in 1591 to be the site of a Protestant educational institute known as Trinity College." That was nearly three hundred years ago. Then all education was absolutely prohibited to the people of Ireland—absolutely, because only Protestants could go to school, and there were scarcely any Protestants in the country. How long did the laws then enacted remain in force? When did England give the masses of the Irish people the privilege of going to school again? Fifty years ago!

Can Americans now understand why the Irish immigrant is illiterate? It will not be fair to say that if the privilege of learning has existed for fifty years, this generation of Irish should be educated. Something more is required to make a people educated than the leave to go to school. Schools are necessary: we shall shortly see how they were provided. Schools are not enough, however numerous: the parent must be so situated that he can spare the time of the child, buy it books and clothe it presentably. The landlords of Ireland extorted such enormous rent from the tenantry—who are, broadly speaking, all the people of Ireland—that the labor of the children was needed on the farms; and if that were not needed, the parents were usually without the means with which to equip them for the schoolroom. Will any but the thoughtless taunt the Irish immigrant with his want of education, with his poverty?

While it is true that the penal laws by which the Irish people were robbed of their schools and compelled to become illiterate were ostensibly directed against the Catholic religion, it is equally true that the Catholic sovereigns of England were as vicious toward their Irish subjects as were the Protestant monarchs in whose reigns the penal laws were passed. It was essential that the masses of the people should be kept ignorant in order to complete the confiscation of their land, to establish absentee proprietary, and to prevent the rise in Ireland of the industries which intelligence and liberty would develop.

Yet some learning, some hope of freedom to acquire learning, lingered among the people, and the traditions of the culture of former days, however rude and meagre their form, were fondly handed down. "By the fireside on a winter night," writes Sir Charles Gavan Duffy, " at fairs and markets, the old legends and traditions were a favorite recreation. The wandering harpers and pipers kept them alive; the itinerant schoolmaster taught them with more unction than the rudiments. Nurses and seamstresses, the tailor who carried his lapboard and shears from house to house and from district to district, the peddler who came from the capital with shawls and ribbons, the tinker who paid for his supper and shelter with a song or a story, were always ready with tales of the wars and the persecutions. A recent historian (Froude) cannot repress his disdain that in these times—for this was the Augustan age of Queen Anne—no great drama or epic poem or masterpiece of art was produced in Ireland; but it is not on the gaolers in this penal settlement, but their prisoners, that the critic's reproaches fall."

What improvement had been made in the beginning of the present boastful century? For the still insignificant Protestant minority education was free, abundant and attractive. There was the great University of Dublin, with its professorships, its scholarships, its patronage and its honors: no Catholic could enter it. For the masses of the people there were still only the illegal hedge-schools; and it is an imperishable proof of the love the Irish people had for knowledge that these open-air schools—as certain to be suppressed, if discovered by the police, as are the Land-League meetings in Ireland to-day —graduated scholars whose attainments were far from contemptible, and whose stores of learning were generously poured out to all with whom they came in contact.

The burdens which the landlords imposed upon the people were heavy enough, but they had also to support a State-Church which they did not attend.

The clergy of that Church maintained themselves in a princely manner at the expense of those who lived in squalor and who believed none of their doctrines. Nor, indeed, were these doctrines obtrusively preached, for in many of the parishes there was no congregation. The ministers had to be supported by those who were not of their religion, and the tithes were as odious as they were oppressive.

In 1832 four-fifths of the population of Ireland could neither read nor write. English law had reduced a nation to illiteracy.

It would be rash for the fair-minded American to assume that, having given the masses of the people of Ireland liberty of conscience in 1829, free schools sustained by Irish taxes in 1832, and abolished the State-Church in 1870, the conscience and the intellect of the masses of the Irish people are now alike free. There is to-day a Catholic university in Ireland, founded by voluntary contributions, but the English government does not permit it to confer degrees. At the same time, the University of Dublin is essentially Protestant; the astounding fact stands forth that without offence to his conscientious convictions a Catholic cannot obtain a university degree in a country of which four-fifths of the taxpayers who sustain the schools are Catholics!

To best extinguish as rapidly as possible the abstract idea of nationality in Ireland, the use of the native language was made penal; but so tenacious were the people of the tongue in which their fathers composed a noble literature that to fifteen per cent. of them Gaelic is still a living speech. The determination of the English government to extinguish the idea of nationality shows itself even now more conspicuously in the national schools. No history of Ireland is permitted to be studied in them.

In spite of the extreme poverty of the country, and by sacrifices which must be heroic, the people are acquiring education by using such advantages as they are allowed: there are to-day more than a million children in the schools, national and denominational; and the tragic and exasperating story of their country's wrongs is fearfully pored over at the humblest firesides, although it is excluded from the schools. The idea of distinct nationality cannot be extinguished; and the method now resorted to to keep it out of the consciousness of the intelligent Irish youth only inspires them with a more determined love of it. If they cannot read the Gaelic of the bards, they can read the English of Thomas Davis.

The eminent English critic—a Protestant of the Protestants—Mathew Arnold thus characterizes the refusal of the English Parliament to allow the majority of the people of Ireland the same rights in higher education which are enjoyed in other parts of the British empire and in every other civilized country:

"All that by our genial policy we seem to have succeeded in inspiring in the Irish themselves is an aversion to us so violent that for England to incline one way is a sufficient reason to make Ireland incline another, and the obstruction offered by the Irish members in Parliament is really an expression, above all, of this uncontrollable antipathy. Nothing is more honorable to French civilization than its success in attaching strongly to France—France Catholic and Celtic—the German and Protestant Alsace. What a contrast to the humiliating failure of British civilization to attach to Germanic and Protestant Great Britain the Celtic and Catholic Ireland!

"For my part, I have never affected to be either surprised or indignant at the antipathy of the Irish to us. What they have had to suffer from us in past times all the world knows, and now, when we profess to practise 'a great and genial policy of conciliation' toward them, they are really governed by us in deference to the opinion and sentiment of the British middle class, and of the strongest part of this class—the Puritan community. I have pointed out this before, but in a book about schools, and which only those who are concerned with schools are likely to have read. Let me be suffered, therefore, to repeat it here. The opinion and sentiment of our middle class controls the policy of our statesmen toward Ireland. That policy does not represent the real mind of our leading statesmen, but the mind of the British middle class controlling the action of statesmen. The ability of our popular journalists and successful statesmen goes to putting the best color they can upon the action so controlled, but a disinterested observer will see an action so controlled to be what it is, and will call it what it is. The great failure in our actual national life is the imperfect civilization of our middle class. The great need of our time is the transformation of the British Puritan. Our Puritan middle class presents a defective type of religion, a narrow range of intellect and knowledge, a stunted sense of beauty, a low standard of manner. And yet it is in deference to the opinion and sentiment of such a class that we shape our policy toward Ireland. And we wonder at Ireland's antipathy to us! Nay, we expect Ireland to lend herself to the make-believe of our own journalists and statesmen, and to call our policy 'genial'!

"The Irish Catholics, who are the immense majority in Ireland, want a Catholic university. Elsewhere both Catholics and Protestants have universities where their sons may be taught by persons of their own form of religion. Catholic France allowed the Protestants of Alsace to have the Protestant university of Strasburg; Protestant Prussia allows the Catholics of the Rhine province to have the Catholic university of Bonn; the Protestants of Ireland have in Trinity College, Dublin, a university where the teachers in all those great matters which afford debatable ground between Catholics and Protestant are Protestant; the Protestants of Scotland have universities of a like character; in England the members of the English Church have in Oxford and Cambridge universities where the teachers are almost wholly Anglican.

Well, the Irish Catholics asked to be allowed the same thing.

"There is extraordinary difficulty in getting this demand of theirs directly and frankly met. They are told that they want secondary schools even more than a university. That may be very true, but they do also want a university; and to ask for one institution is a simpler affair than to ask for a great many. They are told they have the queen's colleges, invented expressly for Ireland. But they do not want colleges invented expressly for Ireland: they want colleges such as those the English and Scotch have in Scotland and England. They are told that they may have a university of the London type, an examining board, and perhaps a system of prizes. But all the world is not, like Mr. Lowe, enamored of examining boards and prizes. The world in general much prefers to universities of the London type universities of the type of Strasburg, Bonn, Oxford; and the Irish are of the same mind as the world in general. They are told that Mr. Gladstone's government offered them a university without theology, philosophy or history, and that they refused it. But the world in general does not desire universities with theology, philosophy and history left out; no more did Ireland. They are told that Trinity College, Dublin, is now an unsectarian university, no more Protestant than Catholic, and that they may use Trinity College. But the teaching in Trinity College is, and long will be (and very naturally), for the most part in the hands of Protestants; the whole character, tradition and atmosphere of the place are Protestant. The Irish Catholics want to have on their side, too, a place where the university teaching is in the hands of Catholics, and of which the character and atmosphere shall be Catholic. But then they are asked whether they propose to do away with all the manifold and deep-rooted results of Protestant ascendency in Ireland, and they are warned that this would be a hard—nay, an impossible—matter. But they are not proposing anything so enormous and chimerical as to do away with all the results of Protestant ascendency; they propose merely to put an end to one particular and very cruel result of it—the result that they, the immense majority of the Irish people, have no university, while the Protestants of Ireland, the small minority, have one. For this plain hardship they propose a plain remedy, and to their proposal they want a plain and straightforward answer.

"And at last they get it. It is the papal answer, *Non possumus*. The English ministry and Parliament may wish to give them what they demand, may think this claim just, but they *cannot* give it them. In the mind and temper of the English people there is an unconquerable obstacle. 'The claims of the Irish Roman Catholics,' says the *Times*, 'are inconsistent with the practical conditions of politics. It is necessary to repeat the simple fact that the temper of the people of Great Britain will not admit of any endowment of Catholic institutions. We should recognize the futility of contending against the most rooted of popular prejudices.' 'The demand for the state endowment of a Catholic university or of a Catholic college,' says the *Saturday Review*, 'may be perfectly just, but at the same time perfectly impracticable. The determination not to grant it may be quite illogical, but it is very firmly rooted.'"

CHAPTER VI.

THE IRISH TENANT TO-DAY.

ENGLISH armies and English penal laws succeeded in establishing foreign landlordism in Ireland: the heirs of the rightful owners are now the tenants of the heirs of those to whom the confiscated lands were given. John Bright fixes the number of these landlords at six thousand; Michael Davitt, who has studied the question still more closely, says the number is more nearly three thousand. These three thousand have an entire nation for tenants. Seventy-five per cent. of these tenants were practically, down to the passage of the Land Act of 1881, tenants-at-will. They could be expelled from their holding at the caprice of the landlord whether they paid their rent or not. Expulsion was for most of them a sentence of death.

The rent extorted was always so high that the tenant, even in the best seasons, could barely live; to save a shilling from year to year was impossible. If the harvest was good, he sold his crops to pay his rent; on a portion of the farm he raised potatoes to feed his family, the labor of all of whom, young and old, of both sexes, was required on the farm. If the potato crop failed, the family was in danger of starvation, because the money obtained for the crops had to go to the landlord and there was nothing left with which to buy food. If the harvest was bad for all the crops—and bad harvests are not uncommon—the rent could not be paid; the tenant was then evicted, and, having neither home nor money, he and his family perished by the roadside.

The rents of Ireland have oftener caused famine than have bad harvests. Did Americans fail to observe, when collections were being taken up in all parts of the United States, two years ago, for the famine-stricken people of Ireland, that it was distinctly stated by all the relief committees that money, not food, was wanted? There was no scarcity of food in Ireland. The famine was not a natural but an artificial one. The food was the property of the landlords, to whom the tenants had to give it for rent; it was necessary that money should be sent from America to buy it for the tenants from the landlords. It was only the potato crop that had failed; all the other fruits of the soil in Ireland are the property of the landlords: they are the equivalent of rent. Food was being exported from Ireland, while money was being sent there in hundreds of thousands of dollars to save the tillers and the rightful owners of its soil from death by famine. The same extraordinary phenomenon was presented in the more awful famine season of 1847, when millions perished of hunger and by fever. Corn was exported that year from the Irish ports to English consignees to be sold in Liverpool to pay Irish rents to absentee landlords.

Sometimes the famines have been natural, the entire harvests being bad; but the rule in Ireland is that famines there are artificial. They are the result of exorbitant rents; they are made, not by God, but by landlords. No land law that does not make the landlord share with the tenant the misfortunes of a bad harvest will be either an act of justice or an act of peace for that country.

The condition to which excessive rents and the possibility of eviction have reduced Irish tenants is unparalleled in any other country, in any other age. When evicted they "will cower, often for days and weeks together," says the English economist Professor Cairnes, "in ditches by the roadside, dependent for their support on casual charity." When permitted to remain on their little farms, what is their condition? One of abject poverty. Its depth is indicated by their food, their clothing and their shelter.

Their food is the potato.

Their clothing is the most meagre covering of nakedness. They rarely have hats or shoes, or a second garment of any kind.

Their shelter? Mud cabins without the simplest conveniences of civilization.

In the latest census the Irish dwellings are divided into four classes. The first are comfortable and substantial; the second are houses of from five to nine

CUSTOM HOUSE, DUBLIN.

rooms, on farms or in towns; the third and fourth are mud houses; the fourth are mud houses of only one room, generally without window or chimney. Of the third and fourth classes there are five hundred and twelve thousand eight hundred and one. Estimating five persons to a family—which is a small estimate for Ireland—there are two and a half million persons living in mud houses, and more than half of them in mud hovels of one room.

To these wretched people the land of Ireland belongs by natural law—law which no economist has assailed, law which English economists have been the most emphatic in asserting.

"The land of any country is the property of the nation occupying that country," says Froude. "The great evil of Ireland," said John Bright, "is this—that the Irish people, the Irish nation, are dispossessed from the soil." "The surplus profit is what the farmer can afford to pay as rent to the landlord," says John Stuart Mill. "Rent is surplus profit," says Bonamy Price. Speaking of those who affirmed that economic laws do not apply to Ireland on account of her unfortunate situation, Professor Cairnes says: "In my opinion, it is a radically false and practically a most mischievous view—one against which, alike in the interest of the peace of Ireland and for the credit of economic science, I am anxious with all my energy to protest." Again he says: "I have already stated what I conceive to be the economic basis of property—the right of the producer to the thing he has produced. . . . I will suppose a farm which owes nothing of any kind to the landlord's outlay, on which the whole capital, fixed and circulating, in buildings, fences, manure and wages, has been advanced by the cultivator, and I will suppose that the soil of the farm is the worst possible quality compatible with profitable cultivation. These conditions being supposed, how much of the wealth produced from the farm represents the due reward of the cultivator's exertions? I answer, The whole."

Let us see how this principle has been applied in the relations of landlord and tenant in Ireland under the laws which began in the confiscations, were confirmed by the penal statutes and have been enforced by the armies of England in Ireland.

Professor Cairnes thinks his imaginary case extreme, but not absolutely impossible; and he modifies his conclusion as to the right of a farmer to all he produces if the landlord had furnished any portion of the capital expended on the farm. But in Ireland there are tens of thousands of farms on which the landlord never expended a penny of capital, and in that country the imaginary case, instead of being extreme, is common. But with what results? The landlord rented the land to the tenant; perhaps there was no cottage or even mud cabin on it. The landlord would neither build a dwelling nor loan the tenant the money to build it; the tenant built some sort of shelter. Was it then the property of the tenant? No; it belongs to the landlord. Perhaps there was not a fence on the land; the tenant built the fences. Did the landlord not allow him the outlay in a rebate of rent? No; the fences have become the property of the landlord. Perhaps the land was wholly without drainage; the tenant drained it. Surely the landlord compensated him for his time and labor? No; the drainage now is part of the landlord's estate. Possibly the soil was not in a favorable condition for the crops; the tenant must first nurse it and feed it and coax it. Did he receive no compensation? Under the law he was entitled to none. Said Lord Sherbrooke: "The Irish tenant knows perfectly well that he has no claim in equity or otherwise to payment for the cabin he may build, the bog he may drain or the stones he may roll away."[1] And after he had built the cabin or the cottage, and drained the bogs, and put up the fences, and wheedled or enticed the mountain-side into geniality, the landlord could step in and say: "When I rented you this farm it was worth only ten pounds a year. It was not drained; it was not fenced; it needed manure and labor before seeding; there was no dwelling on it. Now all these things are accomplished; therefore the farm is worth a higher rent. You must now pay twenty pounds a year."

"But I cannot," plead the tenant.

"Then go," said the landlord. "Go," said the law.

[1] "Legislation for Ireland," *The Nineteenth Century*, November, 1880.

"Will you allow me nothing for the permanent improvements I have made?" begged the tenant.

"Not a farthing," said the landlord. "Not a farthing," said the law.

How long would the American people submit to such a law?

Occasionally there was a landlord who recognized the right of the tenant to compensation for labor which permanently raised the value of the land. But every such landlord has been better than the law. There are not many of them. Lord Sherbrooke is anxious that the world shall not misjudge the landlords. He is willing that legislation should do something for the tenant, but the landlords must not be required to pay the tenants for improvements. In refusing to do so they acted strictly in accordance with the law.

"If a man," inquires Lord Sherbrooke, "is not safe in directing his course by the law of the land, where is he to look for safety?"

"There are no bounds to the tenant's liabilities," says Mr. Thornton,[1] "and no security against his ejection."

It is desirable that Americans should understand precisely what the law has been for the tenure of land in Ireland, and here it is, stated by a distinguished and experienced gentleman, better known in this country as Mr. Robert Lowe.

The law of land tenure, then, was in brief this:

---

[1] *A Plea for Peasant Proprietors*, p. 190.

The labor of the tenant was perpetually confiscated.

When his industry turned his labor into capital in the form of permanent improvements on his holding, his capital was confiscated. What money capital he used in improving the holding was confiscated.

Thrift would have inspired him to improve the farm, but the fruits of his thrift would have been confiscated.

The improvement of the holding would give superior crops; he would have more money when the rent was paid; he could send his children to school. No; the improvement of the farm would have brought with more absolute certainty an increase in the rent. When the increased rent had been paid, there would be less money left to send the children to school or to buy physical necessaries.

"The improvement in the condition of the tenant cannot be brought about," insists a political economist, "except by the improvement of his farm." That is true everywhere but in Ireland. There the improvement of the farm made the condition of the tenant worse. His labor was confiscated; his money was confiscated; his thrift was punished; his industry was turned into misfortune. If he improved his farm, his rent was raised or he was turned off it without the means of procuring shelter. The rent was kept up to the highest competition rates in all seasons. He could not, in good season or in bad, however great his energy or complete his self-sacrifice, save enough to give his children a chance to rise above the squalor in which they were born.

It was the interest of the tenant, therefore, not to be thrifty; it was his interest not to be industrious; it was his interest not to make any effort to better himself; it was his interest to keep his children in squalor; it was his interest to be as wretched as possible.

A law which makes these things the interest of human beings is a law against nature. Blackstone, a most fervent Englishman, who glories, pardonably, in her laws and the greatness which they have produced, and which in turn has produced them, says that laws against nature have no validity. Froude, an Englishman who loves his own land as intensely as he hates its victim-sister, says: "Land is not, and cannot be, property in the sense in which movable things are property. Every human being born into this planet must live upon the land if he lives at all. The land in any country is really the property of the nation which occupies it;" which is true in every country but Ireland.

There has hitherto been slight difference in the land laws of England and Ireland, and that difference, strange to say, was in favor of Ireland. England has never had the advantages of the encumbered estates court or of its twin-tribunal the landed estates court. We shall reach these in time. But how vastly in favor of the English tenant is the operation of the land laws! In England the landlord makes all the improvements. The tenant, generally speaking, has fixity of tenure—so long, at least, as he pays his rent. Not being compelled to make the improvements, or being equitably compensated for such as he does make which increase the permanent value of the farm, his labor is rewarded and he is able to save money. If the lord should be pleased to turn his farm into park or put it to manufacturing purposes, the departing tenant cannot complain for the same reason that exists to the ruin of his Irish brother. His labor has not been confiscated; his capital has not been stolen; his industry has not been punished; his thrift has not been turned into calamity. In his interesting, if not profound, *England, her People, Polity and Pursuits*, Mr. T. H. S. Escott gives an imposing picture of the "Great Landlords and Estate Management." It is altogether too flattering toward them, for the English tenant-farmer has something to say to his countrymen when he shall have obtained adequate representation in Parliament. But it is at least true that the land laws are as leniently administered in England as such laws are likely ever to be. The duke of Devonshire, for instance, makes all the improvements on the farms he rents. Agreements are annual between the duke and his tenants, but there is a revaluation only every twenty-one years. "This arrangement," says Mr. Escott, "comes to very much the same thing as a lease for that term. The tenants know very well that so long as they do their duty by the land they will not receive notice to quit; and here, as elsewhere, the archives of the estate show many cases in which farms have been in possession of the same families, from father to son, for many generations, and not unfrequently for two or three centuries."[1] "There are estates" in Ireland "where a notice to quit," says Mr. Samuelson, "is printed on the back of each half-year's receipt for rent; so that the tenants are under perpetual notice."[2] "When the revaluation is made," Mr. Escott goes on, "a full report of the condition of all the farms and other portions of the property is drawn up. Anything that can throw light on the management of a particular holding and the qualities displayed by a particular tenant are duly noted down, as also are the improvements which it may be considered desirable to institute or which the tenant himself may have suggested as necessary. It is then for the duke and his agents to consider whether the property shall remain in the same hands and what repairs shall be effected. In consideration of such repairs as may finally be carried out, either a permanent addition is made to the rent or else the tenant is charged a percentage on the money expended." "Improvements in the way of drainage," Mr. Escott says, describing the tenancies of Westminster, Northumberland, Cleveland and Devonshire estates, "improvements in the way of drainage, buildings, roads and fences, are either done

[1] *England*, p. 38.
[2] *Studies of the Land and Tenantry of Ireland*, by B. Samuelson, M. P., p. 13.

at the expense of the landlord, or, if the tenant immediately defrays their cost, he receives compensation from the landlord."[1] Mr. Samuelson says of the Irish tenant that, except on the estates of some large proprietors, the tenants have made every improvement. They "have erected the house and steadings, have built every fence, have drained the farm more or less perfectly, in many cases have reclaimed it from the mountain or bog." Yet the rule has been that the landlord allowed the tenant nothing for all this even on eviction. "As far as the law is concerned," it is "entirely at the option of the landlord" to "make an allowance to the tenant for any or all these improvements or let him dispose of them to his successor, or whether he will confiscate them as his own property."

It would be easy to multiply authorities on the different operation of the laws regulating land in the two countries, but these two Englishmen have stated it with sufficient distinctness. In England there is practically security of tenure; in Ireland there has been practically perpetual notice to quit. In England the tenant receives compensation for improvements or the landlord makes them at his own expense; in Ireland the tenant made all the improvements and the landlord confiscated them. In England the rent is not raised, generally speaking, except every twenty-one years, and then after a fair revaluation; in Ireland, generally speaking, the rent has been raised when-

[1] *England*, p. 40.

ever the landlord's agent thought he could extort another shilling out of the tenant. In England capital is permanently united with the land; in Ireland capital has been permanently divorced from the land. In England, if the tenant must give up his holding, there are all the vast industries of his country for him to seek employment in; in Ireland there is only one industry, the land. The tenant turned out of his holding, moneyless, without skill for any other calling, can find no other employment: he must starve, or commit crime and go to jail, or emigrate.

Another feature exclusively peculiar to the condition of the Irish tenant is that in many cases he does not even know who his landlord is; in still more he knows who he is, but never sees him, and any appeal which he might wish to make for justice or for humanity has to be made to an agent whose selfish interest requires that he shall extort the highest possible rent from the tenant. Absenteeism is an old evil in Ireland, and was one of the inevitable consequences of the confiscations, as has been already sufficiently shown. The Irish Parliament undertook to remedy it a hundred and fifty years ago. Taxation was tried; confiscation of a portion of the absentee's estate was decreed. Swift exposed all its hideous features. The free—and the last—Irish Parliament endeavored to grapple with it, but the class at whom the proposed act was levelled had retainers enough to protect their interests. The abolition of the Parliament and the transfer of the seat of legislation for Ireland to the English capital aggravated absenteeism by increasing the inducements to live out of Ireland. One who has no sympathy with the movement, now going on there writes: "This is not a matter upon which one is left to speculate, for there is visible proof of the results of the two systems—the system of residence and the system of absenteeism. Those parts of Ireland which are to-day best disposed to the English government, which are freest from political agitation, which are the most peaceful and law-abiding, and in which the people are most generally enlightened, liberal and tolerant, are just those places where the land-owners have been longest and most constantly resident, and have for generations faithfully performed the duties of their position; those parts of Ireland where the people are most lawless, most ignorant, most superstitious, poor and backward, are the places where absenteeism has thrown its blighting influence, and where the people have been left to themselves. Had absentees but done their duty, the result for many past years and in the present day would have been far different. Unfortunately, as it is, disturbance, crime, political agitation and disaffection to England,—these were, and are, the Nemesis of absenteeism, a Nemesis visited, unfortunately, not on the absentees, but on the kingdom itself."

Morally considered, absenteeism is one of the most powerful agents in reducing the Irish tenantry to poverty and keeping them in it. Many a landlord who resides always, or nearly always, in England or on the Continent would, if he lived upon his own estates, be touched by the distress of his dependents. His representative has the strongest motive to resist every instinct of humanity: he is paid in proportion to the amount of rent he can extort from the tenants and send to his distant master. Absentee landlords draw out of Ireland one-third of the entire rental of the country, not a penny of which returns in any form to the country and the people producing it. Indeed, it is not inaccurate to say that the entire rental of the country is an absentee rental, since even the resident landlords have to send abroad for nine-tenths of the manufactured articles they use on their farms, in their stables and houses, and on their persons. Why there can be no general creation of manufactures in Ireland while the present landlord system prevails has been sufficiently shown in a preceding chapter.

CHAPTER VII.

THE PEASANT-FARMER IN OTHER COUNTRIES.

BY peasant proprietor is commonly meant a farmer who owns the land he tills.

"Since the French Revolution," writes Mr. W. E. Baxter, "the feudal laws in France, Switzerland, Holland, Belgium, Norway, Germany, North Italy and Austria have been abolished. . . . The result of this change in all these countries has been, in many instances, the breaking up of the large, unwieldy, unmanageable estates and the formation of a numerous and powerful conservative class of small proprietors. . . . The change has been highly beneficial wherever it has been brought about, peasants formerly in as miserable a condition as the Irish being now contented and prosperous owners of the soil."[1] "It would be difficult, perhaps," says Professor Cairnes, "to conceive two modes of existence more utterly opposed than the thriftless, squalid and half-starved life of the peasant of Munster and Connaught and

---

[1] *Our Land Laws of the Past*, by the Right Hon. W. E. Baxter, M. P. (London: Cassell, Petter, Galpin & Co.), page 17. Mr. Baxter's brochure is an argument for reform of the land laws of England, especially in relation to primogeniture and entail.

that of the frugal, thriving and energetic races that have over a great portion of continental Europe—in Norway, in Belgium, in Switzerland, in Lombardy—and under the most various external conditions, turned swamps and deserts into gardens."[1]

Let us look first at that "transition between land and sea," that "measureless raft of mud and sand," and discover the miracle of peasant proprietary in the spot where it is most marvellous. In his charming book on Holland, Edmondo de Amicis tells the whole story—what it was in the beginning, what it is now: "There were vast tempestuous lakes like seas touching one another; morass beside morass; one tract covered with brushwood after another; immense forests of pines, oaks and elders traversed by hordes of wild horses; and so thick were these forests that tradition says one could travel leagues from tree to tree without ever putting foot to the ground. The deep bays and gulfs carried into the heart of the country the fury of the northern tempests. Some provinces disappeared once every year under the waters of the sea and were nothing but muddy tracts, neither land nor water, where it was impossible either to walk or to sail. The large rivers, without sufficient inclination to descend to the sea, wandered here and there uncertain of their way, and slept in monstrous pools and ponds among the sands of the coasts. It was a sinister place, swept by furious winds, beaten by obstinate rains, veiled in a perpet-

[1] *Essays*, p. 160.

ual fog, where nothing was heard but the roar of the sea and the voices of wild beasts and birds of the ocean."

And what is the Holland of to-day?

Groningen was the province most difficult to transform, and even in the sixteenth century a great part of it was still uninhabited. De Amicis confirms all that Delaveleye, that capable student of peasant proprietary, has written of it and its towns and people: "Groningen, in fact, is like a species of republic governed by a class of educated peasants; a new and virgin country where no patrician castle rears its head above the roof of the tillers of the soil; a province where the products of the land remain in the hands of the cultivators, where wealth and labor always go hand in hand and idleness and opulence are for ever divided." And to what is this almost ideal state to be attributed? "The description would not be complete if I omitted to speak of a certain right peculiar to the Groningen peasantry and called *beklem-regt*, which is considered as the principal cause of the extraordinary prosperity of the province. The *beklem-regt* is the right to occupy a farm with the payment of an annual rent, which the proprietor can never augment. The right passes to the heirs, collateral as well as direct, and the holder may transmit it by will, may sell it, rent it, raise a mortgage upon it even, without the consent of the proprietor of the land. Every time, however, that this right passes from one hand to another, whether by inheritance or sale, the proprietor receives one or two years' rent. The farm-buildings belong in general to the possessor of the *beklem-regt*, who, when his right is in any way annulled, may exact the price of the materials. The possessor of the *beklem-regt* pays all taxes, cannot change the form of the property, nor in any way diminish its value. The *beklem-regt* is indivisible. One person only can possess it, and consequently only one of the heirs can inherit it. However, by paying the sum stipulated in case of the passage of the *beklem-regt* from one hand to another, the husband may inscribe his wife or the wife her husband, and then the consort inherits a part of the right. When the possessor is ruined or does not pay his annual rent, the *beklem-regt* is not at once annulled. The creditors can cause it to be sold, but the purchaser must first of all pay all outstanding debts to the proprietor." It is unnecessary for the traveller to add that thus the farmers have a continuous and strong interest in their improving land, "secure as they are of the sole enjoyment of all the ameliorations which they may introduce into the cultivation; of not having, like ordinary tenants, to pay a rent which grows higher and higher in proportion as they succeed in increasing the fertility of the land. They undertake the boldest enterprises, introduce innovations and carry out the costliest experiments. The legitimate recompense of their labor is the entire and certain profit that accrues from that labor." And these peasants "practise agriculture, not blindly and as if

COLLEGE ST. AND ENTRANCE TO HOUSE OF LORDS, DUBLIN.

it were to be contemned, but as a noble occupation which demands the exercise of the noblest faculties of intelligence and procures for those that follow it fortune, social importance and public respect."[1]

The working of peasant proprietary in France is most strikingly illustrated by the relation of the agricultural class to the public debt of that country. In 1798 the number of holders of *rente* was 24,791; in 1860 this number had increased to 1,073,381; in 1876 it had risen to 3,473,475; in 1879 it reached 4,380,933. The annual interest which these holders of the national obligation draw on their investment is 748,404,971 francs. "It will be seen that the national debt in recent years has been steadily undergoing the process of complete subdivision among the population of France, *the number of public fundholders having come to approach that of the freeholders of the soil.*"[2] More than half the people of France live by agriculture. Over five millions of the farms are under six acres. There are only five hundred thousand farms averaging sixty acres, and fifty thousand averaging six hundred acres. "The contrast between the land system of France and England," Mr. Cliff Leslie may well assert, "two neighboring countries at the head of civilization, may without exaggeration be called the most extraordinary spectacle which European society offers for study to po-

---

[1] *Holland and its People*, by Edmondo de Amicis, page 382 *et seq.*

[2] *Statesman's Yearbook*, 1880, p. 66.

litical and social philosophy."[1] "Of the soil of England we may say that nobody knows who own it,"[2] but the nominal owners do not exceed thirty thousand persons. Like so many more Englishmen who abhor confiscation when the results are not to their liking, Mr. Leslie finds satisfaction in affirming that, contrary to prevalent belief, peasant proprietary in France did not originate in the confiscation of the French Revolution. That a large proportion of the small farms did, however, get into the hands of working proprietors through those confiscations is undeniable. Confiscation in France was done in behalf of tenants; confiscation in Ireland by England was done in behalf of landlords. The contrast is again an "extraordinary spectacle." England is the only government which in modern times, after the decay of feudalism, confiscated land for landlords. Confiscation has taken place in other countries, but it has generally been for tenants. In the sixteenth century Mr. Leslie finds peasants buying small farms in France. It was not the lack of landed property, he goes on to say, which, two hundred years later, left the peasantry in destitution "and drove them to furious vengeance." What was it, then? "The deprivation of its use by atrocious misgovernment and the confiscation of its fruits by

---

[1] *Systems of Land Tenure in Various Countries*, p. 336. (Cobden Club Essays.)

The Land Question, with Particular Reference to England and Scotland, by John Macdonnell (London: Macmillan & Co.), p. 24.

merciless taxation and feudal oppression." The verdict of the world on the French Revolution does not lack a sense of horror; but if there be any of its consequences which humanity instinctively and unqualifiedly approves, it is the wresting of the land by the people and its distribution among the people. Mr. Leslie describes the cause of the insurrection of the peasantry correctly. They had land, indeed, but it did not keep them from destitution while their noble masters dazzled Europe with their splendid luxury. The peasantry were deprived of the benefits of the land by "atrocious misgovernment." They too suffered confiscation of the fruits alike of the land and of their labor. They finally arose and wreaked a "furious vengeance;" and to-day they present to the world an example of thrift, industry, patriotism and contentment which the appreciative pen of this broad-minded Englishman effectively presents. Is he willing to concede that the historian of the next century shall tell in the same spirit the fate of the Irish peasant? Let us hope that there will be no "furious vengeance" to describe, but that the wrongs of the peasant—wrongs which in France were wiped out by revolution—shall be righted in a peaceful and legal way.

"The subdivision of the French soil," says Mr. Leslie, "which has been the subject of sincere regret and pity on the part of many eminent English writers and speakers, as well as of much ignorant contempt on the part of prejudiced politicians, is really both a cause and an effect of the increased wealth of every part of the population—the seller and buyer of land, the land-owner, the farmer and laborer, the country and the town." But all the people in France who live by agriculture are not land-owners; there are tenant-farmers there. What are the relations between them and the landlords? Mr. Leslie answers fully and briefly. There are two kinds of tenure—by lease for a money-rent and by *métayage*, according to which the proprietor and the tenant work the farm in partnership, each furnishing a proportion of the capital and dividing the produce. The contract for *métayage* is really a lease, and usually extends over a term of years. "The truth is," writes Mr. Leslie, "the system of short tenures common throughout most of Western Europe has a common barbarous origin. It belongs to a state of agriculture which took no thought of a distant future and involved no lengthened outlay, and which gave the land frequent rest in fallow; and it belongs to a state of commerce in which sales of land were rare, changes of proprietorship equally so, and ideas of making the most of landed property commercially non-existent. It is right to observe, however, that in many parts of France, although the stated period of tenure is commonly short, the farm really remains commonly with the same family from father to son, from generation to generation, provided only the rent is paid." The tenant is never in apprehension of eviction. On the contrary, so fortunate is he in the fruits of his toil that he does not like to encumber himself with a long lease, because he intends to buy land and become himself a proprietor. "Again, although no legal customs of tenure for unexhausted improvements remain in France, where the Code has swept away all customary laws, yet compensation for some unexhausted improvements exists under the Code. . . . It is fortunate for France not only that peasant proprietorship already exists on a great scale, but that the tendency of the economic progress of the country, as already shown, is to substitute, more and more, cultivation by peasant proprietors for cultivation by tenants, and to give, more and more, to those who remain tenants or laborers the position and sentiments of proprietors." Why would not this be fortunate for Ireland and England? "France," says Mr. Leslie in conclusion, " has had only three-quarters of a century of anything like liberty, and less than half a century of tranquillity and industrial life." He wrote just on the eve of the Franco-Prussian war. Yet he deems the French land system not only "the salvation of the country itself, but one of the principal securities for the tranquillity and economic progress of Europe."

The result of the brief and disastrous conflict into which the country was plunged by the ambition and folly of the last of the emperors furnishes a remarkable emphasis for this conclusion. It was her peasant proprietors and tenant-farmers who subscribed with such cheerful alacrity so great a proportion of the immense forfeit France had to pay for the fatal imperial venture; it is they who constitute to-day the conservatism and strength of the republic. It is her free land that makes and will keep France free; and it is the well-recompensed, the industrious and the thrifty tillers of the soil that will hold back the politicians at the head of the government from rushing into foreign wars or precipitating either monarchy or anarchy at home. France is stable because her land belongs to those who live by it. For that reason is she rich, prosperous, contented; for that reason is she to-day one of the preservers of the peace of Europe and the most efficient promoter of all industries, all arts, fine and industrial, and all economic progress.

Let us go to Prussia. "A people," says John Macdonnell, "are what their land system makes them; the soil that they till is stronger than they; and the essence of their history records the changes in the ownership of their land. Frugal and industrious or unfixed and unstable in their ways they are according to the nature of their tenure of land. . . . Disappointingly feeble as is most political machinery to alter men for better or for worse, . . . a statesman has one instrument which pierces through all obstacles and uses men as clay: that instrument is legislation affecting land. A Stein or a Hardenberg who knows how to use it may shape the morals and destiny of a people."[1]

[1] *The Land Question*, pp. 4, 5.

Napoleon destroyed the German empire in 1803; the edict of emancipation in 1807 laid anew its permanent foundations. That edict freed the peasant and the land. Two years later the superstructure was begun. The law of 1811 made the peasant a proprietor; then the empire became invincible. The German armies that Napoleon put to rout were serfs who had nothing to fight for but their serfdom; the soldier of the new German empire is a freeman who has his land and his home and his family to fight for.

To whom the credit of the creation of peasant proprietary in Prussia belongs is not historically clear. It should be divided among the king and the ministers by whom he was surrounded at that period. None of them seemed to fully comprehend the scope or the consequences of the momentous step. Even Stein wrote that it was reserved for Hardenberg to take the advice of a dreamer who died in a madhouse, and transform the peasants into landlords;[1] but Stein himself procured the signature of the king to the edict and promulgated it. The law of 1811, by which the peasant was made the actual proprietor and the landlord was indemnified by the state for his loss, was Hardenberg's. But when its operation became clear to Stein he not only adopted it, but provided for its universal application; and when, after the preliminaries were completed, the law received the royal assent, well might a com-

[1] *The Life and Times of Stein; or, Germany and Prussia in the Napoleonic Age*, by J. R. Seeley, vol. i., p. 287.

mentator of the time[1] declare that there had come "the dawn of a golden day upon economic darkness, and a new creation rising out of the ruins of destructive war; never had any public measure been taken which had more happily or more beneficially united the private happiness of many families with the interest of the state."

To-day half the people of Prussia are engaged in agriculture under conditions which insure the permanence of the state more effectually than all the enactments of Bismarck. The first Napoleon easily threw serfs into consternation; the last Napoleon found a phalanx of free farmer-soldiers a wall which he could not shatter, and whose stones flew upon him for his destruction. The French army which the last Napoleon hastily precipitated into a war which the French nation did not solicit was composed chiefly of the undisciplined crowds of the cities; the huge German army was drawn chiefly from the bone and muscle of the German land. The men had their farms and their homes to return to when the conflict was over. They had not sought the war, either; but, since it was thrust upon them, they fought like men who wanted it quickly ended, so that they might return to their homes and their fields. The statement that the hurriedly-augmented French army, whose valor was so superior to their discipline and their generalship, was largely a collection of city multitudes is amply warranted by the

[1] Stagemann, quoted by Seeley, vol. i., p. 462.

time in which it was gotten together and by the statistics showing the transformation of the rural into an urban population in the ten preceding years. Their valor could have been no greater had every man been a veteran, but they fought with dash, not with discipline; with the enthusiasm of national glory, not with the steadiness and endurance of those who have homes and farms awaiting them, and whose commanders know the art of war as well as they the art of husbandry. In the American rebellion whole regiments, composed, probably, of men who had never smelled gunpowder, fought with astonishing bravery and strength. What was the substitute for discipline? The home to which they hoped to return; the citizenship which protected the home, and which was involved in the conflict. Give a man the right and the power to be a proprietor—to acquire and to hold property—and he must be the best of soldiers, because he is defending his own. Make a soldier of the man who cannot own and cannot acquire property, and he is without the highest incentive to bravery. Had the French army of ten years ago been drawn from the farmers of France and subjected to the same drill which the German troops carried to the field, with equal generalship, shall it be prudently said that the result would have been precisely the same? But the supreme virtue of the possession of property is not that it makes a man a soldier: it is that it makes him a man of peace. Property is the police of the world; it is the preserver of the world's peace. Is it not strange that peasant proprietary has not occurred to English statesmanship as the permanent pacifier of Ireland?

Shall we go to Russia? In the cold, slow and barbarous North, England should not find much to learn. Yet she is perplexed with the problem how to make five millions of her subjects owners of twenty million acres of the land on which they live. The czar, with no constitution to restrain him, with no law but his own will, with little statesmanship—for what is statesmanship but the antithesis of despotism?—a Russian czar found a way to take an area equal to one-seventh of the habitable globe, and so transform eight times the population of Ireland that they ceased to be serfs and could become proprietors. Can the Irish problem become insoluble in the light of Russian emancipation and Russian peasant proprietary? Twenty per cent. of the entire cultivable area of Russia is owned and tilled by peasant proprietors. Does any thoughtful reader of history need to be told that the emperor to whom that humane and redeeming act is due thereby saved his throne, postponed revolution—in a country without a constitution it must eventually come—and attached the army of peasants so strongly to his person that they are to-day his preservers and the protection of property and life in the empire?

Nor did the emperor create peasant proprietary by wholesale confiscation: the owners of the serfs were compensated for their land on a scale of payment by which the previous labor of the serf was estimated at a yearly rental of six per cent. Of the sum required to carry out the provisions of the edict the peasant was required to pay twenty per cent.; the government advanced the balance, securing itself at intervals extending over forty-nine years. All these arrangements were completed in 1865; from that time serfdom entirely ceased in Russia, and the progress of peasant proprietary has been uninterrupted. Said the emperor Nicholas to the marshals of the noblesse in 1856: "It is better to abolish serfage from above than to await the time when it will begin to abolish itself from below."[1] Catholic emancipation was not granted from above until Wellington told the king that it would be snatched from below; the Irish Church was not abolished from above until Gladstone saw that the foundations were in imminent danger. Wellington told the king he must choose between emancipation and insurrection; Gladstone has publicly avowed that the much-derided Fenian made the disestablishment a political necessity. In Russia, then, a czar allows reforms from above in order to take the credit to the state for doing voluntarily what it might have to do under compulsion; the English government allows no reforms from above except under stress of compulsion from below—at least, in Ireland.

Certainly at least in Ireland; for let us turn to

[1] *Russia*, by D. Mackenzie Wallace, p. 485.

India. What is the story of British legislation there concerning land?

The area of British India is eight hundred and ninety-nine thousand three hundred and forty-one square miles; the population is one hundred and ninety-one million ninety-six thousand six hundred and three. The government claims the land as its own, and has regularly drawn from it a revenue largely in excess of that from salt and opium together: for ten years past it has averaged twenty million pounds. Before the mutiny the East India Company was so thrifty a landlord that it drew one-half its total receipts from the land. While the imperial legislation concerning land in India was not uniform in all the provinces, much being left to the apparent exigences of situation and time, certain principles, it is asserted, are found to be generally present. An acknowledged deference has been shown to claims of clear title of native origin; the greatest respect has been shown for the rights of working farmers; the tenants have been carefully protected against the oppression of their landlords. The state, as chief landlord in India, has held the land, it is alleged, not as its absolute property, but as a possession in partnership with the tenant, whose right to live off it was the first of all rights.

The pen of the historian will yet point to the fact, already sufficiently apparent, that just in proportion as the imperial government dealt justly with the Indian tenant the government of the empire was submitted to, and that the enormous expenses which the treasury has had to meet for the retention of the Indian domain would have been considerably lessened had the rights of tenants been more sacredly and more judiciously considered.

If we should take the assertions of the government commissioner, Sir George Campbell, the land legislation for India has been in some provinces ideally perfect. How strange, then, that famines are occurring there with dreadful frequency! not famines of food—for the land continues to pay enormous profits on its products—but famines of money. The middleman and the state take everything the land can be induced to yield, and the peasant has neither produce nor money left.

Speaking of the remarkable liberality of the empire in settling disputes of title, Sir George Campbell says: "Renouncing the ordinary *de facto* powers of native princes, we have recognized as valid and binding all grants made by any authority which was at the time competent to make them, and have given the grantees complete and certain tenure, instead of the precarious tenure at the pleasure of the prince at the time being." Insecurity of tenure is obnoxious, it will be observed, in India. "All incomplete tenures having some show of long possession or other equitable claim we have treated very tenderly, either maintaining them or giving them terms of very easy compromise." There are tenures of long possession in Ireland in which there is the claim of bog made into meadow, of mountain turned into pasture, by the industry of the tenant; yet the landlord may eject the man who did it all, and there was no law to compel him to take into account any claim whatever upon him or his property. But the rights of the Mohammedan were most "tenderly treated," lest any injustice should be done him. "We have not only professed this indulgent treatment, but we have embodied these lenient rules in public laws, and have opened the courts of justice to all who wish to appeal to them from the decisions of the executive officers." All lands to which titles were thus procured are revenue-free for ever.

But now as to lands held subject to revenue, lands the title of which resides in the state. Is it absolute title, or is it a partnership with the tenant who occupies and tills, and with the middleman who is a kind of political support of the state and lives off the land and the working tenant?

There were land laws and customs of tenure in India before the British conquered the country. In those laws and customs nearly everything that the Irish tenant is begging to-day were to be found. There was compensation for improvements; there was practically fixity of tenure, so long as the rent was paid.

Bengal was the first province in which the British applied reform. Sir George Campbell points out that the government recognized the tenant as entitled to fixity of tenure while he paid his rent, and as entitled to protection against an increase of rent at the caprice of the middlemen, from whom the government collected the land revenue, and who held a curious position between the tenant and the state. The law became settled that every working tenant who was in possession at least twelve years at uniform rent was entitled to his holding for ever at that rent. Sir George Campbell is of opinion that these arrangements were just, and that the subsequent ground for complaint is to be found in the failure properly to carry them out. But let us get at them more closely. The tenant-farmer is the ryot; the landlord from whom he leased was the zemeendar. The state had nothing to do with the ryot except to protect him against the zemeendar. The latter was the nominal landlord: he executed the lease; he collected the rent from the ryot; but the state claimed to divide with both him and the ryot the real ownership of the land and its produce. The share which the state claimed was ten-elevenths of what the zemeendar got from the ryot. Is it any wonder that the zemeendars were soon engaged in the general enterprise of extracting almost eleven-elevenths of all the ryot could get out of the land? The historian of land tenure in India admits "English ideas of the rights of a landlord and of the advantage of non-interference began to prevail." "It has been epigrammatically said," reports Campbell, "that Lord Cornwallis designed to make English landlords in Bengal, and only succeeded in making Irish landlords."

In the north-west provinces the early legislation differed somewhat from that in Bengal, but in 1822 the regulation was adopted which is the basis of all subsequent land law in Northern India. Occupants were to have long leases with the right of renewal at revaluation, and these rights were to be transferable—a recognition of Ulster tenant right in India, although it was not recognized as law in Ireland. The ryots were to be secure in their holdings so long as they paid their rent. Ryots who had been twelve years in occupancy were deemed to have acquired the right permanently, and eviction was never thought of by any one. If the zemeendar desired to raise the rent, he had to go before a court, prove that the permanent value had been increased in some way other than by the exertion of the tenant, and thus obtain the power to increase the rent. "The course of procedure was, however, difficult; the right hardly known." Occupancy rents continued unvaried until the government introduced a new rent law. But even this did not secure peace. The principles were correct enough so far as they went. Why should mutiny arise? It was found that the principle was better than the practice. It "was found that the position of the ryots had not been sufficiently defined," discreetly remarks Mr. Campbell.

The Punjab did not become British territory until 1849. In settling the land question there the same principles were ostentatiously adopted. The tenants

HOLMES' HOTEL AND QUEEN'S BRIDGE, DUBLIN.

were carefully protected. The legislation of 1859 confers upon ryots for ever their holdings at an unchangeable rent. If any increase is to be allowed the zemeendar in the rent, he can get it only after demonstrating in court that the value of the holding has been permanently improved without expense to or by the labor of the ryot. If a ryot desires to surrender a lease, he may carry away with him everything he placed on the land which is not sunk in the soil. When the thirty years' settlement of the north-western provinces expired a new settlement took place, and the government reduced its proportion of the rent. Instead of two-thirds, it was content with one-half.

In Oude, after the mutiny, a different course was tried. The ryot was no longer to be regarded as having any rights worthy of consideration. The government was going to be a strong one; it should be a government of landlords. So all the land was confiscated, and was assigned again according to the plan followed by Elizabeth in Ireland. A judicial decision was obtained dissipating the principles which the government had professed to follow in all previous legislation. After much discussion it was determined to protect a few families who had hereditary claims or whose loyalty was above suspicion. All other tenants were reduced to tenancies-at-will, and the system of rack-rents went speedily into operation.

Campbell writes: "Already we hear of the service

of notices of ejectment in large numbers, and, on the other hand, of combinations of the tenants to resist these proceedings." And the government lent money to the landlords, not to improve their estates, but to stave off their creditors.

In the central provinces the ryot rights were respected.

Summing up all the legislation affecting the tenure of land in India by Great Britain, Sir George Campbell thus describes its present status:

Oude: Great zemeendars, almost complete owners, with few subordinate rights.

North-west provinces: Moderate proprietors; old ryots have also a measure of fixity of tenure at a fair rent.

Bengal: Great zemeendars whose rights are limited. Numerous subproprietors of several grades under them. Ancient ryots who have both fixity of tenure and fixity of rent. Other old ryots who have fixity of tenure at fair rent, variable from time to time.

Central provinces: Moderate proprietors. Ancient ryots who are subproprietors of their holdings at rents fixed for the term of each settlement. Other old ryots who have fixity of tenure at fair rent.

Madras and Bombay: The ryots are complete masters of the soil, subject only to payment of revenue.

It will be observed, therefore, that, with the exception of a single province, Great Britain has given to its Indian subjects a virtual peasant proprietary, more or less modified, or, where there is tenantry, fixity of tenure and reasonable fixity of rent. Great Britain has done more, therefore, for her Indian subjects in half a century than she has done for her Irish subjects in nearly seven centuries. The principles which she has generally professed in adjusting land-settlements in India are the principles which the Irish tenant has not been able to induce her legislators to recognize in their land legislation for Ireland.

The state is the only landlord in Bombay. There the middleman has been almost entirely dispensed with, and the government deals directly with the tenant. There, then, we shall find the ideal relationship of landlord and tenant according to the standard of modern British statesmanship.

"The survey and assessment of the Bombay presidency has been almost completed on a system introduced and carefully elaborated twenty years ago. The whole country is surveyed and mapped and the fields distinguished by permanent boundary-marks, which it is penal to remove; the soil of each field is classed according to its intrinsic qualities and to the climate; and the rate of assessment to be paid on fields of each class in each subdivision of a district is fixed on a careful consideration of the value of the crops they are capable of producing, as affected by the proximity to market-towns, canals, railways and similar external incidents, but not by improvements made by the ryot himself. This rate was probably about one-half the yearly value of the land when fixed, but, owing to the general improvement of the country, it is not more than from a fourth to an eighth in the districts which have not been settled quite recently. The measurement and classification of the soil are made once for all; but the rate of assessment is open to revision at the end of every thirty years, in order that the ryot, on the one hand, may have the certainty of the long period as an inducement to lay out capital, and the state, on the other, may secure that participation in the advantages accruing from the general progress of society to which its joint-proprietorship in the land entitles it. In the thirty years' revision, moreover, only public improvements and a general change of prices, but not improvements effected by the ryots themselves, are considered as grounds for enhancing the assessment. The ryot's tenure is permanent, provided he pays the assessment."[1]

In Bombay, therefore, where the English government is sole and actual landlord, we find, first, fixity of tenure; second, no increase in rent except once every thirty years, and then after a fair valuation, in which the improvements effected by the tenant are not made the cause of increasing his rent; third, the state makes all the improvements of a permanent kind at its own expense. The rent is fixed on a fair valuation of the producing-power of the farm and the relative cost of getting the crop to market.

[1] *Statesman's Yearbook*, 1880, p. 681.

Such is land law under the English government in Bombay. What has been land law under the Irish landlord, protected by the English government in Ireland? No security of tenure; perpetual notice to quit. No fixity of rent; perpetual liability to increase. No inducement to improve the land; every inducement not to improve it. No assurance that if the tenant spends money and labor in improving the land, he will not be compelled to pay more rent on account of the improvement effected by himself; on the contrary, a moral certainty that the rent will be increased the moment the improvements are discovered. In India the English government recognizes the tiller of the soil as in partnership with the lord of the soil; in Ireland the law recognizes the tiller of the soil as having no rights except what the lord chooses to grant him.

Which stands condemned, the English government in Bombay or the English government in Ireland? Are British subjects to be imprisoned in Ireland for requesting for themselves the rights of British subjects in Bombay? Or is it better to be an Indian than to be an Irishman, to be a Mohammedan than to be a Christian?

This is the question the Irish National Land League put to the most liberal of English ministers, Mr. Gladstone, with whom is officially associated that eminent advocate of peasant proprietary Mr. John Bright. The answer was, first, the arrest of Michael Davitt, the founder of the Land League, a one-armed invalid; next, the arrest of John Dillon; then a coercion act giving to one Englishman in Ireland, Mr. Forster, the power to arrest without accusation, and to keep in prison for an indefinite period without trial, as many men and women in Ireland as he may choose to rob of their liberty; lastly, a Land Act whose provision for peasant proprietary amounts simply to nothing.

CHAPTER VIII.

PECULIAR FEATURES OF IRISH LAND-LORDISM.

THE first organized effort to recover the lands of Ireland for the people to whom they belong was begun in 1879 when the Irish National Land League was formed. Before entering upon the narrative of that constitutional and peaceful but now suppressed organization, it is necessary to consider the condition to which the people of Ireland have been reduced by the exactions of the landlords, who were acting within English law and were protected by English armies—by armies, for the constabulary of Ireland are not policemen: they are soldiers armed with bayonets, equipped better than were the warriors of Napoleon, and drilled more thoroughly than were the English at Waterloo. There are fifteen thousand of these in Ireland, assisting landlords to oppress five millions of unarmed, undrilled, hungry and, it must be said, meek people; for what other epithet can justly be applied to a nation which has submitted for so many centuries to misgovernment without a parallel even in

Russia? The constabulary of Ireland, a landlord-army in time of peace, number more than half the available men of the entire standing army of fifty millions of free people.

It has been demonstrated by the bloodless logic of facts that it is the landlords of Ireland—who obtain their legal rights there by inheritance from land-stealers who had no legal rights—who make the famines in Ireland. It was the famines which led to the formation of the first organized movement to recover the lands for the heirs of their rightful owners.

Famines were frequent in the seventeenth century; they were not unknown in the eighteenth; and Hely Hutchinson, already quoted, describes the condition of the people in even the large cities, reduced to street-begging on account of the suppression of Irish trade and the consequent poverty of all classes. Irish famines—it should be repeated so often that the fact shall be ever-present before the eyes of the American—are not *natural* famines, they are *artificial* famines; they are made, not by the Lord, but by the landlord; they are not famines of food—there is always enough of that in Ireland—but famines of money with which to buy food from landlords who have taken the fruits of the soil as rent for land to which they have generally no moral title. It will be needless to go farther back than to the famine of 1847 to ascertain precisely what "famine" means.

The English government has occasionally appointed commissions to inquire into the condition of the people of Ireland, but it has rarely acted on their advice, which has usually been sound. In 1845 a commission reported as follows: "The agricultural laborer of Ireland continues to suffer the greatest privations and hardships; he continues to depend upon casual and precarious employment for subsistance; he is still badly housed, badly fed, badly clothed and badly paid for his labor. . . . We cannot forbear expressing our strong sense of the patient endurance which the laboring classes have generally exhibited under suffering greater, we believe, than the people of any other country in Europe have to sustain." There was no famine then.

Of the small farmers the report said: "It would be impossible to describe adequately the privations which they and their families almost habitually and patiently endure. It will be seen in the evidence that in many districts their only food is the potato, their only beverage water; that their cabins are seldom a protection against the weather; that a bed or a blanket is a rare luxury; and that nearly in all their pig and their manure-heap constitute their only property." That was in 1845, when there was no famine.

The landlords continued to extort everything that the land and all the labor on it produced. The little farmers sold their crops to pay the rent of their holdings, but they still had potatoes and water on which to feed themselves and their families. The next year the potato blight appeared. Then came famine—not of food, but of money with which to buy it. Let those who saw enacted the scenes of the next two years describe them.

The first witness is John Mitchel: "There is no need to recount how the assistant-barristers and sheriffs, aided by the police, tore down the roof-trees and ploughed up the hearths of village after village; how the farmers and their wives and little ones in wild dismay trooped along the highways; how in some hamlets by the seaside, most of the inhabitants being already dead, an adventurous traveller would come upon some family eating a famished ass; how maniac mothers stowed away their dead children to be devoured at midnight; how Mr. Darcy of Clifden describes a humane gentleman going to a village near that place with some crackers and standing at the door of the house, 'and when he threw the crackers to the children (for he was afraid to enter) the mother attempted to take them from them;' how husband and wife fought like wolves for the last morsel of food in the house; how families, when all was eaten and no hope left, took their last look at the sun, built up their cottage doors that none might see them die or hear their groans, and were found weeks afterward skeletons on their own hearth; how the 'law' was vindicated all this while; how the arms bills were diligently put in force and many examples were made; how starving wretches were transported for stealing vegetables at night; how overworked coroners declared they would hold no more inquests; how Americans sent corn, and the very Turks—yea, negro slaves—sent money for alms, which the British government was not ashamed to administer to the 'sister-country;' and how in every one of these years —1846, 1847 and 1848—Ireland was exporting to England food to the value of fifteen million pounds sterling, and had on her own soil at each harvest good and ample provision for double her own population, notwithstanding the potato blight."

The next is Alexander M. Sullivan, now member of Parliament. The passage is from *New Ireland:* "I saw the horrible phantasmagoria—would to God it were but that!—pass before my eyes. Blank, stolid dismay, a sort of stupor, fell upon the people, contrasting remarkably with the fierce energy put forth before. It was no uncommon sight to see the cottier and his little family seated on the garden-fence gazing all day long in moody silence at the blighted plot that had been their last hope. Nothing could arouse them. You spoke; they answered not. You tried to cheer them; they shook their heads. I never saw so sudden and so terrible a transformation. . . . I doubt if the world ever saw so huge a demoralization, so vast a degradation, visited upon a once high-spirited and sensitive people. All over the country large iron boilers were set up in which what was called soup was concocted, later on Indian meal stirabout was boiled. Around these boilers on the roadside there daily moaned and shrieked and fought and scuffled crowds of gaunt, cadaverous creatures that had once been men or women in the image of God. The feeding of dogs in a kennel was far more decent and orderly. I once thought—ay, and often bitterly said in public and private—that never, never would our people recover the shameful humiliation of that brutal public soup-boiler scene. I frequently stood and watched till tears blinded me and I almost choked with grief and passion. It was heartbreaking, almost maddening, to see. But help for it there was none. . . . Soon beneath the devouring pangs of starvation the famishing people poured into the workhouses, which soon choked with the dying and the dead. Such privations had been endured in every case before this hated ordeal was faced that the people entered the bastille merely to die. The parting scenes of husband and wife, father, mother and children, at the board-room door would melt a heart of stone. Too well they felt that it was an eternal severance, and that this loving embrace was to be the last on earth. The warders tore them asunder—the husband from the wife, the mother from the child—for 'discipline' required that it should be so. But, with the famine-fever in every ward and the air around them laden with death, they knew their fate, and parted like victims at the foot of the guillotine. It was not long until the workhouses overflowed and could admit no more. . . . The first remarkable sign of the havoc death was making was the decline and disappearance of funerals: there was a rapid decline in the number of attendants, until at length persons were stopped on the road and requested to assist in conveying the corpse a little farther. Soon, alas! neither coffin nor shroud could be supplied. Daily, in the street and on the footway some poor creature lay down as if to sleep and presently was stiff and stark. In our district it was a common occurrence to find, on opening the front-door in early morning, leaning against it the corpse of some victim who in the night-time had 'rested' in its shelter. We raised a public subscription and employed two men with horse and cart to go around each day and gather up the dead. One by one they were taken to a great pit at Ardnabrahir Abbey and dropped through the hinged bottom of a 'trap' coffin into a common grave below. In the remoter rural districts even this rude sepulture was impossible. In the field and by the ditch-side the victims lay as they fell till some charitable hand was found to cover them with the adjacent soil. . . . Whole families perished unvisited and unassisted. By levelling above their corpses the hovel in which they died the neighbors gave them a grave. . . . Under the pressure of hunger ravenous creatures prowled around barn and store-house stealing corn, potatoes, cabbage, turnips—anything, in a word, that might be eaten."

The English government was present while these scenes were being enacted. Any one who supposes that no government, even a government of Hottentots or Apaches, would permit such scenes, may rest assured that the government was indeed present. Here is the indisputable evidence: "*Bantry Sessions.* —Timothy Leary and Mary Leary were indicted for that they, on the 14th January, at Oakmount, did feloniously steal twenty turnips and fifty parsnips, the property of James Gillman. Found guilty. Sentence: Transportation for seven years."

The next witness is a landlord's agent. His name is William Steuart Trench, and he has written a book entitled *Realities of Irish Life*. He was a landlord's agent, and his book abounds in cant and self-complacency; he certainly exaggerates nothing at the expense of the class to which he belongs: "When I first reached Kenmare, in the winter of 1849–50, the form of destitution had changed in some degree, but it was still very great. It was true that people no longer died of starvation, but they were dying nearly as fast of fever, dysentery and scurvy within the walls of the workhouse. Food there was now in abundance, but to entitle the people to obtain it they were compelled to go into the workhouse and 'auxiliary' sheds until these were crowded almost to suffocation."

The American reader may marvel why starving men, women and children should not be given food without compelling them to incur the risk of death from fever if they escaped death from hunger; but this was another way the English government had of showing how desirous it was to save the lives of its Irish subjects. The late Earl Beaconsfield said that there were worse evils than Irish famines, meaning that a reduction of the population was a blessing. Some economists, more humane, have urged that emigration should be promoted to reduce the population, on the ground that the country is incapable of supporting so many. But it has been established by those whose testimony is unanswerable that Ireland is able to support twenty millions of people; and it is a fact perfectly authenticated that, while her people were actually dying by tens of thousands in the pangs of hunger, she was exporting, says John Mitchel, "food enough to sustain eight millions."

Mr. Trench, the landlord's agent, continues: "Several of the respectable shopkeepers informed me that at this period four or five dead bodies were frequently found in the streets or on the flags in the morning, the remains of poor people who had wandered in from the country in search of food, and that they dreaded to open their door lest a corpse should be found leaning against it." This was three years after the blight of the potato; the country was still in the famine. The government had had ample time to go to the rescue of the starving; but, says Mr. Trench, "the quantity of food given was so small, and the previous destitution through which they had passed was so severe, that nearly as many died now under the hands of the guardians as had perished before by actual starvation."

A farmer in County Cavan, who is at present visiting with his children in the city of Philadelphia, has told me a famine-fact which I have never seen stated. He was steward of certain public works at the famine-time. So weak had the strongest men become that they were unable to stand upright while laboring on the roads; many women who were glad to do the same work were missing portions of every day, compelled to lie down in the fields from utter exhaustion; and the kind-hearted steward, whose duty it was to report for the receipt of the pittance allowed only those on actual duty, was daily obliged to shut his eyes as he passed the places where the women should have been toiling, in order that he might excuse, to himself at least, his failure to report their absence and thereby save them the few pennies grudgingly granted. That the government agents connived to slay the people is also well attested. This upright and sturdy man informed the writer that to keep down the tax for the support of the poor the next year absolutely necessary food was often withheld by those having it to distribute. Each parish was assessed in proportion to the number of paupers who received relief; the fewer reported, the lower the landlords' taxes the year following. Many victims were undoubtedly sent into famine-graves to diminish the landlords' expenditure.

Mr. Trench promised work to the people at Kenmare: "Three hundred gaunt, half-famished men and nearly as many boys and women appeared in my field the next morning, all of them claiming my

THE ROTUNDA, DUBLIN, WHERE THE VOLUNTEERS OF '82 ASSEMBLED.

promise, but none of them having any tools wherewith to labor." The very hovels had been robbed to raise at auction, for the landlord, some fraction of arrears of rent! "Here was a new dilemma. The offer of employment had been accepted with only too great avidity; but the creatures had not a spade nor a pickaxe nor a working-tool amongst them." He procured some tools, "and, partly by buying, partly by borrowing, and by making some of them work with their hands, I managed to keep them employed."

The agent found that a more economical step would be to pay the passage of a considerable number of the people to America. The landlord agreed to furnish the money, purely as a means of evading the tax which the poor would be on the estate, and three thousand five hundred paupers were shipped by Lord Lansdowne to this country to get rid of them. Perhaps Americans may yet inquire by what right His Lordship manufactures paupers for shipment, and by what clause in international law he is justified in delivering them on American soil, to be supported here until they recover from the effects of His Lordship's process of reducing them from manhood to pauperism.

While the wretched victims of landlordism were dying they were in many instances driven off their little holdings by landlords' commands—not be exported at their expense, but simply to die on the highways. Mr. George Sigerson tells in his *History of Land Tenures in Ireland* that the "tenantry were driven out at the point of the bayonet with a remorseless cruelty which has never been paralleled in any time nor in any country. The transplantation of Cromwell was a merciful and considerate act in comparison with these ruthless devastations; for their authors spared neither babes at the breast, pregnant mothers nor dying men, but from the homes their fathers had erected thrust all forth, and not unfrequently in the midst of rigorous winters and beneath pitiless storms of snow and sleet."

Mr. Sigerson quotes Lord Clarendon, British minister of foreign affairs in 1869, addressing an English agricultural society: "They were practical men, and he would ask any gentleman present if he were to take a farm at will upon which the landed proprietor never did, and never intended to do, anything, and were to build upon the farm a house and homestead and effectually drain the land, and then be turned out on a six months' notice or less, would any language be strong enough to condemn such a felonious act as that?" This very day tenants are being evicted in Ireland by bayonets under precisely these conditions. Many fell behind in the rents two years ago on account of the famine and have not been able to pay up; and Gladstone permitted the House of Lords to so amend the new Land Act as to exclude these unfortunate people from its benefits. There have been at least three thousand evictions in Ireland this year, and we shall learn from eye-witnesses what eviction means in 1881, as we have learned from eye-witnesses what it meant thirty years ago.

If we go back fifty years, we find the Irish landlord the same man that he is to-day. A now rare, but to the humanitarian and the student of political economy quaint and valuable, book, entitled *An Address to the Landlords of Ireland on Subjects connected with the Melioration of the Lower Classes*, by Martin Doyle, and published in Dublin, London and Edinburgh, arraigns the landlords for precisely the evils which exist in Ireland to-day. The volume is not political, but social, and the author defines these to be the causes which had then created universal poverty in Ireland among the workers of the soil:

1. The want of sufficient employment;
2. The indolence and inattention of a large number of the landed proprietary, their want of enterprise, and their neglect of their estates;
3. Absenteeism;
4. The wholesale evictions.

This is the picture Doyle presents of Ireland in the year (1831) in which he wrote: "Vagrancy and suffering, and sometimes famine, on which hang pestilence and every misery at which the heart of philanthropy sickens, are so familiar to their experience that the resident proprietors of the soil are in general little affected by circumstances. . . . If a solitary group of woe-worn, houseless parents, followed by their ill-clothed offspring through the daily cold and wearisome pilgrimage that utter destitution renders necessary to the prolongation of that life to which even misery will cling, clad in the torn and threadbare blanket which at night is to be the only covering of their exhausted frames in some cheerless hovel,—if such a picture were only to be seen in its dismal coloring here and there, it is easy to conceive with what intensity of feeling it would be viewed. . . . But the eye of the resident landlord is accustomed to the aspect of squalid wretchedness; . . . he rolls in his comfortable chariot to the house of mirth and feasting without a sigh for the wretchedness of those to whom the crumbs that fall from his table would be a high-prized boon." As for absenteeism, "its lamentable effects are unhappily too apparent for ingenuity to palliate or selfishness to excuse."

Doyle points out to the Irish landlords the excellent example to be found on certain English estates, and then—a false prophet, as fifty years of misery attest—he says: "The facilities of steam-intercourse with Great Britain are so great that Ireland must rapidly share the advantages which every province of England enjoys." A false prophet; for England has drawn Ireland more closely to her as a bear hugs its victim in its savage embrace. Steam has more swiftly brought from England to Ireland bayonets and coercion laws, and from her rich and generous bosom it has the more speedily borne away the wealth that never goes back by steam or by sail. Not only has closer intercourse brought Ireland no new advantages from her foreign ruler, but it is an almost startling truth that it is the poor of England who have been benefited at the expense of the poorer Irish. No English agitator is in a prison to-day for demanding lower rents for the English tenant-farmers; yet this telegram appears in an American journal with strong English predilections (the quotation is from the New York *Herald*, November 6, 1881): " Lord Fitzwilliam has remitted unconditionally the past half-year's rent of all his tenants. Many other English landed proprietors are making large deductions, thus taking the sting out of the land agitation in England." Thus does history repeat itself. While Irish tenants, for whom the agitation was made, are being evicted for not paying arrears of rent which a season of famine rendered unavoidable, and while three hundred of their leaders are in prison, refused bail and denied trial, the English tenants, who have suffered no famine, receive a half-year's rent as a voluntary gift from their landlords. So in 1829, when four-fifths of the people of Ireland were still without religious liberty, one of the conditions which the English government attached to its concession— a concession yielded only because the country was on the brink of insurrection—was that the voters in Ireland who paid forty shillings rent should be deprived of their votes. This was done, and the suffrage was given instead to the forty-shilling freeholders of England.

Another almost as striking illustration of the truth that time and closer intercourse with her government has done nothing for Ireland is furnished by Mr. Trench, with no intention on his part of doing so. The reader who examines the list of Irish landlords in Thom's *Directory* for the current year will find there this, on page 750: "Shirley, Evelyn Philip, 26,386 acres; valuation, £20,744." The estate is Farney. It doubtless gives him an income of upward of a hundred thousand dollars annually. This estate was placed in Trench's hands forty years ago; he recites its history. On another page it has been affirmed that if a lawyer follows up the record of a great estate in Ireland, he will discover that its present title was born in a confiscation. Mr. Shirley's estate is no exception. Trench asserts, with landlord pride, that it was presented by Queen Elizabeth to her favorite, Essex. Of course Essex was an absentee landlord. The queen had boldly confiscated it from the rightful owners, whose name was Macmahon, and Trench relates that they had the audacity to attempt to disturb those whom the new proprietor placed upon it. Finally, Essex allowed Macmahon to occupy it on condition of his paying annually as rent two hundred and fifty pounds—not at Farney, but in Dublin, the handsome earl not caring to go after his money. If there was any evidence on record that the earl spent money improving the estate, Mr.

Trench would be pleased to reproduce it; we must assume, in the absence of the evidence, that the improvements were made by the tenants, and they so increased its value that when next the rent was raised it became fifteen hundred pounds annually; and a Macmahon had to pay it. This Macmahon was so industrious that a new set of tenants are soon found paying over two thousand pounds a year. When the third earl of Essex died he bequeathed the estate to his two sisters, one of whom married a Shirley, the ancestor of the present landlord. Soon the rent amounted to eight thousand pounds a year. Now the original estate, of which Farney is only a part, brings in forty thousand pounds a year, and it is perfectly reasonable to assume that the entire increase in its value was made by tenants whose labor, time and capital were constantly confiscated. True to the hereditary practice, the present landlord refused to make improvements which would have benefited the tenants as well as himself, and Mr. Trench was compelled to abandon his efforts to control either the tenants or the landlord, whose exactions exasperated the people at times into impotent fury.

The American reader, to whom famine and eviction are unknown, may well inquire whether such poverty, with famine and eviction, as was described by Doyle in 1831 and by Sullivan, Mitchel, Trench and Sigerson in 1847, 1848, 1849 and 1850, occurred during the past two years. The simple truth is that the peasant-farmer in Ireland is no better off to-day than he was fifty years ago.

Mr. James Redpath is well known to the people of the United States as an independent, alert and intrepid man. He bore a heroic part in the struggle to make ours a republic in fact as well as in name, and it would have been impossible twenty years ago to convince him that there was any other human being whose lot was so miserable as that of the black slave in the United States. Ill-health induced him to take a sea-voyage in the winter of 1879, and he went to Ireland to see if there was any truth in the alleged distress. Incredulous and prejudiced against the Land League, he determined to see and hear for himself. He spent the summer of 1880, and again that of 1881, in Ireland. He wrote the results of his tours there; and the following are condensed extracts from his letters:

"One day about three months ago I was riding in an Irish jaunting-car in the parish of Islaneady, in the county Mayo. My companion was the Rev. Thomas O'Malley; he had been the parish priest of Islaneady for more than twenty years. It was one of my first rides in the country, and everything was new to me. As we drove out we met large numbers of the countrywomen—comely maidens, sturdy matrons, wrinkled grandmothers—trudging along with bare feet in the cold mud on their way to the market at Westport: nine women out of every ten go barefooted in the rural districts of the West of Ireland.

Here and there, on both sides of the road, I saw, as you see everywhere in the county Mayo, the ruins of little cabins that had once been the homes of a hardy and hard-working and hospitable peasantry.

"I turned to Father O'Malley and asked him,

"'Have there been many evictions in your parish?'

"'Yes,' said the old man; 'when I was a young priest there were eighteen hundred families in this parish, but'—his face grew sad and his voice quivered with emotion as he added—'there are only six hundred families now.'

"'Well,' I said, 'what has become of the missing twelve hundred families?'

"'They were driven out,' he answered, 'by famine and the landlords.'

"'Famine and the landlords!'

"Now, if this answer had been made by one of the Irish land reformers—by Mr. Parnell, for example, or Michael Davitt—I should have regarded the phrase as an excellent 'bit' of rhetorical art, as a skilful coupling of two evils not necessarily mates, and I should have smiled at the forced marriage and then thought no more about it.

"But the words impressed me profoundly when they came from the lips of an old priest, a cadet of an ancient Irish family, a man of the most conservative temperament, whose training and whose office might have been expected to intensify his natural bias in favor of existing institutions and established authority. For the Catholic Church is the most potent conservative force in our modern society. It teaches its adherents to render unto Cæsar the things that are Cæsar's, and it rarely arrays itself against the civil authority.

"Yet I found that in Ireland, wherever there was famine, there the Catholic priest did not hesitate to declare both in private and in print that the primary causes of Irish destitution were the exactions of the landlords.

"During my recent visit to Ireland I gave both my days and my nights to the study of the famine. I interviewed the representative managers of the duchess of Marlborough fund, the Mansion-House fund, the Philadelphia fund, the *Herald* fund, and the National Irish Land League fund. I interviewed Catholic priests and Protestant clergymen, British officials and American consuls, Irish journalists and Irish drummers, Irish lords and Irish peasants—everybody I met, everywhere, who knew anything about the famine from personal observation. I never had to tell where I came from, because I asked so many questions that nobody ever doubted for a single moment that I was what Father O'Farrell called me the other day—'a pure unadulterated Yankee.'

"I shall not call witnesses from the committees of the Land League, because *they* might be suspected of exaggerating the distress in order to demonstrate the evils of a government by landlords. I shall show the imperative need of the Irish Land

League by the evidence of its enemies and the friends of the landlords.

"From six hundred and ninety districts six hundred and ninety reports made to the Mansion-House demonstrate the appalling fact that there are

In the Province of Leinster	28,000
In the Province of Ulster	180,000
In the Province of Munster	233,000
In the Province of Connaught	422,000
In all Ireland	863,000

persons at this very hour whose strongest hope of seeing the next harvest-moon rise as they stand at their own cabin-doors rests, and almost solely rests, on the bounty of the stranger and of the exiles of Erin. I have not a shadow of a shade of doubt that there are to-day in Ireland one million of people hungry and in rags—and by and by I may show you why—but I can point out province by province, county by county and parish by parish where eight hundred and sixty-three thousand of them are praying and begging and clamoring for a chance to live in the land of their birth. Eight hundred and sixty-three thousand! Do you grasp this number? If you were to sit twelve hours a day to see this gaunt army of hunger pass in review before you in single file, and one person was to pass every minute, do you know how long it would be before you saw the last man pass? Three years and four months!

"Remember and note well that these statistics are

not *estimates*. They are the *returns*, carefully verified, of the actual numbers on the relief rolls, *or* of the numbers reported by the local committees as in real distress.

"But I ought to say that I was not satisfied with the vast volume of documentary and vicarious evidence that I had accumulated. I personally visited several of the districts blighted by the famine, and with my own eyes saw the destitution of the peasantry, and with my own ears heard the sighs of their unhappy wives and children. They were the saddest days I ever passed on earth, for never before had I seen human misery so hopeless and undeserved and so profound. I went to Ireland because a crowd of calamities had overtaken me that made my own life a burden too heavy to be borne, but in the ghastly cabins of the Irish peasantry, without fuel, without blankets and without food; among half-naked and blue-lipped children shivering from cold and crying from hunger; among women who were weeping because their little ones were starving; among men of a race to whom a fight is better than a feast, but whose faces now bore the famine's fearful stamp of terror,—in the West of Ireland I soon forgot every trouble of my own life in the dread presence of the great tidal-wave of sorrow that had overwhelmed an unhappy and unfortunate and innocent people.

"The famine-line follows neither the division-lines of creeds nor the boundary-lines of provinces. It runs from north to south—from a little east of the city of Cork, in the South, to Londonderry in the North—and it divides Ireland into two nearly equal parts. The nearer the western coast, the hungrier the people.

"The western half of Ireland—from Donegal to Cork—is mountainous and beautiful, but its climate is inclement. It is scourged by the Atlantic storms; it is wet in summer and bleak in winter. The larger part of the soil is either barren and spewy bogs or stony and sterile hills.

"The best lands in nearly every county have been leased to Scotch and English graziers; for after the terrible famine of 1847—when the Irish people staggered and fainted with hunger and fever into their graves by tens of thousands and by hundreds of thousands; when the poor tenants, too far gone to have the strength to shout for food, faintly whispered for the dear Lord's sake for a little bread—the landlords of the West answered these piteous moans by sending processes of ejectment to turn them out into the roadside or the poorhouse to die, and by hiring crowbar brigades to pull down the roof that still sheltered the gasping people. As fast as the homeless peasants died or were driven into exile their little farms were rented out to British graziers. The people who could not escape were forced to take the wettest bogs and driest hill-slopes. These swamps and slopes were absolutely worthless; they could not raise enough to feed a snipe. By the patient toil of the people they were redeemed. Seaweed was brought on the backs of the farmers for miles to reclaim these lands.

"The landlord did not spend one shilling to help the tenant. He did not build the cabin; he did not fence the holding; he did not drain the bog. In the West of Ireland the landlord does nothing but take rent. I beg the landlord's pardon; I want to be perfectly just. The landlord *does* two things besides taking the rent: he makes the tenant pay the larger part of the taxes, and as fast as the farmer improves the land the landlord raises the rent. And whenever, from any cause, the tenant fails to pay the rent, the landlord turns him out and confiscates his improvements.

"The landlords charge so high a rent for these lands that even in the best of seasons the tenants can save nothing. To hide their own exactions from the execration of the human race, the landlords and their parasites have added insult to injury by charging the woes of Ireland to the improvidence of the people. Stretched on the rack of the landlord's avarice, one bad season brings serious distress to the tenant; a second bad season takes away the helping hand of credit at the merchant's; and the third bad season beckons famine and fever to the cabin-door.

"Now, the summer of 1879 was the third successive bad season. When it opened it found the people deeply in debt. Credit was stopped. But for the confidence of the shopkeepers in the honesty of the peasant, the distress would have come a year ago: it was stayed by the kind heart of the humble merchant. *Therefore* the landlords have charged the distress to the system of credit!

"There was a heavy fall of rain all last summer. The turf was ruined. Two-thirds of the potato crop was lost, on an average of the crop of all Ireland; but in many large districts of the West not a single sound potato was dug. One-half of the turnip crop perished. The cereal crop suffered, although not to so great an extent. There was a rot in sheep in some places, and in other places an epidemic among the pigs. The fisheries failed. The iron-mines in the South were closed. Everything in Ireland seemed to have conspired to invite a famine.

"But the British and American farmers were also the innocent causes of intensifying Irish distress.

"In Donegal, Mayo, Galway and the western islands the small holders for generations have never been able to raise enough from their little farms to pay their big rents. They go over every spring by tens of thousands to England and Scotland and hire out to the farmers for wages. They stay there till the crops are harvested. But the great American competition is lowering the prices of farm-produce in Great Britain and the prices of farm-stock, and therefore the English and Scotch farmers for two or three years past have not been able to pay the old wages to these Irish laborers. Last summer, instead of sending back wages to pay the rent, hosts of Irish farm-hands had to send for money to get back again.

"These complex combinations of misfortune resulted in universal distress. Everywhere in the strictly agricultural regions of the West the farmers, and especially the small holders, suffered first, and then the distress spread out its ghoul-like wings until they overshadowed the shopkeepers, the artisans, the fishermen, the miners and, more than all, the laborers, who had no land, but who had worked for the more comfortable class of farmers.

"These malignant influences blighted every county in the West of Ireland, and these mournful facts are true of almost every parish in all that region.

"Looking at the physical causes of the distress, every honest and intelligent spectator will say that they are cowards and libellers who assert that the victims of the famine are in any way responsible for it.

"Looking at the exactions of the landlords, none but a blasphemer will pretend that the distress is an act of Providence.

"Let us run rapidly over Ireland. We will begin with the least distressful province—the beautiful province of Leinster. Leinster is the garden of Ireland. There is no finer country in the temperate zone. There is no natural reason why poverty should ever throw its blighting shadows athwart the green and fertile fields of Leinster.

DUBLIN, FROM BLAQUIERE BRIDGE.

"There are resident landlords in the rural districts of Leinster; and wherever in Ireland the owners of the soil live on their own estates, the peasantry, as a rule, are more justly dealt with than when they are left to the tiger-mercy of the agent of the absentee. But it is not the fertile soil only, nor the presence of resident proprietors only, nor the proximity of markets only—nor is it these three causes jointly—that accounts for the absence of such a long procession of distress as the other provinces present.

"In some of the fairest counties of Leinster eviction has done its perfect work. Instead of toiling peasants, you find fat bullocks; instead of bright-eyed girls, you find bleating sheep. After the famine of 1847 the men were turned out and the beasts were turned in. The British government cheered this infamy, for Irishmen are rebels sometimes, but heifers are loyal always. There is less distress in the rural districts of Leinster because there are fewer people there.

"In the twelve counties of Leinster there are 38,000 persons in distress—in Dublin, 250; in Wexford, 870; in King's county, 1047; in Meath and in Westmeath, 1550 each; in Kildare, 1567; in Kilkenny, 1979; in Carlow, 2000; in Louth, 3050; in Queen's county, 4743; in Wicklow, 5450; in Longford, 9557.

"In Carlow, in Westmeath, in Louth and in one district of Queen's county the distress is expected to increase; in Kildare and in King's county it is not expected to increase.

"You see by this list how moderate the returns are—how strictly they are confined to famine or exceptional distress, as distinguished from chronic or ordinary poverty—because there are thousands of very poor persons in the city of Dublin, and yet there are only two hundred and fifty reported as in distress in the entire county. They belong to the rural district of Glencullen.

"Longford leads the list of distressed counties in Leinster. There are no resident proprietors in Longford. Up to the 1st of March not one of them had given a single shilling for the relief of the destitute on their estates. The same report comes from Kilkenny.

"The distress in Leinster is among the fishermen and small farmers and laborers. In Wicklow the fishers are kept poor because the government refuses to build harbors for their protection. In Westmeath 'the laboring class and the small farmers are in great distress.' That is the report of the local committee, and I can confirm it by my personal observation.

"The province of Leinster contains one-fourth of the population of Ireland, but it does not contain more than one-thirtieth part of the prevailing distress. So I shall take you to one parish only—to Stradbally, in Queen's county. It is not included in the reports of the Mansion-House committee.

"Dr. John Magee, P. P., of Stradbally, wrote to me quite recently:

"'In this parish—one of the most favorably circumstanced in Leinster—such has been their misery that for the last three months I have been doling out charities to one hundred and twenty families. Some of them I found in a state of utter starvation—an entire day, sometimes, without a morsel of food in the cabin. But, most miserable of all and what makes the case so affecting, very many of our small farmers (whose pride would hide their poverty) are now reduced to the same plight, the rack-rent (or excessive rent) having robbed them of every available salable chattel they possessed. I had missed for some time one of our farmers holding about thirty-five acres. On inquiry, I found that he was confined to his house for want of clothing, and that he had eaten his last potatoes and the only fowl left on the place. To add to his misery, the rack-warner had waited on him the day before to come in with his rent. In the past week I gave stealthily to one of our farmers—holding over sixty acres of land, and who used to have a stock of eighteen or twenty milch-cows—a bag of Indian meal to save his family from starvation. The man, with tears in his eyes, told me that "his children had not eaten a morsel for the last twenty-four hours;" and I believed him. Of the two hundred and forty families in my parish, one-fifth of them are in the same miserable condition —without food, without stock, without seed for the land, without credit, and without any possible hope from the justice or the sympathy of the English government.'

"Father Magee is not only a good Irish priest, but a profound student of Irish history. Will you let me read to you what he wrote to me about the causes of Irish famines?

"'If I were asked,' he wrote, 'Why is it that Ireland is so poor, with abundance of foreign grain and food in our ports? Whence this famine that alarms even the stranger? my answer would be, "Speak as we may of short and scanty harvests, the real cause is landlords' exactions, which drain the land of money, and which leave nothing to buy corn. Landlord absolutism and unrestrained rack-rents have always been, and are at present, the bane and the curse of Ireland. If the harvest be good, landlordism luxuriates and abstracts all; if scanty or bad, landlordism seizes on the rood or cattle for the rack-rent."

"'I have in my own parish,' he says, 'five or six landlords—not the worst type of their class—two of them of Cromwellian descent, a third an Elizabethan, all enjoying the confiscated estates of the O'Moores, O'Lalors and O'Kellys, whose sons are now the miserable tenants of these estates—tenants who are paying, or trying to pay, forty, eighty, and in some cases one hundred and twenty, per cent. over the government valuation of the land; tenants who are treated as slaves and starved as beggars. If these tenants gainsay the will of the landlord, or even complain, they are victimized on the spot. This land system pays over, from the sweat and toil of our inhabitants, ninety million dollars yearly to six or seven thousand landlords who do nothing but hunt a fox or hunt the tenantry.

"'The [British] government, that upholds this cruel system, abstracts thirty-five millions more from the land in imperial taxation, while there is left for the food, clothing and subsistence of five millions of people not more than fifty million dollars, or about ten dollars per head, yearly.

"'This is the system,' says Father Magee, 'that produces our periodical famines; which shames and degrades us before Europe; which presents us periodically before the world as mendicants, and beggars before the nations. . . . And will any one blame us, cost what it may, if we are resolved to get rid of a system that has so long enslaved our people?'

"It was in this province that I gained my first personal knowledge of the fierce celerity with which the Irish landlords in years of distress rally to the assistance—*not* of their tenants, but the famine. I went down from Dublin to attend an indignation-meeting over an eviction in the parish of Ballybrophy, near Knockaroo, in Queen's county.

"As we drove from the railway-station I noticed that three men jumped into a jaunting-car and followed us. I asked my companion if he knew who they were. 'Oh yes,' he said; 'it is a magistrate and two short-hand writers paid by the government. They follow us wherever we go, to get evidence of seditious language to try and convict us; they have constabulary with loaded muskets at all our meetings: they think they can overawe me, but they only exasperate me.' It was Michael Davitt. .

"Sure enough, when we got to the meeting there was a platoon of armed constabulary at it. No one pretended that there was any risk of a riot at Ballybrophy, for everybody there belonged to the same party. Next week a party of Orangemen threatened in advance to break up a meeting of the Land League in a county in Ulster. Not a constable was sent there, and the Orange rioters were allowed to disperse the audience and shed the blood of peaceful citizens.

"Why was this meeting called at Ballybrophy? Malachi Kelly, a decent old man with a wife and five children, had been turned out of his house into the road by his landlord, a person of the name of Erasmus Dickson Barrows. Mr. Kelly had paid his rent without failing once for thirty consecutive years. All his life long he had borne the reputation of an honest and temperate and industrious man.

"His rent at first was five hundred and thirty-five dollars a year. He made improvements at his own cost; the rent was instantly raised to six hundred and forty dollars. The landlord solemnly promised not to raise the rent again, and to make some improvements that were needed. Relying on this pledge, Mr. Kelly spent fifteen hundred dollars in erecting permanent buildings in 1873; the landlord instantly raised the rent again—this time to seven hundred and seventy-five dollars. In other words, he fined Mr. Kelly one hundred and ten dollars a year for the folly of believing a landlord's pledge and for the offence of increasing the value of his landlord's estate. Last season Mr. Kelly's crop was a total failure, and the old man could not pay the rent, for the first time in his life; so he was turned out in his old age, homeless and penniless, and the buildings that he had erected at his own cost became the property of his landlord.

"Michael Davitt made a speech on this eviction, and I did not notice that the loaded muskets of the constabulary overawed him.

"I am a Protestant of Protestantism. I conciliate nobody, and I ask favors of no man; but I hate with a hatred inextinguishable every form of oppression, and I shall strike at it in the future, as I have done in the past, without waiting to inquire its name or to look at its flag.

"In the province of Ulster, on the first day of March last, the local committees of the Mansion-House, one hundred and thirty-one in number, reported that there were in distress, in eight counties, 160,880 persons—in Antrim, 220; in Down, 800; in Armagh, 10,455; in Monaghan, 7447; in Cavan, 34,709; in Fermanagh, 12,768; in Tyrone, 7447; in Donegal, 87,034. Fourteen of the Ulster committees report that the distress is likely or certain to increase. The most moderate estimate, therefore, of the army of hunger in the province of Ulster, including the county of Londonderry, would put the figures at one hundred and eighty thousand. It is more probably two hundred thousand.

"Yet this vast aggregation of human misery exists in a province in which the Belfast manufactories employ large numbers of boys and girls, and so to a considerable extent relieve the agricultural classes, both by sending back wages to the cabins in the country and by affording a home market for their produce. And in justice to the Catholic provinces let it be remembered that the reason why there are no manufactories in Connaught and Munster is because the English Parliament for several generations by positive legislation prevented their establishment, and because, since these infamous laws were repealed, their disastrous results have been conserved by combinations among the English manufacturers.

"Listen to a report of how one landlord, 'a noble lord,' helped the distress on his own estates in the county Cavan.

"It is the Rev. Father Joseph Flood who speaks: 'In the midst of cries of distress around me, while Protestants and Catholics, here as elsewhere, are struggling to keep together the bodies and souls of this year's visitation, I was hurried off to witness the heartless eviction of five whole families—thirty souls in all—of ages varying from eighty years to two years. At twelve o'clock to-day, in the midst of a drenching rain, when every man's lips are busy discussing how relief can be carried to this home and that, an imposing spectacle presented itself through a quiet part of the parish of King's Court. A carriage containing Mr. Hussey, Jr., son of the agent of Lord Gormanston; behind and before it about a dozen outside cars, with a resident magistrate, an inspector of police, about forty of Her Majesty's force, the sheriff and some dozens of as rapacious-looking drivers and grippers as I ever laid my eyes upon. There is a dead silence at the halt before the first doomed door. That silence was broken by myself, craving to let the poor people in again after the vindication of the law. The sheriff formally asks,

"'" Have you the rent?"

"'The trembling answer is,

"'" My God! how could I have the whole rent—and such a rent!—on such a soil in such a year as this?"

"'" Get out!" is the word, and right heartily the grippers set to work. On the dung-heap is flung the scanty furniture, bed and bedding. The door is nailed. The imposing army marches on to the next holding, till every house has been visited and every soul turned out.

"'At this moment there is a downpour of rain on that poor bed and bedding and on that miserable furniture, and an old man whose generations have passed their simple lives in that house is sitting on a stone outside with his head buried in his hands thinking of the eighty-three years gone by. And are these tenants to blame? No! It is on the records of this parish that they were the most simple-minded, hard-working, honest and virtuous people in it.'

"This is the sort of contribution that the landlords have made to the distress in the province of Ulster.

"Let us now, in spirit, take the shoes from off our feet as we draw nigh the holy ground of Connaught and Munster. There is nothing on this earth more sacred than human sorrow. Christianity itself has been called the worship of sorrow. If this definition be a true one, then the Holy Land of our day is the West of Ireland. Every sod there has been wet with human tears. The murmurs of every rippling brook there, from time out of mind, have been accompanied by an invisible chorus of sighs from breaking human hearts. Every breeze that has swept across her barren moors has carried with it to the summits of her bleak mountain-slopes (and I trust far beyond them) the groans and the prayers of a brave but a despairing people. The sun has never set on her sorrows excepting to give place to the pitying stars that have looked down on human woes that excel in number their own constellated hosts.

"I have heard so much and I have seen so much of the sorrows of the West that when the memory of them rises up before me I stand appalled at the vision. Again and again since I came back from Ireland I have tried to paint a picture of Western misery; but again and again and as often as I have tried—even in the solitude of my chamber, where no human eye could see me—I have broken down, and I have wept like a woman. If I could put the picture into words, I could not utter the words, for I cannot look on human sorrow with the cold and æsthetic eye of an artist. To me a once-stalwart peasant shivering in rags and gaunt and hollow-voiced and staggering with hunger—to me he is not a mere picture of Irish life: to me he is a brother to be helped; to me he is a Christian prisoner to be rescued from the pitiless power of those infidel Saracens of the nineteenth century the Irish landlords and the British government.

"I know not where to begin nor what county to select in either of these unhappy provinces.

"Dr. Canon Finn of Ballymote wrote to me that the priests in his parish tell him that the little children often come to school without having had a mouthful of breakfast to eat, and that vomiting and stomach sickness are common among them.

"Why?

"'I know whole families,' writes the canon, 'that have to supplement what our committee gives by eating rotten potatoes which they dig out day by day.'

"Father John O'Keene of Dramore West wrote to

me that 'there are four hundred families in his parish dependent on the relief committees, and one hundred almost entirely in want of clothing and the children in a state of semi-nudity.'

"Four hundred families! Let us look at the mother of just one of these four hundred families.

"Listen to Father O'Keene: 'On Sunday last, as I was about going to church, a poor young woman prematurely aged by poverty came up and spoke to me. Being in a hurry, I said:

"'"I have no time to speak to you, Mrs. Calpin. Are you not on the relief list?"

"'"No, father," she said, "and we are starving."

"'Her appearance caused me to stop. She had no shoes, and her wretched clothing made her a picture of misery.

"'I asked her why her husband had not come to speak to me.

"'She said:

"'"He has not had a coat for the last two years, and, as this is Sunday, he did not wish to trouble Thomas Feeney for the loan of one, as he sometimes lends one to him."

"'"Have you any other clothes besides what I see on you?"

"'"Father, I am ashamed," was the reply; "I have not even a stitch of underclothing."

"'"How many children have you?"

"'"Four, father."

"'"What are their ages?"

"'"The oldest a boy, eight years; a girl, seven; another, four; and a little one on the breast."

"'" Have they any clothes?"

"'" No, father. You may remember that when you were passing last September you called into the house, and I had to put the children aside for their nakedness."

"'" Have you any bedclothes?"

"'" A couple of guano-bags."

"'" How could you live for the past week?"

"'" I went to my brother, Martin MacGee of Farrelinfarrel, and he gave me a couple of porringers of Indian meal each day, from which I made Indian gruel. I gave my husband the biggest part, as he is working in the fields."

"'" Had you anything for the children?"

"'" Oh, father," she said, "the first question they put me in the morning is: 'Mother, have we any meal this day?' If I say I have, they are happy; if not, they are sad and begin to cry."

"'At these words she showed great emotion, and I could not remain unmoved.

"'This,' adds Father O'Keene, 'is one of the many cases I could adduce in proof of the misery of my people.'

"Are the landlords doing nothing for these people? Certainly. There are nine hundred families in the parish of Bruninadden, in the county of Cork. Canon McDermott is the priest there. Hear what he wrote to me: 'The lands are in part good, but the good lands are chiefly in the hands of landlords and graziers. You can travel miles over rich lands and meet only the herds or laborers of some absentee landlord. Thirty landlords own this parish; twenty-seven of them are absentees. The three resident proprietors are poor and needy themselves. You can judge of the condition of the tenant-farmers and of their relations with their landlords by a statement of facts. There are in my parish two iron huts—one to protect the bailiff of an absentee landlord, the other to protect a resident landlord. Again, in a district containing one hundred and sixty families, eighty-nine processes of ejectment were ordered to be served by the landlords; but in some cases the process-servers declined to act, and in others the processes were forcibly taken from them.'

"It is not always a pastime to serve processes of ejectment on a starving and desperate peasantry.

"The good canon continues: 'Allow me to state the condition of some of those on whom processes were to have been served. Pat Grady, of Lugmore, has fourteen children, thirteen of them living with him in a small hut. He holds about five acres of unreclaimed land, for which he pays at the rate of one pound twelve shillings (eight dollars) an acre. He owns neither a cow nor a calf. He has not a morsel to feed his children except the twenty-five pounds of Indian meal I dole out to him each week. To-day I saw his ticket from a pawnbroker for his very bedclothes. His children sleep on straw or on the bare floor.'

"But the landlord wanted his rent, for all that.

"I have entered hundreds of Irish cabins in districts where the relief is distributed. These cabins are more wretched than the cabins of the negroes were in the darkest days of slavery. The Irish peasant can neither dress as well, nor is he fed as well, as the Southern slave was fed and dressed and lodged. Donkeys and cows and pigs and hens live in the same wretched room with the family. Many of these cabins had not a single article of bedclothing except guano-sacks or potato-bags, and when the old folks had a blanket it was tattered and filthy.

"I saw only one woman in all these cabins whose face did not look sad and care-racked, and she was dumb and idiotic.

"The Irish have been described by novelists and travellers as a light-hearted and rollicking people, full of fun and quick in repartee, equally ready to dance or to fight. I did not find them so. I found them in the West of Ireland a sad and despondent people, careworn, broken-hearted and shrouded in gloom. Never once in the hundreds of cabins that I entered—never once, even—did I catch the thrill of a merry voice or the light of a joyous eye. Old men and boys, old women and girls, young men and maidens—all of them, without a solitary exception—were grave or haggard, and every household looked as if the plague of the first-born had smitten them that hour. Rachel weeping for her children would have passed unnoticed among these warm-hearted peasants, or, if she had been noticed, they would only have said, 'She is one of us.' A home without a child is cheerless enough, but here is a whole land without a child's laugh in it. Cabins full of children and no boisterous glee! No need to tell these youngsters to be quiet: the famine has tamed their restless spirits, and they crouch around the bit of peat-fire without uttering a word. Often they do not look a second time at the stranger who comes into their desolate cabin.

"My personal investigations proved that the misery that my witnesses have outlined is not exceptional, but representative; that the Irish peasant is neither indolent nor improvident, but that he is the victim of laws without mercy that without mercy are enforced; and my studies, furthermore, forced me to believe that the poverty I saw, and the sorrow and the wretchedness, are the predetermined results of the premeditated policy of the British government in Ireland to drive her people into exile. This, also, I believe and say—that Ireland does not suffer because of over-population, but because of over-spoliation; because she has too many landlords and not enough land-owners.

"Americans believe that it is England that rules Ireland, and that the Irish in Ireland enjoy the same rights that the English enjoy in England. The belief is an error. England delegates the most import-

CUSTOM HOUSE AND QUAY, LIMERICK.

ant of all legislative powers—the power of taxation—to the absentee landlord, and he assigns the odious task of impoverishing the people to his irresponsible agents.

"The Irish landlord has no more pity for his tenant than the shark has for the children of the sailor who falls between his jaws. If American landlords, even in law-abiding New England, were to act as the Irish landlords act, they would perish by the eager hands of vigilance committees.

"From 1847 to 1851 one million and a half of the Irish people perished from famine and the fevers that it spawned. This appalling crime has been demonstrated by a man whose love of Ireland no man questioned, and whose knowledge of her history no man doubted—John Mitchel. These victims of landlord greed and British power were as deliberately put to death as if each one of them had been forced to mount the steps of a scaffold. And why? To save a worse than feudal system of land tenure, for it is the feudal system stripped of every duty that feudalism recognized, the corpse that breeds pestilence after the spirit that gave protection has fled; a feudal system that every Christian nation, excepting England only, has been compelled to abolish in the interests of civilization."

Another witness is indeed unnecessary; but an eviction-scene which the bishop of Meath, Right Rev. Dr. Nulty, saw is so representative of all evictions that this record would not be complete without it. It did not occur under Cromwell, it was not in 1847; its date is 1871:

"In the very first year of our ministry as a missionary-priest in this diocese we were an eye-witness of a cruel and inhuman eviction which even still makes our heart bleed as often as we allow ourselves to think of it. Seven hundred human beings were driven from their homes in one day and set adrift on the world to gratify the caprice of *one* who, before God and man, probably deserved less consideration than the last and least of them. And we remember well that there was not a single shilling of rent due on the estate at the time, except by one man; and the character and acts of that man made it perfectly clear that the agent and himself quite understood each other.

"The crowbar brigade, employed on the occasion to extinguish the hearths and demolish the homes of honest, industrious men, worked away with a will at their awful calling until evening. At length an incident occurred that varied the monotony of the grim, ghastly ruin which they were spreading all around. They stopped suddenly, and recoiled panic-stricken with terror from two dwellings which they were directed to destroy with the rest. They had just learned that a frightful typhus-fever held those houses in its grasp, and had already brought pestilence and death to their inmates. They therefore supplicated the agent to spare these houses a little longer; but the agent was inexorable, and insisted that the houses should come down. The ingenuity with which he extricated himself from the difficulties of the situation was characteristic alike of the heartlessness of the man and of the cruel necessities of the work in which he was engaged. He ordered a large winnowing-sheet to be secured over the beds in which the fever-victims lay—fortunately, they happened to be perfectly delirious at the time—and then directed the houses to be unroofed cautiously and slowly; because, he said, he very much disliked the bother and discomfort of a coroner's inquest. I administered the last sacrament of the Church to four of these fever-victims next day, and, save the above-mentioned winnowing-sheet, there was not then a roof nearer to me than the canopy of heaven.

"The horrid scenes I then witnessed I must remember all my life long. The wailing of women, the screams, the terror, the consternation of children, the speechless agony of honest, industrious men, wrung tears of grief from all who saw them. I saw the officers and men of a large police-force, who were obliged to attend on the occasion, cry like children at beholding the cruel sufferings of the very people whom they would be obliged to butcher had they offered the least resistance. The heavy rains that usually attend the autumnal equinoxes descended in cold copious torrents throughout the night, and at once revealed to those houseless sufferers the awful realities of their condition. I visited them next morning and rode from place to place, administering to them all the comfort and consolation I could. The appearance of men, women and children as they emerged from the ruins of their former homes—saturated with rain, blackened and besmeared with soot, shivering in every member from cold and misery—presented positively the most appalling spectacle I ever looked at. The landed proprietors in a circle all around, and for many miles in every direction, warned their tenantry, with threats of their direst vengeance, against the humanity of extending to any of them the hospitality of a single night's shelter. Many of these poor people were unable to emigrate with their families, while at home the hand of every man was thus raised against them. They were driven from the land on which Providence had placed them, and, in the state of society surrounding them, every other walk of life was rigidly closed against them. What was the result? After battling in vain with privation and pestilence they at last graduated from the workhouse to the tomb, and in a little more than three years nearly a fourth of them lay quietly in their graves.

"The eviction which I have thus described, and of which I was an eye-witness, must not be considered an isolated exceptional event which could occur only in a remote locality where public opinion could not reach and expose it. The fact is quite the reverse. Every county, barony, poor-law union, and indeed every parish in the diocese, is perfectly familiar with evictions that are oftentimes surrounded by circumstances and distinguished by traits of darker and more disgusting atrocity. Quite near the town in which I write [Mullingar], and in the parish in which I live, I lately passed through what might be characterized as a wilderness, in which, as far as the eye could reach, not a single human being or the vestige of a human habitation was anywhere discernible. It was only with great difficulty, and much uncertainty too, that I was able to distinguish the spot on which till lately stood one of the most respectable houses of this parish. A few miles farther on I fell in with the scene of another extensive clearance, in which the houses that had sheltered three hundred human beings were razed to the ground some few years ago. That same proprietor desolated, in an adjoining parish, a densely-populated district by batches of so many families in each of a series of successive clearances. Seventeen families formed the first batch."

The American reader will ask, Does not the new Land Act abolish such scenes for ever? It does not, as will be shown when we reach the terms of that measure. Was there not urgent need for the Land League? The proposition the League made to the government is this: That the government should buy out the landlords at a fair price, then sell the lands to the tenants at a fair price and give them thirty-five years to complete their payments, holding a first mortgage until the whole sum was paid, with interest. Thus the landlords, who generally got the lands for nothing, and who have been in the enjoyment of princely incomes from them, would lose nothing by their sale; the government would lose nothing; while the now poor and wretched tenant would become a peasant proprietor.

CHAPTER IX.

THE LANDLORDS SOW THE SEED OF THE LAND LEAGUE.

IT was the Irish landlords who made the formation of the Land League inevitable. The Gladstone Land Act of 1870 was intended to restrain them, but it was a law of excellent intentions and impotent performance. The promise it made to the tenant's wistful ear it broke to his sanguine hope. The biographer of Mr. Gladstone, George Barnett Smith, says very correctly: "It did not confiscate a single valuable right of the Irish landlord." One valuable right of the Irish landlord was to raise rents as often as he pleased; another was to expel a tenant and his family whenever he pleased; another was to confiscate, without compensation, the improvements made by tenants at their own expense

These rights they exercised with uniform energy during the years 1877, 1878, 1879 and 1880. They succeeded in creating another famine, in which there would have been frightful loss of life had not the charity of the world poured into Ireland, chiefly from the United States, to save the stricken tenantry. It was not food that was sent, it was money. The money did not go to the tenantry or do them any permanent good; it went to the landlords: it was paid to them for food for the tenants. The food had been produced by the tenants, but they had given it to the landlords for the rent of their little farms. They had nothing left for themselves but the potato, and the potato crop failed.

It was the free exercise of their legal rights by the landlords during these three years which resulted in the formation of the Land League. The manner in which the rights of the landlords were exercised is most graphically described in a series of episodes which are herewith presented. The newspapers of April 3, 1878, contained the following:

"On the 2d inst. a dreadful event occurred in a remote part of the North of Ireland which has attracted the attention of the civilized world. On that morning an old and haughty nobleman, the earl of Leitrim, accompanied by his clerk, left his residence at Milford to drive to Derry, where he was to meet his solicitor and settle the process of eviction of eighty-nine tenant-farmers and laborers on his estates who were under notice to quit. The earl was armed: he always carried arms. On the road lay men driven to desperation by the earl's grinding cruelty. When he had arrived opposite an empty cottage from which he had recently evicted a poor widow, the men sprang forward and stopped the carriage. A terrible struggle ensued, as proved by the marks; but the desperate assailants were the victors. The earl was shot through the heart; his arms were broken, his skull shattered and his bleeding body flung into the roadside ditch, where it was found. The clerk and driver were also shot dead. The earl's valet was driving about a mile behind, and on coming up found his master and the clerk dead on the road; life was still in the driver. The assassins meanwhile escaped in a boat across Mulroy Bay. The valet drove back to Milford and alarmed the police, who, coming to the place, found the driver alive, but unconscious. He died shortly afterward. The *London Times*' editorial says: 'The news of the murder of the earl of Leitrim has struck this country with as much pain and amazement as an unprovoked declaration of war.'

"The earl of Leitrim was well known as a landlord whose ideas of the rights of property prompted him to stretch the powers given him by the law to the utmost limit, and who was therefore extremely unpopular with his tenantry and with the small-farmer class generally. For over twenty-five years he had been consolidating farms, evicting tenants and turning his lands into immense grass-farms. He owned immense tracts of land in the counties of Donegal, Leitrim and Derry, as well as a small estate in Kildare, and probably evicted more tenants in his lifetime than any man in Ireland. Hundreds of sturdy Presbyterian farmers now settled in Ohio, Indiana and Illinois, as well as Catholics, were forced to give up their homes in Donegal and emigrate. It was his habit to act as his own bailiff, and on horseback, alone and armed to the teeth, to carry out those processes of law which even under the severest necessity are so painful to a tender nature. His tenantry in Leitrim and Galway bore with his savage freaks with the greatest forbearance, believing him to be irresponsible for many of his acts. But to Derry, where this murder was committed, he was comparatively a stranger, his property there being very small; and it will doubtless be found he has committed some terrible act of tyranny to provoke such a crime in a region in which agrarian outrage has hitherto been wholly unknown. It is told of him that his favorite phrase in dismissing any appeal made to him was to bid the applicant 'Go to hell or to America!'

"On more than one occasion, also, he appeared at the local petty sessions in cases which aroused considerable popular indignation and gained him a great deal of newspaper notoriety. Many of his tenantry live on the rocky coast of the Atlantic, where the soil is very poor, and eke out a miserable existence, partly by fishing, partly by gathering kelp on the seashore, which is sold for manufacturing purposes. The right to gather this kelp had been exercised from time immemorial by the tenantry, but some years ago Lord Leitrim and a few other landlords claimed the kelp as the property of the landlord, and in cases where he found them gathering it had them arrested for theft. The irritation caused by these petty prosecutions was very deep, and extended over many parts of Ireland not immediately affected by the litigation. His father had been a mild landlord and a very popular man, and great expectations were formed of the son when, in 1854, he succeeded to the title and estates. The family seats are at Lough Rynn, Dromod, County Donegal, and Killadoon, Celbridge, County Kildare. The family originally obtained from James I. large tracts of confiscated land, and the earl who has just been murdered added largely to his estates by purchase. The earl was unmarried.

"The earl of Leitrim was possessed of vast estates in the counties of Londonderry, Sligo, Donegal and Leitrim. The town of Lifford in the first-named, and the towns of Manorhamilton and Mohill in the last-named, county were his property. He never employed an agent to collect the rents of his immense possessions, but managed all himself with the assistance of the unfortunate clerk who shared his tragic fate. When his tenants went to pay their rents to him, they approached him with fear and trembling, as he made it a rule to treat them like dogs. No kind or encouraging word ever escaped his lips to the poor struggling slaves that contributed his princely income. If a poor tenant had not the full amount of his rent on the appointed day for collecting it, and asked his hard taskmaster for a few days to make up the remainder, he would not grant him an hour, but would immediately hand him over to his lawyer, who would have his effects seized upon by the bailiffs. Many a poor man, with his wife and children, he drove from the house which their industry had built, and from the farm which their toil had cultivated and reclaimed from a barren morass to a fertile plain. There never has been six months since the passing of the Irish Land Act of 1870 without Lord Leitrim's name appearing more than once in the law-courts as the plaintiff in ejectment cases. He made several futile attempts in the House of Lords to nullify the act. He said upon one of these occasions: 'The Land Act of Mr. Gladstone has confiscated my property.' Some years ago a steward of his named Wilson was shot at in the county Donegal and maimed so badly that he is a cripple for life. Wilson had been engaged in putting some of His Lordship's tyrannical evictions into execution when he was fired at. The seat at Lough Rynn was the deceased nobleman's favorite place of residence. The house—or castle, as it is called—is built upon an island in Lough Rynn, and the communication with the main-land is by a drawbridge. He had the island fortified and defended with cannon, making it look more like the stronghold of a feudal baron of the Middle Ages than the residence of a nobleman of the latter part of the nineteenth century."

Rewards were offered for the apprehension of the assassins, and several men were arrested, tried and acquitted, there being no evidence connecting them with the deed.

It transpired, after ample investigation, that the death of the earl was not due to agrarian causes. He had baser passions than avarice and malignity: he was bestial as well as brutal, and had invaded many humble and virtuous families. The brother of one of his victims, a young man who had been driven from his native land and was toiling in the United States, learning of his sister's dishonor, took ship, waited for his opportunity, and returned to his exile.

During the previous winter the *Freeman's Journal* of Dublin sent a correspondent to the Galtee Mountains to investigate rumors of famine and evictions. The following is his report:

"MITCHELSTOWN, CHRISTMAS EVE.—Mr. Patten Smith Bridge told Lord Chief-Justice May that the whole five hundred and seventeen tenants who populate the twenty-two thousand acres of mountain and lowland under his sway had already settled except forty-seven, and he had reason to believe that they would be 'settled' when he went home. There was laughter in court at this. I do not know whether it was intended for grim humor, but the settlement has taken the form of a sheaf of processes of ejectment for the January sessions in Clonmel. Mr. Bridge has left the Galtees for the Christmas holidays, and, however it may have been in the castle, it must be owned that in the cabins singled out for the process-server's visits, as well as in those which are spared for another sessions, the season of Christmas peace and pleasure has little meaning around the Galtees. The exact number of processes served I have yet to cast up one by one as I visit the holdings, but it is certain that a selection of the recalcitrants has been made, and that a large section of those who did not, and declare they cannot, accept the revaluation have been respited, for reasons quite beyond their own comprehension. The question then comes to be once more of cruel urgency, Is this whole wail over the Galtee tenantry a gigantic conspiracy against truth, or is it the cry of honest industry driven to despair? Has public sympathy been trifled with, or has it only been half aroused? Have we here a cunning and secretive peasantry, with rags on their backs and gold in the thatch, striving to shelter themselves by a parade of mendicancy and filth from paying the honest value of their holdings, or are they really a race of humble toilers whose sweat and substance has wrung—alas! not even bread, but—sustenance from the barren bosom of mountains and fens; who have waged a lifelong battle for existence against rocks and heather, against a subsoil of sandy mud, against Nature in her stubbornest and most grudging mood; and who to-day find themselves face to face with strangers who have appropriated and trafficked in their improvements, and sentenced them to rents which will, in due process of law, chase them from the fields they have created? Is their case, in fact, a libel upon a good landlord and a conscientious agent, or is it a damning proof that under the ægis of the Land Act

Irish tenants still owe it to the mercy of their masters that they are not stripped of all that a life's industry has laid up for their declining days, and sent upon the world with only the consolation of a legal viaticum? It will be the business of these letters to make some small contribution of evidence upon this head, such as a person quite severed from the dispute, who uses his eyes and ears cautiously and frankly describes his experiences, may glean from careful investigation on the spot. There is no disguising the diffidence with which I commence the task. I do not for a moment pretend to review the revaluation further than the facts, when brought together, may affect it; and even an inquiry into the actual condition of a community spread over a tract of wild hills some thirty miles round—where there are so many diversities in the quality of soil and stock and habitations and so many exaggerations on both sides to be discounted—is beset with difficulties, the more especially that, as will be seen in the sequel, Mr. Bridge's explanations of what I may see are denied one. The dread that any inaccurate statement or incautious word of mine may be twisted to the disadvantage of creatures whom I have seen bowed to the verge of despair weighs even more heavily than the consciousness that every sentence is written under the sword of a capricious law. My plan is, however, a humble one. It is to visit personally not only the doomed homesteads, but as large a proportion as possible of all others lying in my track over the estate, townland by townland; to describe the peasants' homes and mode of life; to satisfy myself, as far as a layman may, of the nature and value of their crops; to see their stock for myself, and see what quality of land is this for which a few shillings an acre is a rack-rent. The facts thus collected I shall first embody in as plain and succinct a narrative as may be. Afterward I shall state the impressions left upon my own mind, leaving it to the judgment of sober public opinion to say whether they shall have been justified by dry facts.

"The townland of Skeheenarinka extends from the little village-cross of that name over the crest of a bare hump of mountain rising to a height that must be quite two thousand feet above the sea-level, considering that Galteemore, which rises just behind and does not greatly overtop it, is three thousand and twelve. Neither of the peaks looks nearly so high from the level of the adjoining village. On the southern slope, where the sun most rests, the face of the hill is scored with great stone fences, marking out, terrace above terrace, the patches of reclaimed land, until they merge in an untamable belt of heather not a stone's-throw from the top. I saw it on Sunday at its best, when scarcely a breeze stirred below and it was lighted by a sun of very unusual brilliancy for the winter solstice—when, too, the houses and the people were in their Sunday trim and the cattle basking in unwonted warmth. My visit was made, I need scarcely say, without the

COVE OF CORK, NOW QUEENSTOWN.

smallest previous notice. It will be readily understood, also, that, even if a perfect stranger could have threaded his way alone through a maze of mountain-borheens, he could not have penetrated for a moment the suspicious reticence natural to people under the pressure of heavy calamity without the passport of a familiar face.

"I was happy enough in this respect to have obtained the guidance of the Very Rev. Dr. Delany, P. P., of Ballyporeen. His wide parish embraces most of the Buckley estates, and his great heart all their misery. Many a time during the day, as he struck a faint track across some remote glen or greeted some astonished mountaineer with a reminder that he had not been to mass that day, his cheery smile, his gentle reproof, his word of comfort, his complete knowledge of everybody's little troubles, and the whole-souled confidence with which his interest was repaid, recalled the best that I had ever heard or read of the relations of an Irish priest with his people. The dogs in remote highland cabins knew him, while they barked at me. 'Will I tell him, dochtor?' asked one old fellow whom I was questioning about his relations with Mr. Bridge. And when the approval was smilingly given, he who had been taciturn as Jules Verne's Phineas Fogg grew as voluble as the small dressmaker in *Little Dorrit*.

"At the foot of the mountain, where the path begins to be steep, we entered a thatched cabin by the roadside, in front of which, as is usual with cottiers of the more wretched class, a foul pit of liquid manure was smoking. A man with his head between his hands was bent over the fire, and a few children stuck in the chimney-corner. The man started to his feet with a guilty look as the priest entered; he was tall and strong-limbed, but had a cowed and haggard face. 'You weren't at mass this morning, Mick.' The man turned up his broken shoes, which had not, indeed, troubled shoemaker or shoeblack for many a day; he had no coat, a flannel waistcoat and a brown jerry hat, and his shirt was not clean, though it was Sunday. Let me say here that in at least half a dozen other instances during the day we came across similar tenants with similar excuses; and I do not think it was home attractions that kept those men in those noisome dens poring over the fire while the sun was shining and their neighbors going to mass. This was Michael Dwyer, and he had one of the processes of ejectment behind the dresser. 'It is the only Christmas-box we got yet, God help us!' said an old man, later in the day, who had been similarly served. A pot was boiling on the fire. It contained potatoes, the Sunday dinner of the family, ten of them all told. I took up some of the potatoes lying in a heap in the corner; they were many of them rotten, all of them wet and miserably small. Several of them I could bruise into pulp between my fingers. And these were grown on low lands, in a field that looked as rich as the best of its neighbors. Potatoes have been bad everywhere this year; but these are not like any other potatoes I ever saw, except those picked out as refuse for the pigs in more favored spots. I have not yet seen in Skeheenarinka a single potato as large as an orange.

"The cabin forms but one chamber, in which the whole family of ten are somehow accommodated by night. There were two bedsteads; what the other arrangements are I dare not guess. This man's holding is measured at four acres one rod, of which the old rent was £1 2s. 4d. and the new £1 15s. His own belief (which, of course, goes for what it is worth) is that the four acres include large patches which were taken from him to be attached to the schoolhouse. I only mention it as one of several cases in which the tenants profess themselves satisfied that a new survey would show them to be charged (not, of course, wilfully) with more land than they occupy. Dwyer states he twice offered Mr. Bridge the increased rent in full, and it would not be taken unless he signed an agreement as tenant from year to year. He was employed as quarryman by Mr. Bridge up to the time of these troubles, and he states that he was not only then disemployed, but that another tenant—John Jackson—had refused to employ him, alleging instructions which I cannot, without more authority, give currency to. His whole tillage this year was one acre of potatoes, and of these not six baskets were left on Sunday. His whole stock is, in his own words, 'one old cow that my wife bought for twenty-five shillings.' I saw the old cow grazing in the best field in solitary majesty, and, though she was decidedly a bargain at the money, I doubt whether she would bring double the price this moment in any market in Munster. Cheek by jowl with this grassy field, lying flat beside it, separated only by a fence, lay a tract of virgin moor covered with stunted heather and interspaces of utterly barren sand, with here and there a tuft of yellowish grass—a not inapt picture, even in quite civilized latitudes, of what the land was and what the patient dint of industry had made it. This, then, being the sum of Dwyer's ways and means, it only remained for him to show that he is twenty-one pounds indebted to the bank to convince me that, assuming his figures to be correct, the farm would not, as he himself put it, give a meal of yellow stirabout to ten Christians, only that he ekes out his means by doing jobs as road-contractor.

"A pair of horses well skilled in mountain-climbing awaited us on the borheen outside, for the owner of the post-car had made a special clause the previous day against trusting his vehicle into the by-roads. For a couple of hundred feet we ascended a rough but fairly passable mountain-path some eight feet wide. Thence to the top it grew more and more contracted and jagged, as if the mountain-streams had in winter coursed down the centre and torn a channel for themselves, and very quickly the horses had to pick their steps in single file. Our second visit was to the house of Patrick Burke, about the level of Galtee Castle, which lay in its body-guard of woods a little to our left. Burke's old rent for a farm that he believes to be about sixteen acres was £4 18s. 7d.: it has been raised to £8. There has been no movement whatever toward a settlement since the trial; yet, to his amazement, no process of ejectment has been served upon him. He was at mass when we called. His wife appeared as wretched as if the process had already come. The cabin, poor as it was, had the earthen floor neatly swept and the dresser of blue delft shining. A streak of green slime came down the wall where the rain trickled down and collected in a hole in the floor, out of which it had to be baled with a cup; 'and if you scrubbed it three times a day, you could not keep the floor dry under you.' The five members of the family sleep in two beds in the bedroom, whose poverty she shrank from exposing, but stated they had to put a sop of straw under their feet to keep the floor dry.

"This class of accommodation—which may be taken as a fair average of the mountain-cabins, except that I saw only three others in which the rain penetrated the dwelling-house to any appreciable extent—is what I have generally found in the cabins of the poorest sort of laborers elsewhere, neither better nor worse, but the den in which three people are huddled together in the adjoining cow-house is an outrage upon civilization. I had to stoop on entering its crazy door, and as soon as I could make out anything in the gloom (for it is neither lighted by window nor ventilated by chimney) I discovered that I stood up to my ankles in a fœtid pool of rain-water mixed with the droppings of cattle. Propped up on wattles in a corner of this stifling den was a filthy bag of straw littered with some foul rags and a tattered coverlid, and here I was gravely, but with manifest shame, assured that a man, with his wife and daughter, sleeps nightly, while the cow lies down in the sodden manure beside them!

"I met this wretched wife (whose clothing by day was all but as scanty as by night) coming down the mountain barefooted as we were leaving. She was radiant with thankfulness. She was after begging a mess of Indian meal from a neighbor for the Sunday banquet of herself, her husband and daughter, and she had it rolled up in her red cotton handkerchief. And she thanked God more fervently, I am afraid, than most of us do for merry Christmas dinners. But she had another cause of joy: she held out triumphantly to the Rev. Dr. Delany an American letter she had just received, with an enclosure of £1 from her daughter in distant New Haven, Connecticut.

"But to return to her landlady, Mrs. Burke, who was herself without a dress and only wore torn blue flannel petticoats. Her own blanket is pledged for 7s. 'When we were married the poor man's coat was in pawn, and I had to pledge one of my own dresses that I got in service to release it for the wedding; but, sure, it went again, and we never saw the sight of it since. He got a present of a coat six years ago from a neighboring man, and there it is to this day. And, as God is my judge,' she cried, vehemently, 'I never saw that man drunk!'

"I went out upon the farm, and saw it dug in several places. It really looked one of the best holdings on the mountain at that elevation. Yet even in the lowest parts there was a tract of wet rea, and the upper border was still thick with stones and heath. Two large fields were red with potatoes, and I counted six pits. One of the fields, said Mrs. Burke, was sublet as a garden for £1 a year. In his affidavit her husband swore he would not get £3 for the grazing of his whole farm. I drove the spade some eight inches into the upper potato-field; after two efforts I brought up about four inches of dark soil, beneath which there was a miserable compost of wet sand perfectly incapable of secreting the moisture that trickles down eternally from the heights. At another trial I broke—spade, not ground. The upper part of this field was still dotted with boulders and scrubby patches returning to or never wholly recovered from wilderness, and this season's crop of stones (the only bounteous crop on Skeheenarinka) lay thick around. They never, since the famine years, had enough potatoes to carry them through the year, said Mrs. Burke, and she would be very proud if they held during the winter this season. They sowed five barrels of oats, for the seed of which they paid £4 10s.; upon this and other crops they put two bags of superphosphate, at 21s. the bag. They paid 7s. a day, with diet, for ploughing and harrowing (for only two farmers on the mountain whom I met had either a horse or a plough); they paid a half-sovereign for mowing, and she showed me the note from Mr. Sam Burke of Cahir, to whom her husband sold all but five barrels of the oats for £6 1s. 6d. Three small cocks of oaten straw, however, remain, as cattle-food. They tried quarter of an acre of turnips. 'We could not get a mess for the cow out of them,' was Mrs. Burke's summary of the result.

"The stock transactions are more extraordinary still. There is a cow, a heifer, 'an old sheep that I offered yesterday for half a sovereign,' a lamb and a goat. Her husband bought a cow on May 23 for £13 10s. on credit, and had to sell her again for £8 when his creditors clamored for payment. The present cow was bought in Mitchelstown on January 10, two years ago, for £9 17s. 6d., of which £4 is still due. All this is, of course, mere *ex-parte* statement, as is the assertion that a debt of £60 is hanging over their cabin—that 'they were always living on credit, but there is no credit to be had now since this man came down on us.' Bills in the bank and private bills were shown me, but perhaps it is of somewhat more importance that when I questioned the husband some hours later, in a distant part of the townland, his answers tallied almost exactly with his wife's, save that he mentioned two sheep where she had only mentioned one. Burke brought forward at the same

SLIGO ABBEY.

time a man who said he had been his security for the price of one of the cattle, and said he had to give the cows bran every day in the year, or they would run dry. When questioned as to the cost of the bran, he said he did not know how much a hundredweight it was, as he got it 'on time,' but he made the very questionable statement that his cattle used half a hundredweight per week—say 3s. 6d. worth. 'How much money have you in bank now?'—'God help me, I have plenty of it to pay there!' was the immediate response.

"One word more of Mrs. Burke. I spoke of Christmas. She pointed to a neck of mutton, about three pounds of it, that hung over the fireplace. This was to be the Christmas dinner of the family. ' 'Tis only four or five times in the year we get that same, and then 'tis only a pig's heart or a bone of pork that we could get cheap for a festival.'

"At the other side of the borheen lives one of the 'settled' tenants, the most wretched I had met yet. This is the woman, Johanna Fitzgerald, whose husband has gone to England as a laborer to earn bread for her four children. Mrs. Fitzgerald had not been seen at the chapel that morning, but her bare feet and coarse petticoat made a pretty eloquent apology. The children, who played about the door, had clean faces and clean rags, and the earthen floor was newly swept. A mess of Indian meal was in the pot for dinner. The family, of course, slept in one room; and a man and wife, who are lodged in consideration of help on the farm, stretched by night on the floor inside the doorway. Except a few blue plates the dresser was stocked only with marmalade pots, whose contents were never emptied on the Galtees. Mrs. Fitzgerald said she had not heard from her husband these five weeks, and a shilling was all the money she had in the world. Her rent was raised from £2 10s. 4d. to £4 4s. Her stock of potatoes was out this month past, 'except a handful of seed,' and from this to August yellow stirabout must be bought on credit. Her other tillage was half an acre of oats, which cost her £1 for seed, 7s. for labor, and 10s. for a hundredweight of superphosphate (which she has not paid for yet). The whole crop was sold to James Fitzgerald, a neighbor, for £2, straw and all. Two geese and some hens made the total of her livestock. It was pitiful to see the open-mouthed surprise with which a woman supposed to be the mistress of some twenty acres gloated over the couple of pieces of small silver given to the children, the eagerness with which she pounced upon them, and the extravagant thanks with which she repaid them.

"An ascent of ten minutes more brought us to a point at which we had to dismount and toil across a rocky track, while the horses were led by an easier path higher up the mountain. We were upon the farm of Darby Mahony, and our way lay across a stony field upon which the process of reclamation had commenced. Long rows of tough scraws delved out of the heather lay with the heath turned downward for burning, and the best side uppermost. Anything like soil was not three inches deep; patches of verdure, however, appeared elsewhere in the field. Great heaps of sandstone were collected in the centre, which had been dug out with crowbars, and were waiting to be smashed with a sledge-hammer previous to either being piled on the fences or the biggest of them buried underground. All the fences on this part of the mountain are built stouter than Roscommon stone walls, with the boulders dug out of the fields. 'Sure, we would not mind,' said Darby Mahony, 'if they let us alone; but we have no sort of spirit to root a stone or put on a bit of thatch, owing to this man always promising to turn us out.' His son is a powerfully-built young man—a patient and hard-working drudge, I can easily believe—but dulled and broken-spirited as I have seen few young men at his age.

"Mahony has been served with a process of ejectment. His rent was raised from £2 to £4, and he says, 'If I was obliged to go into the poorhouse, I could not pay it.' So strongly persuaded is he that the measurement of 16a. 1r. 27p. is double the extent of his actual holding that, according to his own statement, he waited on Mr. Bridge twice with an offer to pay the expense of a survey himself if he should turn out to be wrong, Mr. Bridge paying the expense in the other event; the answer was that no credit would be allowed for a survey, and none was made. The bulk of his farm is semi-reclaimed pasture, but the rest melts into the unbroken mass of rock and heather which crowns the mountains. 'What's there is but little,' said the tenant, 'but whatever is there we made it.'—'I am old enough to recollect,' said another old fellow, who had been to the metropolis during the late trial, 'when you might as well graze a cow down the middle of Sackville street as turn her loose on that mountain.'

"Mahony tilled altogether two acres this season: so his statement runs. He paid £1 for seed-oats for half an acre, and 7s. for the plough. Yet he never threshed a grain, and a swathe which he pulled out of a stack showed the ears had never filled, while the straw was scarcely a foot long at its best. His livestock is made up of two cows and a stripper, two yearlings, a donkey, a sow, with eleven bonnives, and one sheep 'nearly as old as himself.' I saw this gaunt and ragged bellwether toddling among the stones, and, making the usual allowance for exaggerated language, it was a miserable mountaineer. Mahony says he gets but two and a half pounds of wool off her yearly, and that these are expended in knitting stockings. The cattle are average mountain-cattle, and an affidavit made by Mahony's son states that a firkin and a half of butter per dairy-cow is their utmost produce, with constant hand-feeding.

"The cabin and its appointments are of the average poverty and cleanliness. The out-office is tottering and covered with rotten thatch, through which the green trail of the water runs down the walls—a cosey shelter for dairy-cattle during the week or fortnight yearly when the farm is snowed up.

"The Rev. Dr. Delany rallied the old fellow on a congenial topic when he pointed to the distant Commeragh Mountains and said, 'Darby, the O'Mahonys were not always on the top of Skeheenarinka.' But, proud as the little old man is of his sept and its glories, he was not to be roused; he shook his head heedlessly, and pulled out a notice of a bill in the bank for £6, to be met the next day, while he had not half the amount. He made me out in Mitchelstown to-day to show that he had discharged the debt by borrowing the money from a neighbor. A horse, he asserted, would not draw more than four hundredweight to the height of his farm, and the horse would cost 4s. a day.

"Michael Regan's is the adjoining farm, verging on the top, in character almost exactly the same, and in extent about 47 acres, as he himself roughs it—74a. 2r. 35p. statute measure, according to the figures in the valuation. He also has been served with an ejectment. His rent was raised from £5 9s. 6d. to £15 16s. 6d. He was out when we called, and, although he came into Mitchelstown to-day to proffer me his statement, inasmuch as his evidence was extracted, no doubt fully, at the trial, I do not care to return to it further than to say he swore that he had ten children; that his father and himself built the house and reclaimed the land; and that his stock consisted of six mountain-cows, six yearlings, three calves, a horse, ten sheep, two pigs and nine bonnives.

"Close by lives the widow English, whose rent was raised from 19s. to £2 1s., and who, although she has accepted the new tariff from the beginning, is as poorly housed and as earnest as any of her neighbors in declaring that the farm would not give them stirabout only that two of her sons have been taken into the employment of Mr. Bridge. One of her sons fills poor Hyland's place as coachman at a wage of 10s. a week, without diet or other perquisites than clothes, and his brother is a laborer on the same terms.

"The next cabin on our way was that of another of the arranging tenants, Edmund Fitzgerald, who accepted an increase from £1 7s. 6d. to £2 17s. 6d. Not a soul was within except four pretty children, the eldest of whom was not six years old. Three of the little creatures were stowed into a high wooden cradle, in which they were rocking themselves joyously at some distance from the fire, while the eldest, with the aid of a big dog, was gravely mounting guard over the tiny trio in the cradle. The place was scrupulously clean; there were even touches of a rude elegance here and there. The bedroom had been roughly boarded in the good old times, though the timber was in many spots displaced or rotting of age and damp. The bed-furniture, though poor, was clean. A half-pint champagne-bottle transformed into a medicine-bottle was on the shelf.

Imagine the adventures of that bottle from the moment it was primed with glowing liquor in some sunny vineyard of the Vosges until fate made it the receptacle of castor-oil in a thatched cabin on Skeheenarinka! There was a little fireplace also in this bedroom, and on the mantelpiece two plaster-of-paris statuettes of the Blessed Virgin, the solitary representatives of the fine arts that have yet crossed my view. Yet the young mistress of the house, whom we met in the borheen, a tidily-dressed, fair-faced, though careworn housewife, looked and spoke as despondingly as if her fate too were to be decided at the Clonmel sessions.

"We were now able to resume the saddle for a ride through a narrow and broken causeway, bordered by a deep channel, around the shoulder of the mountain, where the sight of the cultivated plains disappeared, and we were gazing into the gloomy and forbidding chasms that opened between Lyreen and the bold front of Galteemore—places where the gamekeeper and a stray sportsman alone penetrate.

"Here I came across a farmer with the only good frieze coat I saw on the mountain. This was Patrick Slattery, whose farm in parts looks warmer, and is, at all events, better cultivated, than those of his neighbors. He has accepted the increased valuation, and says he can pay it but badly. For forty-one years all his labor and capital have gone into the land, and, to use his own words, 'it was a fright to look at when I came there.'

"Slattery's next neighbor, Patrick Carroll, who came up in flannel jacket and shabby hat while we were speaking, made a sad contrast. 'He is the most industrious creature on the mountain,' said Slattery. Carroll's holding is one of the highest, and his soil the most thankless. The heather makes constant inroads upon his pasture-lands, and I saw one field off which he had himself built up a thick and almost continuous wall of large stones five feet high. His rent had been raised from £3 8s. to £8 7s. 6d. He has not settled, and says he cannot; but no process of ejectment has yet been served. He spoke in a tone of indescribable wretchedness of his outlook. His oats this season cost him 16s. a barrel for five barrels of seed, upon credit; he paid 7s. a day for the ploughing, with oats for the horse and bread, butter and tea for the ploughman (for in those regions the ploughman is a superior being); yet he never threshed the crop. The potatoes, upon which he spent £4 in manure, will last him three months more. 'Yellow meal from that to August, and where will I get the price of it?' His fields are grazed by three milking-cows, a heifer and two calves—nothing more. His dairy transactions for the year were these: three firkins of butter (three quarters), two of which he sold in Mitchelstown for £3 apiece, and the third, which he sent to Cork, returned him but £2 14s. profit.

"Striking a faint and boggy track across the heather, we passed sheer over the summit of the mountain,

KILKENNY CASTLE.

turning our backs upon that dismal congress of glens and precipices known in old topography by the cruelly-ironic name of Paradise, and descending by a new system of dry watercourses upon the townland of Coolegarranroe. The portion of it over which we had time to range before darkness descended covers the face of a sister-ridge to that of Skeheenarinka, sloping upward, with somewhat better-sheltered pasture-lands, to a point at which its crest rises precipitously like a wall of rock. The cattle here bore marks of better feeding, but the oat and potato crops were, if anything, more blighted.

" Michael Noonan is one of those who have bowed under the valuation. His rent was raised from £2 14s. to £5 14s., and he has undertaken to pay it, 'though God knows I might as well pay for my own coffin.' I spoke with his sick wife as she stood at the door of her miserable cabin, which is sunk in a crevice of the hill, with rain-marks coursing down the walls within and the usual slough of rotting abominations steaming in front. She spoke of her affairs in a mood of settled despondency, as of a fate which it were hopeless to expect to better. Her husband has three strippers and two calves. 'We did not get two firkins of butter out of the three of them, and we have not a supper of potatoes in the house. Every meal we eat from this out will be on credit, and nobody gives us credit now that can help it.' The tottering little cow-house is her dairy. 'We would not make the bit of butter at all, only the doctor, when he said mass here, brought us luck; but, sure, what is the use of it all?' Her husband we met crossing the fields shortly after, and he pointed out in the middle of his pasturage a wall of stones—some of them seemingly half a ton in weight—which had been rolled down from the higher ground after being rooted by his own hand.

"Thomas Kearney's farm of 105a. 35p., upon which the rent has been raised from £5 12s. 6d. to £17 10s., lies close by, part of it smothered with heath, part laid down in scanty but fairly sweet grass, and 16 acres of light, cold soil on an exposed slope, with a subsoil of sand and marl reddened for tillage. Kearney has been served with an ejectment. I saw his seven cows. 'I wish I took them up to Dublin to give evidence in place of myself,' Kearney remarked as he pointed to his gaunt and shrunken stock. They were really poor mountain-cattle. He states that he made six firkins of butter this season, which fetched £3 5s. to £3 6s. per firkin. 'Put against that,' he added, 'that I must buy hay and hand-feed them from the 1st of November to the 15th of May, or they would die in the cold.' The rest of his stock comprises twelve sheep, six heifers and two sows—those which he told the Dublin jury would frighten them to look at. Upon cross-examination in Dublin he admitted that he made up a fortune of £80 for his daughter and paid £38 for the interest of part of his holdings. Yet this lord of a hundred acres was dressed in flannel, and his family of ten souls were after a dinner of Indian meal and will be so regaled for nine months to come. His potatoes are gone, and his oats were never threshed.

"Terence Murphy, Sr., is another of those under process of ejectment. He holds 14a. 1r. 14p. statute measure, the poor-law valuation of which is £3 10s., the old rent £3 15s., and the new demand £7 7s. His farming operations have been these: An acre of potatoes cost him £4 8s., paid for seed to James Neill, £1 paid for ploughing, and £5 10s. for eleven hundredweight of special manure, still unpaid for. He will have potatoes for six weeks to come, and the rest must be reserved for seed. He put down two barrels of seed-oats, which the neighbors sowed gratis in return for like little services done by him, and never threshed a grain of it. His livestock is made up of three dairy-cows and three goats—neither sheep nor lamb nor donkey. His butter is sold in lumps. His family circle numbers seven, and counts absent ones in America and Australia.

"Maurice Gorman has a lease of 116 acres. He is tenant from year to year of another holding of 29a. 1r. 21p., and from this he is under notice of ejectment. Gorman appeared to be one of the strong farmers of the mountain—one who was not likely, therefore, to let any plot of land slip through his fingers for the sake of two guineas a year if any profit were to be had by keeping it. The holding now in question is perched highest upon the Galtee range, and is grazed only by cows. It has not been broken for twelve years, and is fast sinking back into barrenness. The man whom Gorman succeeded in possession made his living by cutting turf and selling heath for litter. The rent used to be £2 2s., and was fixed by Mr. Walker at £4 4s.

"The short day was already near its death when we recrossed to Skeheenarinka. Our passage lay across a steep and rocky gorge between whose jagged sides tumbles down a mountain-stream which might easily enough become a torrent. This is the precipice to the brink of which Denis Murphy invited the lord chief-justice, with the promise of a 'Niagara megrim,' and in sober earnest a few days after the trial a neighboring tenant named Thomas Leonard was precipitated down the gorge, and lies abed to this day with his injuries. I did not experience any American variety of dizziness in the passage, but I would have thought twice of clambering up the opposite height without a safe guide or in wet weather.

"We had only daylight for two visits more. One was to the house of William Neill, who has been under notice to quit, but has for the moment been spared process of eviction. Another cleanly little peasant home is this, and another half dozen dejected people inhabit it. Neill has a horse, which, according to his own assertion, must be fed on kindlier soil than his. The story of his tillage experiments is the same tale of blight and loss that was dinned into my ears in every cabin on the mountain. He has a milch-cow and three heifers. He offered the cow at the last fair of Ballyporeen for £2, and nobody closed with him.

"Maurice Fitzgerald is under process of ejectment. He holds 15 statute acres, the old rent of which was £1 18s. 6d., and the new demand £6 10s. He offered Mr. Bridge £4 in vain. His crop of oats was sown under the double advantage of having the seed himself and having the ploughing done by his neighbors; yet he exhibited the note from Mr. Burke of Cahir for £1 18s. 5d. for the crop, less about ten stone, reserved for himself. He has to pay Lord Lismore for the grazing of his six sheep and six lambs. The dairy-stock comprises three milch-cows, with a heifer in calf. The produce last season was four firkins of butter, to make up the fourth of which Mrs. Burke had to purchase fifteen pounds. Two of these fetched £3 9s., and the two others, sold in Cork, yielded a united profit of £5 12s. 6d.

"Thus far a first excursion around Skeheenarinka. Great portion of it has yet to be traversed before turning to the five or six other townlands embraced in the estate."

"I thought it my duty to repair to-day to the Mountain Lodge to lay before Mr. Bridge, if he should be so minded, a frank statement of what I had heard and seen, and to receive with scrupulous respect whatever denial or correction he should have wished to see placed side by side with evidences inevitably tinged with onesidedness. Owing to his departure to Roscrea for the Christmas holidays, this intention has been frustrated, and these sheets must go forth without the possible explanations which I know you will readily give Mr. Bridge an opportunity most fully of making. The Mountain Lodge is picturesquely seated on a sunny southern slope overlooking a picturesque wooded gorge, through which the meandering course of the Funcheon marks the division between Limerick and Tipperary, opening on one side over the far-reaching plains bounded by the Knockmeldown Mountains, and upon the other side into the gloomy heart of the Galtees. It is approached by a long by-road outside the village of Kilbeheny.

"At the base of the mountain lies the model farm of the estate—that of Mr. Holywell, the only English tenant, I believe, on the property, and manifestly the most skilled agriculturist. But, then, his fields are the fat of the lowlands, and were thoroughly drained at the expense of the land company before Mr. Holywell set foot there. His farmhouse is a little mansion fronted by a well-timbered lawn and backed by extensive slated stables, barns and outoffices. His cattle and his tillage are of a totally different order from any other I have seen upon the estate. Both are excellent, and do him infinite credit. Higher up there are large nurseries of young firs, larches and beech trees, with which Mr. Bridge carried on an extensive system of plantations on the mountain-sides. His own avenue is thrown open to the many, for whom it is a short-cut into the glens. The way is bordered on each side by dense clumps of rhododendrons, whose flowers, in hundreds of thousands, make this, I am told, in summer, another Pass of Roses. The avenue winds steeply up until a bend brings one in full view of the Lodge in its eyrie on the Tipperary side of the river. It is in winter a lonesome-looking place, but the elements of theatric scenery lie all round, and the woods are richly stocked with pheasants, hares, woodcocks and the numerous herds of wild deer that infest the heights of the Galtees. The Lodge is a plain sandstone, two-story building, with a short, foolscap tower, on a little gravelled plateau.

"The iron hut in which Mr. Bridge's body-guard of constabulary, under command of Constable Carraher, are housed, is pitched in the yard to the rear, between the Lodge and the woods, which stretch over the mountain toward Tipperary. It is a low, squat, iron-proof compartment, in which three of the men have their hammocks swung. Their meals are cooked in a wooden hut facing it, and their comrades sleep in an adjoining stable.

."As I rapped at the hall-door of the Lodge an affectionate little beagle rushed up to be fondled. The servant from whom I inquired whether I could see Mr. Bridge informed me that he had left for Roscrea two days before, and would not be back before Monday next. To the suggestion that I might leave my card to say who called, I replied that it was not necessary.

"As I jumped on the car the head-bailiff, O'Loghlen, sprang out of the house, bareheaded and somewhat flurried, and commenced to gyrate around me in a very amusing way. I found it necessary to inquire whether there was anything I could do for him. Very sheepishly he replied,

"'I thought you wanted to see Mr. Bridge, sir.'

"'Well?'

"'Mr. Bridge is from home, sir.'

"'Well?'

"He stopped for a moment hesitatingly:

"'I think, sir, it would be well you left your name, to let him know who called.'

"'I don't.'

"Mr. O'Loghlen moved backward, and the car forward. It had not gone far down the avenue when the coachman was at our back on horseback, and I hear that my visit to Mountain Lodge is exercising the curiosity of some of the authorities there mightily these leisure times.

"It is stated that altogether twenty-six processes of ejectment have been served, but I have as yet traced only sixteen. Two more of the tenants have settled. The rest declare that acceptance of the revaluation is impossible. Snow is falling to-night on the mountains."

In September, 1879, the same journal sent a commissioner to Mayo. The estate visited was that of

BLARNEY CASTLE, CO. CORK.

the earl of Lucan, who owns sixty thousand acres. He is an absentee landlord; he goes to the estate twice a year to collect his rents. None of the money goes back to the country. The commissioner reports:

"In order to the understanding of the thoughts which in this hour of their misery are fermenting in the Irish farmers' minds, there are certain phases of the past which will not brook concealment. The peasant who passes along the cheerless road from Castlebar to near Westport cannot choose but think that he is, as it were, traversing a cemetery of dead villages among the undistinguishable homesteads of thousands who appear there no more. These are the bleak monuments of 'the famine clearances.' It is only old inhabitants who can identify even the sites of villages such as the Kilvrees, Caillogue, Cloghernach, Clugan, Rahinbar, Derryharney, Corhue, Bohess and Lapplagh, which used to send forth their thousands to O'Connell's monster meetings less than forty years ago. The thousands rotted of hunger, died in the ditches, were flung overboard the fevership or 'went with a vengeance' to the ends of the world. A few thorn-bushes, a clump of trees or a naked gable-wall here and there are the only gravestones of those buried villages. The very stones of their huts are built into the roadside walls, as though to obliterate all traces of the dark events that levelled them. An Irish-American who revisited this desolate district a few days ago, after thirty years' absence, was for days poking through the country without discovering any old friend or landmarks except the graveyard, and he said bitterly he wondered they had not turned that too into grazing-ground. To show that I do not exaggerate, one parish which I could name once supported one thousand eight hundred families; it counts six hundred now. Another, farther westward, has had its population shorn down from two thousand two hundred to seven hundred. And the peasants, who told me they remembered seeing the roof-trees sawn through and hearing the thud of the crowbar, remarked with bitterness that every spot which nature or the labor of generations of tenants had rendered fertile was appropriated to the bullocks and sheep of the lords of the soil, while the remnant of the small holders (except those who were safe in the possession of ancient leases) were driven into swamps to commence their weary work of reclamation anew.

"'This makes the madmen who have made men mad
By their contagion.'

"The merchants of Westport had precisely the same dejected tale to tell as the merchants of Castlebar. One of them, as I have already told you, who could only collect fifteen per cent. on his last year's debts, has had to increase them this year to five thousand pounds. Another has distributed eight thousand five hundred pounds' worth of Indian meal on credit, another over four thousand pounds' worth, and so on through every shopkeeper or wayside huckster in or around the place.

"In a potato-plot underneath Croagh Patrick we stopped to talk to a poor old fellow bent and shaking who was digging potatoes in a field of flourishing-looking stalks. These imposing-looking fat stalks, I am sorry to say, when they were dug out, had only a small and wet and scanty family of potatoes at their roots, and it took a long strip of ground to furnish the poor old fellow's basket for dinner. 'But, God be praised! they might be worse,' and 'Who knows what God is doing for us, if it howlds dry for another while?'—it had been 'howlding wet' with a vengeance for eighteen consecutive hours previously—and 'Maybe we'd reap the oats about Michaelmas, if there's any ripening,' were his dismal consolations. For all his clinging to hope, I don't think his hope was much in this world; and as he stood there with his arms crossed on the head of his spade, and told us that he paid six pounds a year for two acres of land to a middleman, that he owed a year's rent and had not a halfpenny to pay it, that he owed for eleven bags of meal, which had supported him since Christmas, that his share of two pounds of pork on Christmas day was the only element of variety in his dietary since, as he rubbed his hand wearily across his forehead and recalled all the years of famine and struggle and hopeless slavery that had gone over his head in this forgotten spot, and, looking across the hill, fixed his eyes upon the place where the village of Thornhill had stood, and stands no longer, and, striving to look on into the future, could only draw his arm across his eyes and shake his head,—I longed for some power of pencil or lens that would fix him as he stood as an image of the fate of the Irish small farmer.

"A ragged old woman in a shred of red petticoat, and with a certain air of sunny resignation under all her yellow wrinkles, came up while we were speaking. She had been paying ten pounds a year for a plot of land. Being unable to scrape together the rent, she was forced to surrender the land, and was now living, God knows how, with a disabled husband in a dark little cabin by the roadside, the rent of which she is obliged to pay by giving up one day's labor in the week for the benefit of a mighty lord. Just as we parted, three policemen in their fine clothes strolled in superb idleness down the road, the only other creatures visible in the silent gray landscape. If I were a great painter, I would spend half a life trying to realize that scene.

"Some miles farther on, where a belt of Sir Roger Palmer's property (which runs in a broken, zig-zag line through some thirty miles of country from near Croagh Patrick to near Killala, eighty-one thousand acres in all) again intersects the road at Lecanvey, we met numbers of the tenantry. They all owed a year's rent at least, and were hopelessly crushed down with other debts. 'We have not a shilling if it were to save us from starvation,' exclaimed one

'They might as well put a rope around our necks at wanst as ask us for it,' said Number Two. And a third, with a vehement oath, declared that the people would have been dead and rotten long ago only for the charity of the Westport merchant and a local trader, whom the man named with flashing eyes. The agent gave them time until August to pay the November rents. His reckoning was that the cottier-farmers, who almost universally throughout this country-side go to England yearly to reap the harvest and return in time to reap their own, would have ere that time earned sufficient tribute for the landlord.

"But even here misfortune dogged their wretched steps. The labor market in England is flooded with hands from other depressed industries; besides that, there, too, the harvest is late and bad. The poor Irish harvester is crowded out. I am told at the post-offices that the post-office orders sent home hitherto have not amounted to more than a quarter of the usual average. I am told in the cabins that many of the harvesters are sick or idle in the great English cities, applying at the workhouse-gates for passage home.

"The little village of Louisburg, down by the Atlantic, we found seething with a sort of stunned and speechless excitement. Several hundred men were congregated upon the street in front of the rent-office conversing low with downcast heads, as if each of them had a near friend dead. These were the marquis of Sligo's tenantry, of the parish of Kilgeever. They had been convoked by summons from the bailiff to pay the May gale and the arrears into the hands of the agent, Mr. Sydney Smith, who, they say, is a near relative of Mr. Patten Smith Bridge, sometime of the Galtees (though, of course, that could not be fairly called his fault even if it were true).

"Mr. Smith attended, so did the tenants, headed by their faithful priests, the Rev. William Joyce, P. P., and the Rev. Father Lavelle, C. C.; but instead of rent they presented him with a respectful memorial, which they asked him to forward to the marquis of Sligo as their apology. In this document, which was worded with studied moderation, they expressed their willingness, but their utter inability, to pay even the rents that their holdings bore in former years. 'As to the increased rent, it is altogether an impossibility. We have worked and toiled,' they declared with touching eloquence, 'to the utmost of our strength in order to make a soil by its nature cold, barren and swampy fertile and productive, and yet, with all our efforts, we cannot procure from the land the bare necessaries of life.' Then, after stating in plain terms that for years it has been only the consideration of the shopkeepers that has kept many of them from 'starvation' or from 'the workhouse,' there came this fearful fact: 'You will doubtless feel surprised to hear that so great is our indebtedness that the property of the greater part of the tenants on His Lordship's estate in this parish, if sold out, would scarcely pay the creditors.' And the poor people wound up their appeal with a very handsome compliment to 'the noble house of Westport' and its motto, which, it appears, is 'Live and let live.'

"Mr. Sydney Smith listened with a grave face, intimated that there were some unpleasant phrases in the memorial which must be expunged before he could place it under the eyes of His Lordship, but finally blurted out roundly (as I am given to understand) that, from a communication of His Lordship's views which he had received lately, he was afraid that the memorial might just as well remain unamended and unpresented. The rentless tenantry, having nothing to pay and nothing more to urge, were bowed airily into the street, where they were crouching helplessly at the time of our arrival."

The following is from the Connaught *Telegraph:*

"A letter appeared recently in the *London Times* and the *Dublin Freeman's Journal*, signed by Charles Ormsby Blake of County Mayo, asserting that numbers of his tenantry had been taken from their beds in the night and been compelled to swear not to pay their rents to Mr. Blake. To this charge the tenantry make reply in the following terms:

"'CLAREMORRIS, June 23, 1879.

"'We the undersigned, tenant-farmers, residents of Coolcon and Ballyglass, County of Mayo, and tenants to Charles Ormsby, Esq., do impeach the veracity of the letter which appeared over Mr. Blake's name in the *London Times, Freeman's Journal* and the provincial papers, etc.

"'We emphatically deny that we were, "on the night of May 11, 1879," taken off our beds and sworn by strange men not to pay our rents to Mr. Blake, as stated by him in his memorial to His Grace the duke of Marlborough, lord-lieutenant of Ireland.

"'Neither did we threaten a process-officer or ejectment-server, as stated by Mr. Blake, as such an individual, to our knowledge, did not put in an appearance in our townlands.

"'We deny owing three half-years' rent, as stated by Mr. Blake. The majority of his tenantry have paid Mr. Blake a year's rent over their agreement, on his promise of giving leases—a promise he has failed to keep.

"'It is true we in a body refused to pay Mr. Ormsby Blake's agents, Messrs. Stewart & Kincaid, a rack-rent; but we offered those gentlemen a full and fair rent, which we are at any moment ready to hand them over.

"'Owing to the great depression in trade and reduction in the value of agricultural produce, we are not able to pay the exorbitant rent imposed on us, as the following tabular statement will show to the world:

Sexton. Biggar. Collins. Davitt. Egan. Healy. Brennan.

AGITATORS OF THE PRESENT.

Tenants' names.	Gov't valuation.	Rack-rent.
John Joyce, Ballyglass	£8 0 0	£11 2 6
Wm. Joyce, Ballyglass	8 10 0	12 0 0
L. Joyce, Ballyglass	8 5 0	14 0 0
D. Slattery, Ballyglass	17 0 0	32 10 0
M. Hannon, Ballyglass	15 0 0	22 0 0
Widow Coyne, Ballyglass	61 0 0	90 0 0
Widow Hahigan, Ballyglass	6 0 0	8 0 0
M. Hannon, Ballyglass	15 15 0	22 5 0
P. Mangan, Ballyglass	7 10 0	10 12 6
Widow McDonagh, Ballyglass	9 12 0	12 12 0
M. Green, Ballyglass	9 4 0	12 10 0
Widow McHugh, Ballyglass	12 0 0	18 0 0
J. Donohue, Ballyglass	10 0 0	17 15 0
P. Corcoran, Coolcon	8 10 0	12 11 0
Thomas Hessian, Coolcon	9 5 0	17 0 0
J. Mullan, Coolcon	8 5 0	15 9 0
D. Walters, Coolcon	15 5 0	22 10 0
Pat Flanigan, Coolcon	10 0 0	13 4 0
J. Walters, Coolcon	15 13 0	24 0 0
M. Heanue, Coolcon	12 10 0	23 0 0
P. Prendergast, Coolcon	22 10 0	45 10 0

"'Before the stripping of the land, some eight years ago, when the excessive rent was imposed upon us, we will give an instance of what the old rent was and the present rent extorted out of us: James Hessian, government valuation, £12; old rent, £14; present rent, £26 13s. 6d.; and the majority are in like proportion.

"'We, the above-named tenantry, empower and authorize Mr. James Daly, proprietor of the Connaught *Telegraph*, to publish this letter in vindication of our characters.

"'Signed in presence of P. J. Gordon, J. W. Nally and others, etc.'"

It would be easy to multiply such testimony; during the years mentioned the newspapers were full of similar narratives. One more will suffice. On November 19, 1879, the editor of the Connaught *Telegraph*, James Daly, Michael Davitt and John Bryce Killen were arrested in Dublin for speeches alleged to have incited a breach of the peace. The next day the following placard was posted throughout Mayo:

"To the People of Mayo—

"Fellow-Countrymen: The hour of trial has come. Your leaders are arrested. Davitt and Daly are in prison. You know your duty. Will you do it? Yes, you will. Balla is the place of meeting, and Saturday is the day. Come in your thousands, and show the government and the world that your rights you will maintain. To the rescue, in the mightiness of your numbers, of the land and liberty. God save the people! Balla, Balla, Saturday next."

The day of the meeting this placard appeared:

"Parnell and Davitt to the People of Mayo: Men of Mayo, we earnestly counsel such of you as intend to be witnesses of the eviction scene to be dignified, orderly and peaceful in your conduct. The future of our movement depends upon your attitude this day. Give no excuse for violence on the part of the government, and our great cause is won."

Mr. Parnell, Mr. Dillon and Mr. Sexton were present at the meeting. The proceedings were thus reported:

"One vast procession was formed in Balla for the march to Dempsey's farm at Loonamore. That procession was one of the most remarkable ever seen. The men were compacted four deep in a dense column spread over a mile and a half of road, a couple of hundred mounted men bringing up the rear. Passing the house of Sir Robert Blosse's agent, the cry of 'Three groans for tyrants!' was taken up all along the ranks. During the march home the band played the 'Dead March' in this neighborhood.

"Dempsey's farm is situated on the crest of a steep hill overlooking for more than a mile the Balla road. When the head of the procession reached the foot of the hill, the fields overhead were seen to be full of armed policemen, who fell into rank at the approach of the procession. The intentions of the police were even then in considerable doubt.

"Mr. Parnell and the leaders were the first to scale the hill. They were informed by Dempsey that the sheriff had promised to give him more time. The police had been by this time drawn up in a body at the rear of the house, under command of Major Wyse, R. M., Castlebar.

"A rath within fifty yards of Dempsey's house on the brow of the hill was immediately fixed as the place of meeting. Now another very singular scene took place. The whole road below for more than a mile was covered by this huge peasant-procession. As the head of the column reached the foot of the hill it parted, two to either side, and climbed the hill in an immense semicircle extending over the whole face of the hill. The two horns of this vast crescent advanced quickly and simultaneously, as if with the intention of surrounding the house and with it a large body of the police. The police immediately prepared to retire, but Mr. Parnell exerted himself to stop the movement, and both sides of the advancing procession, having halted, came quietly together around the speakers. There must have been quite eight thousand men in that extraordinary array, and their self-possession, orderliness and enthusiasm were even more remarkable than their numbers. The Ballinrobe brass band arrived during the meeting.

"Mr. Thomas Brennan (afterward arrested) said:

"We are here to-day for a threefold purpose. We are here, in the first place, to protest against the eviction and possible death of nine of God's creatures. We are here to protest in the name of our country and of justice against the unconstitutional arrest of our leaders, who are now paying the penalty of their devotion to the people's cause (cheers for them), and we are here also to declare our determination to go on with this movement until victory is secured (cheers).

"A VOICE.—Victory or death!

"MR. BRENNAN.—And until the last trace of feudal landlordism is swept from the country. The English government has come to the rescue of that accursed institution (groans), but it cannot save it. The old crumbling edifice is going, and it must fall (cheers). Prison-bars cannot hide the light of God's truth, and, though you or I may have to follow Mr. Davitt or Mr. Daly, our cause cannot be imprisoned (cheers). That cause is just, and it must triumph (cheers).

"A VOICE.—We won't fail you, any way.

"MR. BRENNAN.—My friends, our lives are no longer our own. They now belong to our country and to justice (cheers). We must consecrate them to-day (cries of 'So we will!') to the advancement of that cause for which our friends are suffering. I, for one, am not here to-day to withdraw anything I have ever said in this movement since I first stood upon that platform in Irishtown (cries of 'Never!' and cheers). And whatever may be the words which Mr. Davitt used at the Gurteen meeting, I here adopt them to-day (cheers); and if I knew them, I would repeat them for you, believing in my soul that they are the words of justice and truth (loud cheering).

"A VOICE.—My life on you!

"MR. BRENNAN.—It will become us here not to make long-winded orations to-day. The time for mere speech-making is gone by. The hour of resolve and act has arrived (cheers).

"A Voice.—Stand together!

"Mr. Brennan.—The speech to-day is the indignation which I see flashing from your eyes and the determination which rests upon your brows (cheers). Think of the possible scene which we might be called upon here to-day to witness. Think of the poor man who lies in yonder cabin, the hot fever darting wildly through his brain; think of the poor child who every time he asks for a morsel of bread sends a pang worse than a bayonet-thrust through its mother's heart (cries of 'True!'). Think of this, and then think of the evictor (groans, and cries of 'Down with him!') who has fled the country that his ears may not catch the execrations of the people.

"A Voice.—That his eyes may never see, either (laughter).

"Mr. Brennan.—Think of him as he enjoys all the luxuries of life and pockets the money which the sweat of the poor man has wrought from the land (groans), for in this enlightened nineteenth century God's first decree to fallen man is contravened by human law, and the majority of mankind must work and toil to support the few in idleness (groans).

"A Voice.—It won't be so any longer.

"Another.—Groan every tyrant (groans).

"Mr. Brennan.—Think of the scene of '47; think of the blazing roof-tree; think, oh think! of the workhouse and the emigrant ship; think of the starvation and the death and the coffinless graves; and then tell me to-day, will you be true to the preaching of our friends in prison? (Loud cheering, and cries of 'We will!')

"A VOICE.—Our blood is up.

"MR. BRENNAN.—Shall one generation witness two such scenes as '47? (Cries of 'Never!') Forbid it, Heaven! I call upon every one of you who can to-day to do everything in your power to avoid it. Organize for the protection of your own rights; combine that you may offer an unbroken front to the common enemy (cheers). Surely, if ever you are to be earnest, it is now, when your best and bravest are in prison; now, when liberty of speech is proscribed in the land; now, when the gaunt spectres of famine and death are standing by your thresholds (cheers). I appeal to one class in the community especially. I appeal to the men of the royal Irish constabulary, and I ask them, Are they content to remain or to become the destroyers of their people, of their own kith and kin? (cheers). Turning toward the police, the speaker continued: Look at a possible future; look at your own brother lying in yonder ditch dead and naked: the last garment was sold to buy a measure of milk for the poor child in whose body the teeth of the lean dog is now fastened (groans). Are you human nature? Can you look upon such scenes, strong men as you are, without feeling your knees tremble and a curse gurgling in your throats? Need I remind you that in '47, when you were called on to do work similar to that with which you are now threatened, when one of your force fired upon an unhappy crowd, to find five minutes later that his bullet had lodged in the breast of the mother that bore him? You are Irishmen, and I doubt not that beneath many a policeman's jacket a warm Irish heart beats (cheers). Are you content, then, to be the destroyers of your own people, or will you rather twine hands with them and snatch victory from death, and save the lives of the people? (cheers).—As for you, my friends, your course is clear. Keep before your minds the great fact that the land of Ireland belongs to the people of Ireland (cheers). Follow the teaching of the apostles of our creed, who are now its martyrs and its confessors. We tell you here to-day what has been told you from every platform in your country. We tell you to pay no rent until you get a reasonable reduction. We tell you to take no land from which another man has been evicted (cheers).

"A Voice.—Down with those that do!

"Mr. Brennan.—Should such a mean wretch be found in Mayo to snatch such a farm, then, I say, go mark him well, cast him out of the society of men as an unclean thing.

"A Voice.—Yes, as a mad dog.

"Mr. Brennan.—Let none of you be found to buy with him or sell with him, and watch how the modern Iscariot will prosper (cheers). The loss of each comrade but throws new duties on us who are left behind. Therefore we must all take off our coats and go to work earnestly in this movement. John Mitchel said from the dock in Green Street that

O'Connor. Phillips. Mitchel.
Redpath. Dillon. Murdock.
O'Reilly.

AGITATORS OF THE PRESENT.

there were one, two, three—ay, a hundred—prepared to follow him. Ay, and Mr. Davitt must know in his prison-cell to-day that there are not hundreds, but hundreds of thousands, prepared to take up and carry out the work which he began (great cheering).

"The resolution was carried with acclamation.

"Mr. Parnell, M. P., on coming forward to propose the second resolution, was tremendously cheered. He said:

"Mr. Chairman and men of Mayo, after the magnificent speech of Mr. Brennan it would ill become me to occupy your time with many words of mine. As he has told you, these are days not for words but for action (cheers); and upon your action to-day in coming here in the face of every intimidation, calm and determined to do your duty by your suffering fellow-creatures in yonder cabin, you have shown that you know how to distinguish what your duty is to your country to-day (cheers). I alluded just now to Mr. Brennan's magnificent talent, but it is too true that in these days Ireland's most devoted and talented sons are marked out for imprisonment, and I very much fear that the result of the lead that he has taken in this movement will be that he may be also sent to share the fate of Messrs. Davitt, Daly and Killen ('No, no!'). Lord Beaconsfield has shown that he knows how to appreciate the strength of this movement (groans for him). The whole landed aristocracy of England, and of Ireland also, recognize that the movement that was begun last February on the plains of Mayo, at Irishtown, has set the handwriting on the wall for the downfall of the most infamous system of land tenure that the world has ever seen (cheers). I congratulate you upon your attitude to-day—calm, determined, self-reliant and within the law (cheers). In this way we shall teach our rulers that although they may violate the constitution, although they may rush into illegal acts, we are not going to be induced to follow them ('No, no!' and loud cheering). It is no use for me to repeat the advice that I gave the people of Mayo in February last. You have shown that in keeping a firm grip of your homesteads (cheers, and cries of 'So we will!'), and in refusing to pay an unjust rent, you have shown that you know well that in that advice is your only safety (cheers).

"But I would exhort you with all the little power or force that I may possess to maintain the attitude that you have maintained up to the present (cheers, and cries of 'Never fear us!'), and not to allow any provocation to draw you away from your duty (cries of 'Never!'). Even if your leaders are torn from your midst, let them go: others will take their places (enthusiastic cheering); and by showing that you understand your rights and the way in which you can win them, you will reduce the pride of this haughty government, which, after having beaten the disunited Afghans, after having conquered the naked Zulus, has the temerity to come to Ireland and to place us on a level with these savages (groans).

"A Voice.—They will find us more formidable enemies.

" Mr. Parnell.—I am not going to detain you. I merely wished to come into your midst to-day, for I feared that a terrible event was going to happen before our eyes. I could not feel that I would have done my duty if I had allowed the people to come into danger and had remained away myself (loud cheering). It is the part of a coward to encourage others to take a position that he is not prepared to maintain himself, and I wished to come here to-day to join you in whatever fortune might befall you (prolonged cheers). Thank God that the eyes of the cruel landlord who was threatening a black—a terribly black—deed upon this day have been opened to the reality of the position! Thank God that we, on the eve almost of what appeared to be the first eviction in this land agitation, have been spared that terrible infliction! (cheers). I look upon this meeting, and the result of this meeting—I look upon the fact that the owners of that house are in possession of it—as the harbinger of the speedy and triumphant success of our movement (cheers). Had it been otherwise, had you been placed in that position when it would have been almost impossible for human hearts and hands to forbear, I tremble to think what might have been the result; but, thank God! we have been spared this, and that we have as the reward of the calm determination of the people of Mayo the magnificent triumph of this evening (loud cheering). Bring home, then, with you this lesson—that a man, however powerful he may be, respects his fellow-men when they respect themselves (cheers), and that as you have shown that you know how to respect yourselves, so you may expect in the future that your right to the soil of Ireland will be respected by those who attempt to deprive you of it (cheers). Let us, then, not hesitate in our great work. Let us press forward (cheers). Let us recollect that we are the inheritors of a great past, that our country is a great country and worth fighting for, that we in these days have opportunities which were denied to your fathers when they struggled against tithes, and that the power of no man can prevail against a self-respecting and self-relying people (cheers). Let us, then, maintain our dignified attitude. Let us remain within the law and within the constitution, and let us stand, even though we have to stand on the last plank of the constitution; let us stand until that plank is torn from under our feet (loud cheering). I have to propose for your adoption this resolution:

"'That we, the people of Mayo, protest against the recent arrests as an attempt on the part of the government to stifle the voice of constitutional agitation and drive the people into acts of violence' (cheers).

" Mr. John Dillon seconded the resolution.

" Mr. T. Sexton proposed the third resolution:

"'That we earnestly call upon the people of Ireland to continue to maintain their attitude of dignified self-restraint, and to carefully abstain from giving the government any excuse for inaugurating the policy of coercion which we believe they have in contemplation.'

" Mr. John Walsh, Balla, seconded the resolution.

" Mr. Costelloe, Kiltimagh, proposed the fourth resolution:

"'That we hereby pledge ourselves to persevere in this movement until we have succeeded in securing for the Irish farmer free land.'

" Mr. James O'Connor, Dublin, seconded the resolution, which was adopted with acclamation."

The Irish National Land League was now in full operation. Its aim and its policy were fully indicated at Balla. It proposed a peaceful, constitutional agitation to recover the lands of Ireland for the people to whom they naturally belong.

CHAPTER X.

THE MEN WHO GATHERED THE CROP.

THERE is an impression in the minds of many Americans who read only British literature filtered through a small class of American newspapers that the Irish agitator is an ignorant ruffian. It is a singular fact that every man who has risen to sufficient distinction to be abused, imprisoned or slain for Ireland by the English government has been a man of high personal character, and that the leaders of Irish agitation have been almost invariably men of exceptional intellectual gifts and educational training. The character and culture of Wolfe Tone may be judged by his autobiography. The agitators of a hundred years ago—the men who compelled England to concede the independence of the Irish Parliament—were the first thinkers in the country and had no superiors in the British empire. Many of them became distinguished members of the British Parliament after the passage of the act of legislative union. Robert Emmet, gentle and accomplished, would have graced the most polished society of any country. His brother, Thomas Addis Emmet, and his companion in exile, Dr. Macneven, became equally distinguished in their respective professions of law and medicine in New York; and their monuments on Broadway proclaim for all time their services to the country which gave them home and opportunity.

Those who led the agitation for Catholic emancipation were scholars and literary men. Sheil wrote *Evadne*, which still keeps the stage; his speeches are studied by all who wish to become adepts in elaborate forensic art. The magnificent oratory of O'Connell richly displays his classical studies in France; for, being a Catholic, he could get no education in Ireland. The letters of Bishop Doyle, his coadjutor in agitating for emancipation, are of singular literary beauty and remarkable argumentative power; and the late Archbishop MacHale of Tuam, who was a young priest when O'Connell was leading his people out of bondage, and who enthusiastically supported him, was possessed of attainments in the languages and the arts which even the universities of England rarely confer on the sons of hereditary wealth.

The agitators of 1848 are so fully described in Sir Charles Gavan Duffy's *Young Ireland* that they need not be more than mentioned here; they constituted a brilliant group whose genius is indelibly stamped on the thought and will for ever adorn the literature of their country. The Fenian movement of 1866— so frequently sneered at, and yet so effectual for the good of Ireland that it wrung from the first minister of Great Britain not only the bill abolishing the State-Church in Ireland, but the public confession of that momentous fact—contained men of culture whose motives were as high as their judgment was faulty, and the speeches delivered by some of them on their trial for treason betray not only sublime courage and the purest patriotism, but evidences of culture which would have been eminently useful in private pursuits.

The leaders of the present agitation are also men of education. They are not brilliant men, as were the group of '48; they do not include great orators like Grattan, Sheil or O'Connell; but they are men of clear conception of economic principles, able to discuss the questions of land tenure and peasant proprietary, of home rule and the development of the natural resources of their country, with a cogency which their opponents have been wholly unable to match. They are engaged in serious business—the accomplishment of a vast economic and social reform by strictly peaceful and constitutional means. They ask no soldiers from France, as Wolfe Tone did; they organize no conspiracies of reckless youth and undrilled yeomen, as poor Emmet did; they have no thousands of armed and eager volunteers at their backs, as Grattan had; and as contrasted even with O'Connell, who relied on the same methods, they have not the advantage he had in touching the sympathy of mankind in behalf of re-

Emmet. Curran. Wolfe Tone. Grattan. O'Connell. Fitzgerald. Davis.

AGITATORS OF THE PAST.

ligious equality. Their task is more difficult: they address themselves to the intellect of a hostile power on an economic and social problem perplexing to all, unintelligible to many, and they must overcome without a·battalion the army and navy of that vast empire whose "drum-beat is heard around the world," and whose colonial dependencies, excluding Ireland, cover a third of the surface of the globe and comprise a fourth of its inhabitants. The men who undertake a moral and political enterprise of such magnitude cannot be ignorant ruffians; they must be more than average men, well informed, sagacious, self-controlling, patient, resolute, enlightened, self-sacrificing and prepared for incessant calumny.

The founder and organizer of the Land League, Michael Davitt, is of peasant birth and self-educated. Indeed, it is probable, had not his family been evicted while he was a lad and compelled to seek in an English manufactory the bread denied them in their native land, that he would have been deprived of the chance of education which still another misfortune increased. He was born in Straide, County Mayo, in 1845: those who saw him in this country would suppose him a much older man. He has been aged, not by time, but by the walls and cruelties of British prisons. A year or more after the eviction of his family from the farm which his father tilled he went with his parents to Haslingden, near Manchester, in Lancashire, and the extreme poverty to which they had been reduced made it necessary that he should go to work in the nearest cotton-factory. A whirring wheel caught the sleeve of his right arm; in a moment the arm itself was so severely injured that amputation became necessary. No longer able to work at manual labor, in five years at a Wesleyan school, and still later at an institute, he laid the foundation of an education to which each succeeding year has contributed, even while in prison. At fifteen he was employed as bookkeeper and letter-carrier. A few years afterward he engaged in mercantile occupations and became a travelling agent for a house which sold arms.

It was about this time that fanaticism threatened to burn the Catholic churches of Lancashire; and Mr. Davitt, who was devoutly attached to his faith, led a defence-party which dispersed a mob in Haslingden by firing over their heads, thus saving the church and doubtless many lives. Nearly ten years later, when he returned to Haslingden after his release from imprisonment, the people of the town went out *en masse* to welcome the " ticket-of-leave," and among those who greeted him most warmly were some of the men whom his intrepidity and coolness had restrained from disgrace during that excited period.

"Driven forth by poverty," says John Bright, "Irishmen emigrated in great numbers; and in whatever part of the world an Irishman sets his foot, there stands a bitter, an implacable enemy of England." Another Englishman, Professor Cairnes, says: "Men leaving their country full of such bitter recollections would naturally not be forward to disseminate the most amiable idea respecting Irish landlordism and the power which upholds it. I own I cannot wonder that a thirst for revenge should spring from such calamities; that hatred, even undying hatred, for what they could not but regard as the cause and symbol of their misfortunes—English rule in Ireland—should possess the sufferers; that it should grow into a passion, into a religion to be preached with fanatic zeal to their kindred and bequeathed to their posterity—perhaps not the less effectually that it happened to be their only legacy."

That was the only legacy Michael Davitt carried from the eviction scene to the English factory. He did not nurse the brutal sight to inspire his manhood with a thirst for revenge, but he studied the social condition of the Irish peasantry for the purpose of discovering in what way, by what method, they might be emancipated from the slavery of landlordism—a slavery deeper than any which the feudal barons had imposed on the meanest of their dependants, who, in exchange for labor or military service, were sure of protection; meaner than the slavery in which the negro was held in the Southern States of the American Union. The black slave had food enough; the Irish tenantry died, to the number of millions, of starvation. The black slave was in a climate which required little clothing, and he had enough; the Irish tenantry have perished in thousands from nakedness and exposure. The black slave always had shelter; the Irish tenants have been thrust by bayonets out of their cottages into the highways and left to die under the pitiless sky. The black slave had not the gnawing consciousness that his master's land was his land: he was born a slave; the Irish tenant, even when he could not read, knew the traditions of the confiscations, and he endured the agony of believing that the land off which he was driven through no fault of his own belonged by right to his people and that he should have a share of its fruits. The slave's labor was confiscated by his master; so was the labor of the Irish tenant. But the slave always had subsistence out of his labor; the Irish tenant had not. Was it marvellous that while the sentiment of two continents was heated by the emancipation of the black slave in America the son of the evicted Irish tenant should dream of the emancipation of the Irish peasantry?

Success is the only thing in this life which defies criticism. Had the movement of forty years ago for the repeal of the legislative union succeeded, O'Connell would be deemed another Washington. The repeal movement failed; criticism is glib with reasons for the failure. The rash and silly attempt of Robert Emmet, the too sanguine ardor of Tone, the enthusiasts of '48, all failed, each failure doing Ireland some good by teaching the people patience and the strategy of incessantly worrying an enemy who cannot be fought. Had any of these episodes bloomed into successful revolution, criticism would apotheosize those whose failure it derides. Fenianism failed —not utterly, indeed, for it taught the people three lessons: the folly of premature attempts, the cruelty of wasting precious lives and blasting happy homes, the worthlessness of sublime sacrifices for Ireland made on the scaffolds of Great Britain. But when its ranks were first formed it attracted many a young Irishman whose heart was full of fire, whose head was hot with the memory of personal and national wrong; and it is not surprising that Michael Davitt, one-armed but otherwise strong and able to do a man's part, should have become a member of the organization. That he ever committed any act of treason need not be denied: he never had the opportunity. But the spy and the informer were at work; it was true that he attended secret meetings. He was arrested in London in 1870; the infamous traitor Corydon was the witness against him.

Had Davitt actually been guilty of the offence charged, he would have manfully avowed it at the bar, as did Emmet, as did Mackay. A man who joins an organization avowedly revolutionary is prepared to accept the consequences of his conduct; and the Irish revolutionists, if impracticables sometimes, have never been cowards. Corydon swore that he had been at several meetings where Davitt was present, and had heard him arrange the plans for the capture of Chester Castle; Davitt declared on oath that he was not at the meetings described by Corydon, whose perjuries in relation to others were already exposed; but the government was bound to convict, with or without testimony, and Davitt was sentenced to penal servitude for fifteen years. John Wilson, an Englishman, who was not connected in any manner with the organization, and was wholly innocent even of treasonable intentions, was found suspiciously in Davitt's company, and was sentenced with him. Knowing his innocence and feeling deeply the painful situation in which Wilson's family would be left, Davitt arose and addressed the court in his behalf. He affirmed Wilson's innocence, and, finding that of no avail, asked that the Englishman's sentence be added to his own, that he might be spared to his family. His appeal was not wholly unheeded: Wilson's sentence was lightened.

An incident which occurred just when his trial was about to begin, and which illustrates the disposition of the British government to be fair to Irish political prisoners, deserves to be reproduced here: "A few days previous to being committed for trial I drew up instructions for my solicitor as to the mode of my defence, and this I had done in exact accordance with the rules suspended in my cell; which rules also specified that such instructions could be handed by prisoners to their legal advisers without previous inspection by the governor or other prison officials. When my solicitor's clerk visited me for the purpose of receiving those instructions, I handed him the envelope containing them in the presence of the warder who presided at the interview, and who had brought me from my cell to the visitors' or solicitors' room. Two days afterward I was again visited by my solicitor's clerk, and astounded to hear that the governor had demanded my letter after the previous visit, as the officer had reported that he saw me draw a plan of the prison upon a piece of paper and give the same to the clerk! When I saw the governor on the following morning I demanded an explanation of this strange proceeding, and had to remain satisfied with being told that it was the officer's fault, and that if I had no objection to his (the governor's) reading my letter it would be given to my solicitor. I replied that I had not the least objection, owing to what the officer had reported, but that I protested against the whole proceeding as unfair and directly opposed to the rules hung up in my cell. Now mark what transpired within those two days. A sensational paragraph had appeared in one of the London dailies announcing that another plot had been discovered to blow up the house of detention, and that on this occasion it would be attempted from within the prison. It is unnecessary to say what effect this would have upon the public mind and how small the chance would be of my obtaining an unprejudiced jury and an impartial trial in London after this. Two great points had by this heartless canard been made against me: the plan of my defence had been discovered, and the public feeling directed adversely toward me by the report that I had intended to effect another explosion."

Before citing any passage from Davitt's account of the treatment he received in prison it is proper to consider what manner of man the son of the evicted peasant had become. Of irreproachable character, without a vice or careless habit, his leisure had been wholly devoted to the cultivation of his mind. He had studied political economy thoroughly; and it is a circumstance which has almost escaped attention that the principles he has laid down in the land-reform agitation are those he imbibed from the works of English moral and social philosophers and political economists. We shall discover this when we reach his writings and speeches. He had studied the status and history of the peasant-farmer on the Continent, and to do this more satisfactorily had acquired several languages. He is fond of music and poetry, and has written smooth and graceful verse. His industry had supplied him with the comforts of life and with the means of indulging a refined taste. He had committed no crime; he was only a political conspirator. To such a man what must have been the loathsome situation in which the barbarity of his jailers soon placed him? Of tall, active figure, his face is pale, his features regular, his head large, well shaped and intellectual, his eyes, hair and beard dark. He impresses one as being reserved, passionate and obstinate. He speaks flowingly, using excellent diction, and when in public discussion exhibits a strong, homely, rugged and compact style, never employing mere rhetoric, never failing to make himself under-

(*Reverse of Medal.*)
THE LAND-LEAGUE BADGE AND MEDAL.

stood. His voice is clear, but not powerful; his gesticulation scant, but appropriate. His speeches are uniform in their solidity and simplicity of structure. In private intercourse he is modest, courteous and refined, slightly given to humor at times; but his habit of thought is essentially serious. Unmarried, his devotion to the peasantry of his country is absolute; he has no aim but their emancipation, and in consecrating his life to this he makes a self-sacrifice whose completeness is as apparent as its motive is pure. It is a sacrifice which hopelessly excludes human reward. His only compensation thus far has been to spend nearly ten of the best years of his life in prison.

He is writing of Millbank prison: "A description of the cells, together with an account of the daily routine and work that had to be done, will suffice to form some idea of what punishment has to be borne in what is termed 'probation class.' The cells are some nine or ten feet long by about eight wide, stone floor, bare whitewashed walls, with neither table nor stool, and of course with no fire to warm by its cheerful glow the oppressing chilliness of such a place. My bedstead was made of three planks laid parallel to each other at the end of the cell and raised from the stone floor but three inches at the foot and six at the head of this truly low couch. The only seat allowed me was a bucket which contained the water supplied me for washing purposes, this bucket having a cover, so as to answer the double purpose of water-holder and stool. The height of this sole article of furniture allowed me was fourteen inches exactly, including the lid, and on this 'repentance-stool' I was compelled to sit at work ten hours at least each day for ten months.

"The punishment this entails upon a tall man can be easily conceived. The recumbent posture and bent chest necessary while picking oakum, with nothing to lean one's back against to obtain a momentary relief, is distressing in the extreme. The effect upon me, in addition to inducing a weakness in my chest, was singular, but not surprising.

"On entering Millbank my height was exactly six feet, as measured by the prison standard for that purpose; but on my departure for Dartmoor, ten months after, I had illustrated the saying that some people can grow downward, for I then measured but five feet ten and a half inches.

"The bedding supplied was miserably insufficient during the winter months; and owing to this and the sitting posture during the day, with feet resting upon cold flags, with no fire and with a prohibition against walking in the cell, many prisoners have lost the use of their limbs from the effects of a Millbank winter. But one hour's exercise in the prison-yard was allowed each day, and that was forfeited if the weather proved unfavorable. Owing to my health beginning to break down, I was permitted an extra half-hour's exercise after I had been eight months in the prison. This was granted by the doctor's order.

"I had to rise at six each morning, fold up my bed very neatly, and afterward wash and scrub my cell-floor quite clean with brush and stone used for that purpose. This washing and scrubbing was, I need scarcely remark, very distressing upon me, owing to my physical infirmity; but I was compelled to do it, nevertheless, once each day during the whole term of my imprisonment. After cells were cleaned in the manner I have described work was then commenced, and continued until a quarter to nine at night, allowing, of course, for meals, exercise, and prayers in chapel each morning.

"The work I was put to in this prison was coir- and oakum-picking. I was not tasked, but had to sit working all day and pick a reasonable share of my coir or oakum, as the case might be. When I inquired, on being first ordered to this sort of work, how I could possibly do it with but a limited number of fingers at my disposal, I was told by the warder that he had known several 'blokes' with but one hand who had managed to pick oakum very well with their teeth. As I declined to use my teeth to tear old ropes to pieces, I had to do the work as best I could.

"During the whole of my stay in Millbank my conversation with prisoners—at the risk of being punished, of course—as also with warders and chaplains, would not occupy me twenty minutes to repeat could I collect all the scattered words spoken by me in the whole of that ten months. I recollect many weeks going by without my exchanging a word with a single human being.

"The food allowed me for daily rations was as follows: Breakfast, eight ounces of bread and three-quarters of a pint of cocoa; dinner, four ounces of meat (including bone) four days a week, with six ounces of bread and a pound of potatoes; one day in the week I was allowed a pint of shin-of-beef soup in lieu of meat, and on another one pound of suet-pudding ditto. Dinner on Sunday was twelve ounces of bread, four ounces of cheese and a pint of water, and for supper each night I received six ounces of bread and a pint of 'skilly,' containing—or rather supposed to contain—two ounces of oatmeal.

"This was the ordinary prison allowance.

"After subsisting for three months on this diet I applied to the doctor for a little more food, on the ground that I was losing weight owing to the insufficiency of the quantity allowed; but my application was of no avail.

"The books supplied me while in Millbank were almost exclusively religious, and but one library-book was allowed to each prisoner in a fortnight.

"I asked to have mine changed once a week, but was promptly told I could not be favored beyond other prisoners. The class of books supplied to the Catholic prisoners was such as would be suitable to children or people ignorant of the truths of the Catholic faith.

"I had often no book to read but one that might

answer the requirements of a child, such as the history of 'naughty Fanny' or 'Grandmother Betty,' and like productions, which, though doubtless good in their way, were not what could lessen the dreary monotony of such an existence.

"A circumstance in connection with the situation of Millbank may (taken with what I have already said on that prison) give some faint idea of what confinement there really means. Westminster Tower clock is not far distant from the penitentiary; so that its every stroke is as distinctly heard in each cell as if it were situated in one of the prison-yards. At each quarter of an hour, day and night, it chimes a bar of the 'Old Hundredth,' and those solemn tones strike on the ears of the lonely listeners like the voice of some monster singing the funeral-dirge of Time.

"Oft in the lonely watches of the night has it reminded me of the number of strokes I was doomed to listen to, and of how slowly those minutes were creeping along. The weird chant of Westminster clock will ever haunt my memory and recall that period of my imprisonment when I first had to implore divine Providence to preserve my reason and save me from the madness which seemed inevitable, through mental and corporal tortures combined.

"That human reason should give way under such adverse influences is not, I think, to be wondered at; and many a still living wreck of manhood can refer to the silent system of Millbank and its pernicious surroundings as the cause of his debilitated mind.

"It was here that Edward Duffy died, and where Richard Burke and Martin Hanly Carey were for a time oblivious of their sufferings from temporary insanity, and where Daniel Reddin was paralyzed. It was here where Thomas Ahern first showed symptoms of madness, and was put in dark cells and strait-jacket for a 'test' as to the reality of these symptoms. Ten years have passed their long and silent courses since then, but that same Thomas Ahern is still a prisoner and his mind is still tottering on the brink of insanity. I have anxiously watched him drifting toward this fate for the past six years, unable to render him any assistance, and I can predict that if he is not soon liberated he will exchange Dartmoor for Broadmoor lunatic prison, like so many other victims of penal servitude."

From Millbank, Mr. Davitt was transferred to Dartmoor, in the barren Devonshire moors; he was detained there six years and six months. An extract from his account of the treatment he received there will serve as a description of the boasted English prison system:

"So much attention having been directed to these veritable iron cages by the exposure of poor McCarthy's treatment and his confinement in such cells, I purpose giving an accurate description of them, and removing any doubts, if such exist, as to the account already given of their size, construction and ventilation. The dimensions of one of them will answer for that of the whole, as they are uniform in almost every respect. Length, seven feet exactly; width, four feet; and height, seven feet one or two inches. The sides (or frames) of all are of corrugated iron, and the floor is a slate one. These cells are ranged in tiers or wards in the centre of a hall, the tiers being one above another, to the height of four wards, the floors of the three upper tiers of cells forming the ceilings or tops of those immediately beneath them. Each ward or tier contains in length forty-two cells, giving a total of one hundred and sixty-eight for one hall. The sole provision made for ventilating these cells is an opening of two and a half or three inches left at the bottom of each door. There is no opening into the external air from any of those cells in Dartmoor, and the air admitted into the hall has to traverse the width of the same to enter the hole under the cell-doors. In the cells on the first three tiers or wards there are about a dozen small perforations in the corner of each, for the escape of vitiated air; but in those on the top or fourth ward—or, speaking more confidently, in those on that ward in which I was located a portion of my time—there were no such perforations, no possible way of escape for foul air except where most of it entered as 'pure,' under the cell-door. In the heat of summer it was almost impossible to breathe in these top cells, so close and foul would the air become from the improper ventilation of the cells below, allowing the breathed air in each cell to mix with that in the hall and thus ascend to the top.

"I on one occasion begged the governor of Dartmoor to remove me from such a situation, for the additional reason to those I have given that I had not sufficient light to read in the cell I was in; but I begged in vain. I was, however, soon after removed to a lower tier, after foul eruptions began to break out upon my body through the impure air I had been breathing. It has been since denied by Chatham prison officials that Charles McCarthy ever slept with his bed across the inside of his cell-door in order to catch sufficient air to breathe. From my own experience I can fully believe the necessity of his doing so, as it was quite common in Dartmoor for prisoners to sleep with their heads toward the door for a similar reason; and I have often, in the summer season, done this myself, and had repeatedly to go on my knees and put my mouth to the bottom of the door for a little air.

"The light admitted to those ordinary iron cells is scarcely sufficient to read by in the daytime; and should a fog prevail, it would be impossible to read in half of them. The cells are fitted with a couple of plates of thick intransparent glass about eighteen inches long by six inches wide each, and the light is transmitted through this 'window' from the hall, and not from the extern of the prison. I have often laid the length of my body on the cell-floor and placed my book under the door to catch sufficient light to read it.

"The food in Dartmoor prison I found to be the

BEFORE THE MAGISTRATE.

very worst in quality and the filthiest in cooking of any of the other places. I had been in. The quantity of daily rations was the same as in Millbank, with the difference of four ounces of bread more each day and one of meat less in the week. The quality, as I have already remarked, is inferior to that of any other prison; but from about November till May it is simply execrable, the potatoes being often unfit to eat and rotten cow-carrots occasionally substituted for other food. To find black beetles in soup, 'skilly,' bread and tea was quite a common occurrence; and some idea can be formed of how hunger will reconcile a man to look without disgust upon the most filthy objects in nature when I state as a fact that I have often discovered beetles in my food and have eaten it, after throwing them aside, without experiencing much revulsion of feeling at the sight of such loathsome animals in my victuals. Still, I have often come in from work weak with fatigue and hunger and found it impossible to eat the putrid meat or stinking soup supplied me for dinner, and had to return to labor again after 'dining' on six ounces of bad bread.

"It was quite a common occurrence in Dartmoor for men to be reported and punished for eating candles, boot-oil, and other repulsive articles; and, notwithstanding that a highly offensive smell is purposely given to prison-candles to prevent their being eaten instead of burned, men are driven by a system of half-starvation into an animal-like voracity, and anything that a dog would eat is nowise repugnant to their taste. I have seen men eat old poultices found buried in heaps of rubbish I was assisting in carting away, and have seen bits of candle pulled out of the prison cesspool and eaten after the human soil was wiped off them!

"The labor I was first put to was stone-breaking, that being considered suitable work for non-able-bodied prisoners. I was put to this employment in a large shed, along with some eighty or ninety more prisoners; but, my hand becoming blistered by the action of the hammer after I had broken stones for a week, I was unable to continue at that work, and was consequently put to what is termed 'cart-labor.' This sort of work is very general in Dartmoor, and I may as well give some description of it.

"Eight men constitute a 'cart-party,' and have an officer over them armed with a staff if working within the prison-walls, and with a rifle and accompanied by an armed guard if employed outside. Each man in the cart-party is supplied with a collar, which is put over the head and passes from the right or left shoulder under the opposite arm, and is then hooked to the chain by means of which the cart is drawn about. The cart-party to which I was attached was employed in carting stones, coals, manure and rubbish of all descriptions. In drawing the cart along each prisoner has to bend forward and pull with all his strength, or the warder who is driving will threaten to 'run him in,' or report him for idleness. It was our work to supply all parts of the prison—workshops, officers' mess-room, cook-house, etc.—with coals, and I was often drawing these about in rain and sleet with no fire to warm or dry myself after a wetting. I was only a few months at this sort of work, as I met with a slight accident by a collar hurting the remnant of my right arm, and was in consequence of this excused from cart-labor by the doctor's order. I was again set to breaking granite, and remained at that job during the winter of 1870-71.

"I may remark that in June, when I was first put to stone-breaking, I was employed in a shed, but during the winter I was compelled to work outside in the cold and damp, foggy weather. I was left at this work until spring, and was then removed to a task from the effects of which I believe I will never completely recover. My health on entering prison was excellent, never having had any sickness at any previous period of my life. The close confinement and insufficient food in Millbank had told, of course, on my constitution, though not to any very alarming extent; but the task I was now put to laid the germs of the heart and lung disease I have since been suffering from. This task was putrid-bone breaking.

"On the brink of the prison cesspool, in which all the soil of the whole establishment is accumulated for manure, stands a small building, some twenty feet long by about ten broad, known as the 'bone-shed.' The floor of this shed is sunk some three feet lower than the ground outside, and is on a level with the pool which laves the wall of the building. All the bones accruing from the meat-supply of the prison were pounded into dust in this shed, and during the summer of 1872 (excepting five weeks spent in Portsmouth prison) this was my employment. These bones have often lain putrefying for weeks in the broiling heat of the summer sun ere they were brought in to be broken. The stench arising from their decomposition, together with the noxious exhalations from the action of the sun's rays on the cesspool outside, no words could adequately express: it was a veritable charnel-house. It will be noted that I was at work outside the previous winter, and when the bright days and summer season came on I was put in a low shed to break putrefying bones. The number of prisoners at this work varied from thirty to six, and I may remark that the majority of these were what are termed 'doctor's men,' or prisoners unable to perform the ordinary prison-labor. When all the bones would be pounded, we would then be employed in and around the cesspool mixing and carting manure, and at various other similar occupations.

"I made application to both governor and doctor for removal from this bone-breaking to some more congenial task, but I would not be transferred to any other labor. After completing a term of my imprisonment which entitled me to a pint of tea in lieu of 'skilly' for breakfast, I was then removed to a hard-labor party, as, owing to my being an invalid, or 'doctor's man,' I could not claim the privilege of this slight change in diet without becoming attached to some hard-labor party, invalids, or 'light-labor men,' not being allowed tea at any stage of their imprisonment. I very willingly consented to a heavier task, in order to be removed from the abominable bone-shed, in which I had worked and sickened during the summer."

When accused of subjecting Irish political prisoners to exceptional hardship and personal indignities, the government officials have been vehement in their denials. But Mr. Davitt relates incidents in his prison experience whose loathsomeness renders them too offensive for republication; and the rank injustice of cruelty to him was so much the greater because he never violated a prison rule, however odious or onerous. In 1872 he was transferred to Portsmouth prison, where for a month he endured frightful suffering; then he was taken back to Dartmoor. December 19, 1877, he was released on "ticket of leave" for the remaining portion of his sentence.

Charles McCarthy, of whom he speaks, and several others were liberated soon afterward. When they reached Dublin, the delight of the people was manifested in wild street-demonstrations, in processions, public meetings, songs and speeches. It was clear that, if the government considered them felons, the populace deemed them heroes. At one of the public receptions tendered to them the following address was presented:

"ADDRESS OF THE PEOPLE OF DUBLIN

"*To Messrs. Charles McCarthy, Thomas Chambers, John Patrick O'Brien and Michael Davitt, on their Release from Imprisonment, suffered for Ireland:*

"FELLOW-COUNTRYMEN: We approach you, on your release from the sufferings which you have for many years so cheerfully and heroically borne for our country in the prisons of England, to offer you our warmest congratulations, to bid you, with all the fervor and affection of our hearts, welcome home to Ireland, and to thank you for your courageous and uncompromising devotion to the national cause.

"Roman history reveres the tradition which tells of the heroic self-sacrifice of the patriot Marcus Curtius, who saved the city by casting himself into the yawning abyss opened in the Forum. With a self-denying patriotism equal to his you have made an offering of life, fortune and liberty on the altar of your country; and if by such sacrifices as yours her freedom has not been achieved, her honor has been saved, the manhood of her sons vindicated and a fund of public virtue created amongst us which will yet redeem and regenerate the land.

"Mindful of this, and of all the horrors of penal servitude through which you have been condemned to pass, the capital of your country rejoices in your liberation to-day, and stretches forth its hand to receive you with delight and gratitude.

"The pleasure which we feel, however, is diminished by the recollection that some of your brave companions are still held in captivity, and we cannot conclude without expressing the hope that they too may soon be restored to liberty.

"Wishing you every blessing and prosperity in the future, and assuring you of the gratitude of all your countrymen, we again say to you from our inmost hearts, *Cead Mille Failthe*.

"Signed on behalf of Reception Committee: Charles S. Parnell, M. P., J. G. Biggar, M. P., John O'Sullivan, John Dillon, J. Taafe, Patrick Egan; Treasurer, James Carey; Hon. Secretary, Thomas Brennan; John Burns, Robert Woodward, R. J. Donnelly, Daniel Curley, Edmund Hayes, J. Brady."

Mr. McCarthy died two days afterward from the effects of the brutal treatment inflicted on him in an English model "reformatory" prison. He was buried in Glasnevin, and sixty thousand persons followed his remains to the grave, their tears for the death of a gentle and noble soul mingling with their execrations of the government which had killed him by slow torture.

Mr. Davitt visited various parts of Ireland and was received everywhere with popular welcome, bonfires blazing on the hills to announce his presence in a neighborhood. This circumstance inspired Mr. Lowther, chief secretary, to tell the Irish people a year later, when the fuel was scarce in the West of

Ireland, that "they could find plenty of turf to give bonfire receptions to an ex-convict."

When Mr. Davitt visited London he was received in Parliament by Mr. Parnell and other Irish members, and devoted his time there to securing the release of the political prisoners still detained. Just at what period he resolved upon organizing the Irish people for land reform is not known; he had thought upon it for years; and if the recollections of his own family history and his observation of the wretched state of the peasantry in general had not awakened the determination in his mind, his reading of John Bright, Richard Cobden, John Stuart Mill, Mr. Gladstone, and other English statesmen and economists, could not have failed to do so.

He sailed for America in 1878, and was soon in consultation with the exiled Irish nationalists. Chief among these were Mr. John Devoy and Mr. John J. Breslin. After frequent meetings to devise a plan by which the energy of the Irish people in both countries should be effectively put to work for the emancipation of the peasantry, they drew up and transmitted to the Irish members of Parliament the following proposition (it was the original formulation of the now historic movement to recover the land of Ireland for the Irish people and to establish there peasant proprietary):

"*First.* Abandonment of the federal demand, and substitution of a general declaration in favor of self-government.

THE DEFEAT OF OBSTRUCTION IN THE HOUSE OF COMMONS.
Removal of Mr. Parnell by order of the Speaker.

"*Second.* Vigorous agitation of the land question on the basis of a peasantry proprietary, while accepting concessions tending to abolish arbitrary eviction.

"*Third.* Exclusion of all sectarian issues from the platform.

"*Fourth.* Irish members to vote together on all imperial and home questions, adopt an aggressive policy and energetically resist coercive legislation.

"*Fifth.* Advocacy of all struggling nationalities, in the British empire and elsewhere."

In a lecture in Boston, December 8, 1878, Mr. Davitt fully outlined the programme of new agitation:

"*First.* The first and indispensable requisite in a representative of Ireland in the Parliament of England to be a public profession of his belief in the inalienable right of the Irish people to self-government, and recognition of the fact that want of self-government is the chief want of Ireland.

"*Second.* An exclusive Irish representation with the view of exhibiting Ireland to the world in the light of her people's opinions and national aspirations, together with an uncompromising opposition to the government upon every prejudiced or coercive policy.

"*Third.* A demand for the immediate improvement of the land system by such a thorough change as would prevent the peasantry of Ireland from being its victims in the future, this change to form the preamble of a system of small proprietorships similar to what at present obtains in France, Belgium and Prussia, such land to be purchased or held directly from the state. To ground this demand upon the reasonable fact that, as the land of Ireland formerly belonged to the people (being but nominally held in trust for them by chiefs or heads of clans elected for that among other purposes), it is the duty of the government to give compensation to the landlords for taking back that which was bestowed upon their progenitors after being stolen from the people, in order that the state can again become the custodian of the land for the people-owners.

"*Fourth.* Legislation for the encouragement of Irish industries; development of Ireland's natural resources; substitution as much as practicable of cultivation for grazing; reclamation of waste-lands; protection of Irish fisheries and improvement of peasant dwellings.

"*Fifth.* Assimilation of the county to the borough franchise, and reform of the grand-jury laws, as also those affecting convention in Ireland.

"*Sixth.* A national solicitude on the question of education by vigorous efforts for improving and advancing the same, together with every precaution to be taken against it being made an anti-national one.

"*Seventh.* The right of the Irish people to carry arms."

In a remarkable letter to a Dublin journal, Mr. John Devoy, representing the Irish revolutionists, gave their support to the new movement. He said touching the union of all Irishmen for the recovery of the land:

"The object aimed at by the advanced national party—the recovery of Ireland's national independence and the severance of all political connection with England—is one that would require the utmost efforts and the greatest sacrifices on the part of the whole Irish people. Unless the whole Irish people, or the great majority of them, undertake the task, and bend their whole energies to its accomplishment —unless the best intellect, the financial resources and the physical strength of the nation be enlisted in the effort—it can never be realized. Even with all these things in our favor the difficulties in our way would be enormous; but if firmly united and ably led, we could overcome them, and the result achieved would be worth the sacrifice. I am not one of those who despair of Ireland's freedom, and am as much in favor of continuing the struggle to-day as some of those who talk loudest against constitutional agitation.

"I am convinced that the whole Irish people can be enlisted in an effort to free their native land, and that they have within themselves the power to overcome all obstacles in their way. I feel satisfied that Ireland could maintain her existence as an independent nation, become a respectable power in Europe, provide comfortably for a large population within her borders, and rival England in commerce and manufactures. I contend she can never attain the development to which her geographical position, her natural resources and the moral and intellectual gifts of her people entitle her without becoming complete mistress of her own destinies and severing the connection with England. But I am also convinced that one section of the people alone can never win independence, and no political party, no matter how devoted or determined, can ever win the support of the whole people if they never come before the public and take no part in the every-day life of the country. I have often said it before, and I repeat it now again, that a mere conspiracy will never free Ireland. I am not arguing against conspiracy, but only pointing out the necessity of Irish nationalists taking whatever public action for the advancement of the national cause they may find within their reach—such action as will place the aims and objects of the national party in a more favorable light before the world and help to win the support of the whole Irish people.

"No party or combination of parties in Ireland can ever hope to win the support of the majority of the people except it honestly proposes *a radical reform of the land system.* No matter what may be said in favor of individual landlords, the whole system was founded on robbery and fraud and has been perpetuated by cruelty, injustice, extortion and hatred of the people. The men who got small farms in the times of confiscation settled down in the country, and their descendants, no matter what their political party, are now 'bone of our bone'—have become Irish—and perform a useful function in the land. No one thinks of disturbing them. If the landlords had become Irish and treated the people with humanity, the original robbery might be forgiven, though a radical change in the tenure of land must come of itself some day; but when, as a class, they have simply done England's work of rooting out the Irish people, when the history of landlordism is simply a dark story of heartless cruelty, of artificial famine, of evictions, of rags and squalid misery, there is no reason why we should forget that the system was forced upon us by England, and that the majority of the present landlords are the inheritors of the robber-horde sent over by Elizabeth and James I., by Cromwell and William of Orange, to garrison the country for England. It is the interest of Ireland that *the land should be owned by those who till the soil*, and this could be reached without even inflicting hardship on those who deserve no leniency at the hands of the Irish people. A solution of the land question has been reached, to a large extent, in France, in Prussia and in Belgium, by enabling the occupiers to purchase their holdings. Let the Irish landlords be given a last chance of settling the Irish land question amicably in this manner, or wait for a solution in which they shall have no part. Let a beginning be made with the absentees, the English lords and the London companies who hold stolen land in Ireland, and there will be enough of work for some years to come. *Let evictions be stopped at all hazards* and the rooting-out process come to an end. But I shall be told the English Parliament will never do any of these things. Then, I say, these things must only wait till an Irish Parliament can do them better; but in the mean time sound principles will have been inculcated and the country will be aroused.

"To those who are alarmed at language like this in regard to the land question I would say, Look at France, at Prussia and at Belgium, and you will find that the secret of their prosperity lies in the number of tillers of the soil who own their holdings. Listen to the mutterings of the coming storm *in England*, and ask yourselves what is going to become of the land monopoly after a few more years of commercial and manufacturing depression—a depression sure to continue, because the causes of it are on the increase. The English are a very practical and a very selfish people, and will not let any fine sentiment stand in the way when they think it is their interest to redistribute the land. What, may I ask, would become of the Irish landlords—especially the rack-renting, evicting ones—in case of a social convulsion in England? It is a question which they themselves must decide within the next few years. With them or without them, the question will be settled before long, and many who now think the foregoing assertions extravagant will consider them very moderate indeed by and by."

Meanwhile, the proposition sent over by Mr

Davitt and the Irish nationalists in America had reached its destination. It was received by the Home-Rule party, of which the patriot Irish members of the British Parliament were the leaders, and foremost among these was Charles Stewart Parnell. The Parnells were originally English. As we saw in the chapter on "How the People lost their Land," some of the English who had obtained estates in Ireland from Elizabeth were driven off them by her successors, who wished to distribute the Irish soil to their own favorites or for their profit, and many of the earlier English colonists had become so attached to their new home and the genial and kind-hearted people around them that they were "more Irish than the Irish themselves." The English government viewed this with open alarm, and to prevent the commingling of the natives and the colonists forbade, in severe penalty, all intercourse between them, and even confiscated the lands of any Englishman who married an Irish wife. The beauty of the Irishwomen and their virtues won the heart of more than one English aristocrat, who sacrificed his fortune to his love. It was the statute making an outlaw of the Englishman who married an Irishwoman that furnished Thomas d'Arcy McGee with the subject of his beautiful little poem "My Irish Wife:"

> "I knew the law forbade the banns;
> I knew my king abhorred her race;
> Who never bent before their clans
> Must bow before their ladies' grace.

> Take all my forfeited domain—
> I cannot wage with kinsmen strife—
> Take knightly gear and noble name,
> And I will keep my Irish wife."

The estates which were confiscated for this and other offences against the English law were eagerly sought by English and Scotchmen, who, knowing the fertility of the soil, expected to become rich by its cultivation. Thomas Parnell of Cheshire bought one of these at the time of the Restoration, and then the family, which soon became "more Irish than the Irish themselves," was planted in the island.

John Parnell had two sons, John and Thomas; the first became a judge, the second a minister and a poet. The poem by which he is best known now is "The Hermit." The Parnells were and are Protestants. Thomas drew a handsome income from the Catholic Irish to whom he did not preach; as he had no congregation to speak of to preach to, he became an absentee, and spent much of his time in the literary society of London. He was an intimate friend of Dean Swift, who used his once-powerful influence at the English court to advance the temporal interests of Thomas Parnell.

John, the judge, married an Irish wife—her name was Anne Ward—but he was not outlawed on account of it; on the contrary, he was created a baronet in 1766. This Sir John Parnell had a son, Sir John, who was one of the patriots in the Irish Parliament a hundred years ago; it is he of whom Cornwallis

MRS. DELIA TUDOR STEWART PARNELL.

speaks in the chapter on "How the People lost their Parliament." His son, Sir Henry Parnell, became a member of the British Parliament after the destruction of that of the Irish, and distinguished himself as a sympathizer with the miseries of his countrymen. The brother of Sir Henry Parnell, William, a country gentleman, left a son named John Henry Parnell, who while travelling in America met Delia Tudor Stewart, daughter of Admiral Stewart, " Old Ironsides." A mutual attachment followed, and they were married in Grace church, New York, by Rev. Dr. Taylor. Charles Stewart Parnell is their son. He was born in 1846, at Avondale, Rathdrum, the estate which he now owns, and received his early education in England. Sickness compelled his family to bring him back to the milder air of his native land, and when he had fully recovered he was sent over again to England and placed under the care of a tutor to be prepared for Cambridge, at which he remained for two years. In 1872 he visited the United States as a tourist.

It is not strange that he felt little interest in the affairs of his country. His education and his social status had practically alienated him from home; he did not imbibe Irish sentiments from his English schoolmasters, and he heard no impassioned argument at Cambridge for the redress of Irish wrongs. English society has always been the deadliest foe of Irish nationalism. Had Swift spent less time in London he would have been a better Irishman; for, although he did much for the Irish tradesman and the Irish manufacturer, he was a religious bigot and as violently opposed to extending political privileges to four-fifths of the Irish people as he was bitter in his denunciation of the restrictive commercial laws, the chief victims of which in his time were the men of his own creed. London society tainted even Tom Moore, whose adulation of the aristocracy—who sneered at him as an Irish grocer's son—was so flunkeyish that Byron in pique wrote of him the never-forgotten taunt, "Tommy dearly loves a lord."

The real basis of the enduring fame of Moore rests on his immortal Irish melodies, and for the resources upon which he drew for them he was indebted to a suggestion by Robert Emmet. Moore was not, however, poisoned by the companionship of the enemies of his country. It is true that for the birthday of the prince of Wales he wrote "Our Prince's Day" to the air of "St. Patrick's Day," and even indited the line,

"A curse on the minion who calls us disloyal,"

to ingratiate himself with the princelings and snobs who always constitute the convivial retinue of a king that is to be; but he amply compensated for these trivial infidelities, and his verse was a valuable aid in winning for Ireland the sympathy and the pity of the generous in every part of the globe in which the love of rhythm and of melody exists.

A still more remarkable instance of alienation is

furnished in the person of the newest of the present generation of poets. When Sir Charles Gavan Duffy was on trial for loving his country—he was one of the patriots of '48—among the treasonable articles read by the prosecution was an editorial clipped from the journal of which he was the conductor. It was a bold, powerful and persuasive denunciation of the government of England in Ireland, and it was enough, probably, to secure conviction at an earlier day and to send Duffy to the scaffold of Robert Emmet. But when the reading had been finished a quiet voice spoke from the ladies' gallery: "If that be treason, I am the culprit." The speaker was Lady Wilde, one of the most eloquent poets of that brilliant period, the mother of Oscar Wilde, who has become so English in London circles that in the recently-published first volume of his poems, whose pages are full of tears for the sorrows of other lands, the name of his own miserable country is not mentioned.

English society had not Anglicized Charles Stewart Parnell. An incident which occurred in Manchester in 1867 had set him thinking. An attempt had been made by a small party of excited Irishmen to release from a prison-van as it rolled through the streets the Irish political prisoners enclosed in it. A pistol-ball was fired into the lock of the door to open it. Three men, Allen, Larkin and O'Brien, were hung for the offence which George Washington committed against the English Crown. They were tried for the murder of a policeman; they were not guilty of that crime, but they were hanged because they were convicted of loving Ireland and of hating her brutal foe. The last words of each were "God save Ireland!" These words rang in the ears of Charles Stewart Parnell until he studied the testimony and found that the Manchester three had been legally and judicially assassinated. The sombre hours of reflection which he bestowed on that episode changed the current of his thoughts; henceforward they flowed toward his country. The elegant gentleman became the patriot; the quiet and studious lover of the æsthetic became the agitator.

When the proposition which the Irish nationalists in New York sent to the Home Rulers reached them, Charles Stewart Parnell was the head of that party. He entered Parliament as a Home Ruler in 1875, member for Meath. The following description of the man and his manner is in the main correct; but his experience in public speaking has made him much more effective and interesting than he was at the time of entrance upon a parliamentary career. It is taken from a London journal not friendly to the neighboring country. It was written nearly three years ago:

"'If Parnell does not draw the rein,' remarked a friend to me the other day, 'the country will soon have to put him under lock and key.' It is not my intention to justify the observation or to discuss the anti-rent agitation in Ireland in any shape, but it seems to me that when a politician comes to be regarded by a great many people as a rather dangerous man—and there are a great many people of my friend's way of thinking—it is well the country should know something about him.

"Now for the man himself. I do not know that previous to 1875 either Ireland or England had ever heard of Mr. Parnell. His father was a quiet, unobtrusive man of no mark at all, except that he was once high sheriff for the county of Meath, in which the family property is situated. The first appearance of our friend on any stage was when he made his bow to the Speaker of the House of Commons in April, 1875, with the return for the county of Meath in his pocket. A tall, thin, fair, studious young man of nine and twenty at that time, nobody then suspected in him the future leader of a 'party of exasperation.' He had not long finished his studies at Cambridge, and politics were practically an unknown field to him, his chief article of faith being 'Home Rule.'

"That session, after the manner of most new members, Mr. Parnell was mute. He heard vote after vote of the estimates passed, and clause after clause of bills discussed in committee, and said not a word. The idea of obstruction was then as far from his mind as from, say, Admiral Edmonston's. The following session he began to find his feet and to interest himself in small details of estimates, and it seems to have been about this time, on his seeing the success which attended persistent criticism, that he thought of obstruction. It was only by degrees, however, that the policy of obstruction was developed, and the House itself is, perhaps, in some degree responsible for it. Everybody knows that the House, or rather the ministerial portion of it, is somewhat impatient of criticism, especially of persistent criticism, of the estimates. Dillwyn, Whitwell and a few others have a sort of prescriptive right to make the same remarks and ask the same questions year after year; but no sooner does any new member betray a disposition to pry into the secrets of the public purse than the mechanical majority proceeds to sit on him after its own fashion. A hum of conversation arises as soon as the new man gets upon his legs. The new man, being under the impression that members are merely careless, and not malicious, raises his voice; the talkers raise theirs, till at length, if the trial of strength is continued long enough, the House is a perfect Babel of sound. This was Mr. Parnell's experience.

"Now, few men have the temerity to brave the House of Commons. Ninety-nine members out of a hundred, finding that they cannot get a hearing, are content to accept the inevitable. Not so Mr. Parnell. Under a slim and almost effeminate exterior he has an iron will. He refused to be put down. The more the House would not listen, the more he would talk, even although he could not be heard more than a couple of benches off, and his persistence gradually attracted the support of the sympathetic Biggar and one or two kindred spirits in the same direction, who looked upon him as an Irish martyr. By and by he began to retaliate by talking when he had nothing to say, and so during the sessions of 1877 and 1878 the merits of obstruction as an engine for extorting concessions from the government gradually dawned upon him and his faithful adherents, whose appearance in the character of financial and administrative critics the House resented in pretty much the same way as his own.

"Perhaps had Mr. Parnell possessed in some degree the oratorical faculty, the House would have treated him more kindly; but he has a harsh, monotonous voice which at once destroys all sympathy between him and his hearers, and his manner is stiff and, so to speak, wooden. Since he has been in Parliament he has never, so far as I recollect, spoken upon any question of general politics excepting flogging, and that he took up more, perhaps, for obstructive purposes than on conscientious grounds.

"I have spoken of Mr. Parnell's personal appearance. He is a standing wonder even to his friends. Calm, cool, bloodless, he is a man whom nothing can move. O'Connor Power grows savage under the exasperating treatment of the House and O'Donnell hisses his words through his teeth with ill-disguised resentment, but Parnell remains invariably imperturbable. A contest between him and the House is a comedy in itself. 'Mr. Speaker,' says Mr. Parnell, rising to his feet, amid overpowering cries of "Vide! 'vide!' Then comes a lull, in which Mr. Parnell edges in the words, 'Mr. Speaker, sir.' Here there is a renewed chorus of voices, on the subsiding of which Mr. Parnell utters the words 'I rise,' which are followed by another outburst. In this way he contrives, bit by bit, to proceed with his speech, the House unconsciously serving his purpose by forcing him to pause at every word. Though a man of this resolute and unbending stamp, he has in personal intercourse the mildest and most gentle manner conceivable. He is almost womanly, and Sir Wilfrid Lawson has long since noted that he is an inveterate water-drinker.

"There is a belief abroad that Parnell is a wealthy man. This is a mistake. His property does not bring him in more than fifteen hundred pounds a year, and, true to the principles he has recently been preaching up and down Ireland, he has within the past few weeks reduced his own rents some twenty per cent.

"It is a question of some importance how a man of this stamp stands in popular estimation. From inquiries I have made, I am convinced that Mr. Parnell is at present the most popular man in Ireland. He is almost worshipped by the masses."

The third of those popularly recognized as the leaders of the Land League is John Dillon. In 1866, John Bright—whose repeated expressions of sympathy with Ireland on the floor of the House of Commons had endeared him to a people who should have learned from cruel disappointments that the opinions of a man out of office may be very different from the opinions of the same man in office—was invited to a public banquet in Dublin. Twenty-two members of the House of Commons from Ireland

MEDAL AWARDED COMMODORE CHARLES STEWART, U. S. N.

had signed the invitation. In his speech at the banquet John Bright said: "I speak with grief when I say that one of our friends who signed that invitation is no longer with us. I had not the pleasure of a long acquaintance with Mr. Dillon, but I shall take this opportunity of saying that during the last session of Parliament I formed a very high opinion of his character. There was that in his eye and in the tone of his voice—in his manner altogether—which marked him for an honorable and a just man. . . . I believe, amongst all her worthy sons, Ireland has had no worthier and nobler son than John Blake Dillon."

The man thus justly characterized was adjudged by the English government fit only to be hung or banished, for John Blake Dillon was one of the "Young Ireland" party of '48, and when its aspirations had grown too bold for the English government it sought to wreak the same vengeance on the leaders which had been inflicted on all their predecessors in that cause.

John Blake Dillon escaped to this country, and was for a time the law-partner of Richard O'Gorman, also a rebel and recently elected judge of the superior court in New York. Mr. Dillon returned to Ireland, and was elected to Parliament by the same constituency which his son now represents.

Sir Charles Gavan Duffy, who had the best means of knowing him intimately, as he furnished much of the brains of *The Nation*, of which Sir Charles was editor, says of him: "He was tall and strikingly handsome, with eyes like a thoughtful woman's, and the clear olive complexion and stately bearing of a Spanish noble. His generous nature made him more of a philanthropist than a politician. . . . Codes, tenures and social theories were his familiar reading. . . . He followed in the track of Bentham and De Tocqueville, and recognized a regulated democracy as the rightful ruler of the world; and he saw with burning impatience the wrongs inflicted on the industrious poor by an aristocracy practically irresponsible. . . . He was grave with the sweet gravity which comes from habitual thought. . . . Thackeray assured me in later years that among the half-dozen men in the United States whom he loved to remember the modesty and wholesome sweetness of Dillon, then a political refugee, gave him a foremost place. . . . Dillon was a man of remarkable talents carefully cultivated, of lofty purpose sustained by steady courage, and of as pure and generous a nature as ever was given to man." While a member of Parliament he was conspicuous for the zeal with which he sought to secure the attention of that body to the crying evils of Ireland, and his knowledge of economic matters, especially in relation to land tenure, was frequently exhibited. It was on his motion that many of the "inquiries" were made which resulted in laying before both countries facts which hastened the day of land reform. He died in 1867.

John Dillon, his son, studied in the Catholic University of Dublin, and is a lawyer; his brother William, who has also been active in the land movement, is a physician. The sons inherit their father's ability with his opinions; John resembles him somewhat in personal appearance. Of delicate health, he has had to struggle bravely to maintain vigor enough for the exhausting functions of a public orator to whom neither night nor day can bring assurance of repose. He speaks slowly, carefully choosing his words, and does not at first make a deep impression on those who see and hear him. But in a few minutes the strength and tenacity of his thought becomes apparent. He reveals the mind that has been studying its subject to the ultimate conclusions; he does not tarry midway nor trifle with the incidental to the neglect of the essential. He speaks with clearness, force and determination. He does not temporize or compromise in the course of an address, and never permits the logical end to get out of view. In private life he is a charming conversationalist, never garrulous, but so well equipped with ideas that his conversation is at once interesting, informing and convincing without being in the least strenuous or persistent.

Such are the men who are the recognized leaders of the land agitation in Ireland. Neither in their antecedents, in their associations, in their personal character nor in their ambition do they suggest the "ignorant ruffian."

CHAPTER XI.

A PEACEFUL AND CONSTITUTIONAL MOVEMENT.

THE Irish National Land League was founded October 21, 1879, in the Imperial hotel, Lower Sackville street, Dublin. The parliamentary Home-Rule party had accepted the proposition sent from America by the Irish nationalists, and upon that as a platform all divisions of Irishmen who wish for the good of their country united. The following is the official record of the first meeting:

"The Rev. Father Behan, C. C., proposed, and Mr. Wm. Dillon, B. L., seconded, 'That an association be hereby formed, to be named "The Irish National Land League."'

"Proposed by Mr. W. Kelly, seconded by Mr. Thomas Roe: 'That the objects of the League are, first, to bring about a reduction of rack-rents; second, to facilitate the obtaining of the ownership of the soil by the occupant.'

"Proposed by Mr. Parnell, M. P., seconded by the Rev. Father Sheehy, C. C.: 'That the objects of the League can be best attained by promoting organization among the tenant-farmers, by defending those who may be threatened with eviction for refusing to pay unjust rents, by facilitating the working of the Bright clauses of the Land Act during the winter, and by obtaining such reform in the laws relating to land as will enable every tenant to become the owner of his holding by paying a fair rent for a limited number of years.'

"Proposed by Mr. John Sweetman, seconded by Mr. T. D. Sullivan: 'That Mr. Charles S. Parnell, M. P., be elected president of this League.'

"Proposed by Mr. George Delany, seconded by Mr. W. H. Cobbe, Portarlington: 'That Mr. A. J. Kettle, Mr. Michael Davitt and Mr. Thomas Brennan be appointed honorary secretaries of the League.'

"Proposed by Mr. Patrick Cummins, P. L. G., seconded by Mr. Laurence McCourt, P. L. G.: 'That Mr. J. G. Biggar, M. P., Mr. W. H. O'Sullivan, M. P., and Mr. Patrick Egan, be appointed treasurers.'

"On the motion of the Rev. Father Sheehy, seconded by Mr. Michael Davitt, it was resolved 'That the president of this League, Mr. Parnell, be requested to proceed to America for the purpose of obtaining assistance from our exiled countrymen, and other sympathizers, for the objects for which this appeal is issued.'

"Proposed by Mr. Thomas Ryan, seconded by Mr. J. F. Graham: 'That none of the funds of this League shall be used for the purchase of any landlord's interests in the land, or for furthering the interests of any parliamentary candidate.'

"*Committee.*—Charles Stewart Parnell, M. P., President, Avondale, Rathdrum; P. O'Gorman, M. P., Waterford; John Ferguson, Glasgow; W. Quirke, P. P., dean of Cashel; A. Cummins, LL.D., Liverpool; M. Harris, Ballinasloe; U. J. Canon Bourke, P. P., Claremorris; J. O'C. Power, M. P., London; Rev. J. Behan, Dublin; Richard Lalor, Mountrath; J. L. Finegan, M. P., London; Rev. R. Sheehy, Kilmallock; J. J. Louden, B. L., Westport; O'G. Mahon, M. P., London; John Dillon, Dublin; W. Joyce, P. P., Louisburgh, Mayo; N. Ennis, M. P., Claremount, Meath; T. Roe, *Dundalk Democrat;* J. R. McCloskey, M. D., Derry; Geo. Delany, Dublin; T. D. Sullivan, *Nation*, Dublin; J. Byrne, Wallstown Castle, Cork; J. E. Kenny, Dublin; M. Marum, J. P., Ballyragget; P. F. Johnston, Kanturk; Rev. M. Tormey, Painstown, Beauparc; T. Canon Doyle, P. P., Ramsgrange; P. J. Moran, Finea, Granard; O. J. Carraher, Cardestown, Louth; J. White, P. P., Milltown-Malbay; P. Cummins, P. L. G., Rathmins; J. Daly, P. L. G., Castlebar; Rev. P. M. Furlong, New Ross; Thos. Ryan, Dublin; James Rourke, Dublin; R. Kelly, *Tuam Herald;* Wm. Dillon, Dublin; I. J. Kennedy, T. C., Clonliffe Terrace, Dublin; M. O'Flaherty, Dunoman Castle, Croom; John Sweetman, Kells; M. F. Madden, Clonmel; J. C. Howe, London; T. Lynch, P. P., Painstown, Beauparc; J. F. Grehan, P. L. G., Cabinteely, Dublin; D. Brennan, P. P., Kilmacow, Kilkenny; W. Kelly, Donabate, Dublin; C. Reilly, Artane, Dublin; L. McCourt,

P. L. G., Dublin; S. O'Mara, Limerick; Thos. Grehan, Loughlinstown, Dublin; Rev. M. K. Dunne, Enniscorthy; M. J. Kenny, P. P., Scariff; R. H. Medge, Athlumney House, Navan; M. A. Conway, P. P., Skreen, Sligo.

"*Treasurers.*—W. H. O'Sullivan, M. P., Kilmallock; J. G. Biggar, M. P., Belfast; Patrick Egan, Dublin.

"*Honorary Secretaries.*—A. J. Kettle, P. L. G., Artane, Dublin; Michael Davitt, Dublin; Thomas Brennan, Dublin.

"COMMITTEE ROOMS, 62 Middle Abbey Street, Dublin."

This record is presented in full for two reasons: to answer the charge that the conservative element in Ireland—the Catholic clergy—did not sympathize with the objects or approve of the methods of the Land League, and to establish the fundamental character of the League as it was defined in its official organization. The objects for which the League was organized were kept constantly in view from its inception until its attempted suppression by the English government. These objects were strictly moral, humane and constitutional, and the methods employed to accomplish them were peaceful and legal. The League was in active existence for two years when the English government suppressed it. It accomplished these, at least, among its objects:

1. A reduction of excessive rents.
2. The protection of tenants evicted for not paying excessive rents.

3. It compelled the English government to pass a bill taking away from the Irish landlord for fifteen years the power arbitrarily to raise rents, or to evict when rents are paid according to the terms of the lease.

It accomplished two objects not originally contemplated: it saved from death by famine hundreds of thousands of the Irish people during the winter and spring following its organization, and it blended all classes of the people of Ireland into a compact and homogeneous mass resolved to win by constitutional means the right of Ireland to make her own domestic laws on her own soil.

So much has been written on this side the water about the hostility of the Catholic clergy, as well as of the ministers of Protestant denominations in Ireland, to the Land League, that a word may be said upon this subject. The complaint is made, on the one hand, against ecclesiastics entering into Irish politics at all, and, on the other, the most has been made by the English government of whatever hostility it could arouse among the religious elements against any popular movement with the ultimate object of compelling the foreign government in Ireland to be more just to the people. Americans cannot understand why "the priest should be in politics" in Ireland any more than in this country, in whose party contests he never participates. It is undoubtedly true that in Ireland, as in the United States, the clergyman would prefer to escape the embarrassment

Patrick Egan, Treas.   C. S. Parnell, M. P.   T. Sexton.   T. Brennan, Sec.
T. D. Sullivan, M. P.   Reporters.   M. O'Sullivan.   J. G. Biggar, M. P.   T. M. Healy.

inseparable from such contests; but it should not be forgotten that it has always been the policy of the English government in Ireland to foment religious dissensions there as a powerful means of perpetuating its own domination. If the Catholics could be made odious and detestable to the Protestants, and if the Protestants could be made vicious and intolerant toward the Catholics, violent collisions, breaking the peace of the country, would inevitably ensue—as, indeed, they have ensued, to the discredit of all responsible for them. These collisions, endangering life and property, justified the foreign government inciting them in claiming that the Irish people are incapable of governing themselves, and must have strong government from abroad to make them respect the laws of the country. This has been a distinct feature of English government in Ireland since the Reformation.

That it is wholly unwarranted by the facts of Irish history is indisputable. The first seed of these dissensions was sowed by the English government in the laws imposing dreadful penalties upon the Roman Catholics, who, as late as 1800, comprised seven-tenths of the population. The object of the penal laws, as already fully stated, was not to save the souls of the Irish people, but to get their lands, ruin their industries and reduce the country into a vast farm whose soil and products should be owned in England, and whose tenants should be patrons of the English manufacturer. That plan succeeded, and to insure the permanence of its success the schools of the Catholics were destroyed and they were forbidden to educate their children at home or to send them abroad for education. The only schools which existed in Ireland from the Reformation until a few years ago were schools in which the Creed of the Church of England was taught, and which all who attended them had to accept; and, as the seven-tenths of the people could not in conscience send their children to them, they had to go without education. These schools were conducted in some cases by sincere and benevolent persons who held the doctrines to be essential to the attainment of salvation; in others by brutal and hypocritical demagogues who were especially obnoxious to the mass of the people.

The system of tithes was also calculated to excite the deepest antipathy among the majority of the people. Every Irishman, whatever his real religious opinions, was required to contribute toward the support of the foreign Church, whose ministers often had no congregations, but were in receipt of large incomes; and it was lawful to seize and to sell the property of the Catholic, the Methodist, the Presbyterian or the Baptist to pay the tithes of the minister appointed by the state—one whose theology and person were alike offensive and detested. Is it any wonder that there should have been ill-will on the part of those who were its victims toward those who profited by this injustice? Yet it was only ten years ago that the Irish people were relieved of the burden of maintaining this alien Church and each denomination left free to support the clergy it preferred. If there have been religious dissensions in Ireland, let the blame rest where it belongs.

The special penalties of the laws being laid on the Catholics, they became poor, ignorant, timid; and occasionally they arose in madness and by sudden and frenzied efforts—which were always crushed with the utmost cruelty—endeavored to throw off the yoke which held their necks to the ground. Sometimes the Protestants, stung to fury by the injustice constantly visited upon their country, organized secret revolution, arose, were put down, and the leaders who escaped the bayonet or the ball went to the scaffold. Robert Emmet's insurrection was a Protestant movement; Wolfe Tone's conspiracy was a Protestant movement; the threatened revolution of 1782, which won the independence of the Irish Parliament—only to lose it altogether eighteen years later—was a Protestant movement; but in all these the Catholics cordially united with the Protestants and assisted them so far as their limited means allowed. Wolfe Tone declared that it was only the Catholics who were faithful to him to the end. It was inevitable that in the movement for parliamentary independence a hundred years ago the leaders should be exclusively Protestant, because during a long preceding period the English government had shut out the Catholics from the right to be members or to vote for members. But the Catholics subscribed cordially to the volunteer fund, by which, no less than by the eloquence of Grattan, the victory was won.

The instinct of the patriotic people of Ireland of all creeds has been precisely what the instincts of all human beings are who have a common political object to accomplish—to unite for the accomplishment of that object. The politicians who have conducted the government of Ireland for the English manufacturer understand this, and they have always strenuously sought to arouse sectarian animosity and to perpetuate the miserable spirit of bigotry. For instance, during the time that Cornwallis and Castlereagh were endeavoring to abolish the Irish Parliament, they told the Protestants that if the act of legislative union did not pass the Catholics would obtain from the Irish Parliament the right to vote and to be members, and that then the Protestants would be persecuted and driven out of the country; while, at the same time, they insidiously circulated the assurance among the Catholics that if they would favor the act of union they would be granted the political and civil rights enjoyed then only by the Protestants, who, as long as they controlled the Irish Parliament, would continue to exclude them from participation in the government of their country. Doubtless many of the credulous on both sides believed these libels—gross libels, for the people were rapidly drawing together for the common good. Again, when

O'Connell, twenty years later, was leading the agitation for Catholic emancipation, the Protestants were led to believe that if the agitation succeeded the ascendency which they had so long enjoyed would be destroyed, and that, with their new privileges, the Catholics would become so insolent that the lives and property of the Protestants would be endangered. Many even of the intelligent among them believed this calumny and opposed Catholic emancipation, thereby arousing the suspicion and dislike of the Catholics, who had worked so heartily with them to obtain parliamentary independence. The same arguments were employed against the proposition to abolish the State-Church and leave the people free to pay church assessments according to conscience; the ten years that have passed since that event have proved that the assumption was false.

The Orange society was established in Ireland—doubtless at English instigation—for the purpose of oppressing Catholics and dissenters and of perpetuating foreign government in the country; yet so steady was the inclination of all classes of the people to unite on a common political platform for the good of their country that the idea of running Daniel O'Connell for Parliament, and thereby forcing the English government into an encounter directly with the then almost solid and almost revolutionary body of the people, originated with a famous Orangeman, Sir David Roos, the high sheriff of Dublin. The petty conflicts which have occurred at various times since between mobs of different creeds have always been exaggerated for obvious effect, and, if the truth could be gotten at, were probably instigated by English agents for the ultimate benefit of English taxpayers; for Ireland pays much more than her rightful proportion of the taxes of the empire.

The Land League has been from the beginning formidable to the English government, because from the beginning all classes of the people, clergy and laity, have united on its platform. The "Young Ireland" party of 1848 was the first national effort from which sectarianism was excluded, and of which the leaders were both Catholic and Protestant; it was the noble songs of one of these—Thomas Davis, a Protestant—that sank deeply into the hearts of the Catholic people and inspired them with new determination to drive religious dissensions out of Ireland and despoil the English government of its sectarian quiver. The two peers of Davis, John Blake Dillon and Charles Gavan Duffy, were Catholics, and their superb prose supplemented the powerful verse of Davis. The abolition of the State-Church and the placing of the clergy of all denominations on the same footing, so far, at least, as support was concerned, removed the impassable barrier which had previously kept them apart; and when the Catholic Davitt and the Protestant Parnell united in the organization of the Land League, all classes of the people entered into the ranks, and the most truly national movement which Ireland has seen in recent times was under way.

Clergymen of all creeds spoke on the same platform in advocacy of its objects and in approbation of its peaceful and legal methods, and some of the immediate results were that overwhelmingly Catholic parliamentary constituencies sent Protestant representatives to Westminster, while such eminent members of the Roman Catholic hierarchy as the venerable and lately deceased patriot Archbishop MacHale of Tuam and Archbishop Croke of Cashel wrote and published strong letters of encouragement and endorsement of the League. Before it was in existence a year a large majority of the clergy had become silent sympathizers or open advocates; few held aloof. The archbishop of Dublin even assailed it; he had certainly a right to his opinion—the same right as any other ecclesiastic or any other man. But while the English agents of the American press in London and Dublin were scrupulously careful to send over here, for the purpose of influencing American sentiment, and especially Irish feeling, in this country, every word uttered by an individual ecclesiastic against the League, equal diligence was exercised in suppressing the constant utterances of other ecclesiastics in its support. The truth is that all elements of the population of Ireland have been practically a unit for the objects of the League. The extreme nationalists supported it as a step in the right direction, their judgment being expressed in the letter of Mr. John Devoy; the extreme conservatives supported it in the persons of so many of the clergy; and the great body of the people supported it as a movement whose immediate purpose was moral, urgent and humane. The League was soon in operation throughout the country. Branches were everywhere organized; in a short time hundreds of thousands were enrolled. A small weekly fee was paid by each, and this created a fund a fund for the support of tenants who might be evicted for non-payment of rent, or whom the landlord cast into the highways for no cause whatever.

The landlords found themselves in an entirely new position. Previously they had raised rents whenever they pleased, and had expelled rent-paying tenants whenever they pleased; now they had to think before doing either. If they raised the rent and the tenant could not pay, they thrust him out without any compensation for the improvements he had made; but they were surprised to find that their victim was promptly provided with shelter and necessaries for himself and his family, and they were still more surprised at the second consequence of the eviction: they could not rent the farm to a new tenant. The word had gone to the three hundred thousand, "Rent no farm from which a tenant who belongs to the League has been evicted." Formerly, so great was the competition for small farms that as soon as it was known that one was in the market enough applicants appeared to keep rent up to the highest competitive figure. The consequence of eviction, after the Land League was organized, was not only to gradually induce a lowering of rents, but to keep

THE NOTICE TO QUIT.

idle the property of those landlords who evicted for failure to pay rack-rents. The League was the first antagonist the Irish landlord was compelled to respect.

The entire body of the people were not, of course, members of the League, and its word was not at first universally complied with. Then it endeavored to bring to reflection those who took the farms of the evicts: it forbade its members to have any social or business relations with them. This method of hastening reform in land tenure proved highly effectual. When the patriots of America were engaged in driving the English government out of their country in order that, after their expulsion, some of the benefits of the British constitution—of which so much had been heard and so little seen—might be secured, there was a class who believed that the Revolution could not succeed, and their cunning prompted them to remain loyalists. They were subjected to precisely the treatment which the Land League gave those persons in Ireland who remained servile to the landlords. The American patriots said in substance to the loyalists, "So long as you are perfectly neutral you shall not be molested; the moment you give any countenance to the English we shall treat you as traitors." So the Land League said to those who opposed its peaceable campaign, "So long as you are perfectly neutral you shall not be molested; the moment you aid landlordism we shall treat you as enemies of the people and of the country."

The promise was fulfilled: the man who took a farm from which an evict had gone forth to subsist upon public charity was cut off from social intercourse. His neighbors would sell him nothing; they would buy nothing from him which they could get elsewhere or could do without. One now historic case soon attracted the attention of the entire country—indeed, of the world. It was the case that sent a landlord's agent into the dictionary—a place to which he was quite a stranger.

The approach of famine, with all the horrors which had followed in its ghastly train in '47 and the subsequent years, compelled the Land League to take prompt measures to save the lives of the people. The potato crop is an infallible guide to the condition of the Irish peasantry. In 1876—a fair year—its value was over sixty million dollars; in 1877 its value was twenty-five million dollars; the next year it was thirty-five million; but in 1879 it shrivelled to fifteen million dollars. That meant death to a million of the Irish tenantry. Whatever their little holdings had produced besides potatoes had gone to pay the previous year's rent. Now the crop that they depended on for food was also gone. The general crops had been poor throughout the country, and many of the tenants had not been able to pay their rents in full; others were totally unable to pay; and evictions increased as famine slowly crept after the trembling tenantry. In 1876 the evictions officially reported were one thousand two hundred and sixty-nine; in 1877 there were one thousand three hundred and twenty-three; in 1878 the number rose to one thousand seven hundred and forty-nine; but the figures in 1879, thanks to the determined stand taken by the Land League, showed a diminution: the total was one thousand three hundred and forty-eight. The Land-League leaders saw that if the people who had the means to do so paid their rents in the autumn of 1879, they would swell the number of the possible famine-victims beyond the power of charity to save them from starvation; and, as a man's first duty is to preserve his life and the lives of his family, the tenants were advised to hold back the rents if that was the only way by which they could escape starvation until spring. The Land League never taught the doctrine of no rent; it never taught the doctrine so repeatedly practised by the English government—that of confiscation; it never taught the doctrine of the abolition of private property. The proposition of the Land League was that of John Bright—that the landlords should be bought out by the state, receiving fair prices for their lands, and that the state should sell to actual working tenants at fair prices and on reasonable time, holding a first lien on the lands until the purchase-money and interest were paid. There is nothing communistic or confiscatory in the entire history of the League.

The advice to the tenants to withhold the rent as a means of saving the lives of their children and of themselves commends itself to every just mind; but the landlords were not disposed so to look upon it, and troops began pouring into the country to aid the landlords in enforcing rent-collections and in making evictions, although hundreds of the tenantry were already in want. The notice to quit was soon presented at many a cabin-door; armed with a revolver and backed by soldiery, the process-server forced his way into the bare and wretched cottage and thrust the fateful paper into the thin fingers of its outraged but helpless occupant. In 1846 no less than three hundred thousand starving human beings were thus expelled from their huts to die: they did die. Now note the difference in the results under the manly and stubborn menace of the Land League. In October, 1879, Davitt said to the tenants, "If, to save your families from death, you must keep back the rent, keep it back; you are bound before God to save them. You must not imagine that you will be turned out on the roadside to die, as your fathers were in '46. There is a spirit abroad in Ireland to-day that will not stand that a second time in a century."

The words rang through the humble cabins and were listened to in the mansions of the landlords. The process-server was not from that moment in so great demand, although the country had been filled with English troops to force starvation and eviction. Davitt's menace was not misunderstood. It did not mean armed insurrection: there was not in all Ireland a thousand rifles, probably, with which to make an attack on the whole army of the British empire. But there are methods which, under certain circumstances, are more powerful than cannon—methods absolutely peaceful; and those which the Land League had adopted were already in operation. No man would take a farm from a landlord who had evicted tenants who refused to pay rent, because they needed the money to save themselves from starvation, and no man would hold any social intercourse with those who violated this rule. Against three hundred thousand evictions in the former famine year, we see thirteen hundred and forty-eight in 1879.

But it soon became apparent that the people would perish if money were not obtained to buy food for those who had neither money nor crop. Instead of coming promptly to the relief of the famishing, the government devoted its energies to breaking up the Land League, and in November, 1879, Michael Davitt and two of his associates were arrested. The government failed to make out a case against them, and, personal liberty not having yet been entirely abolished, they were released.

Meanwhile, in accordance with instructions from the Land League, Charles Stewart Parnell and John Dillon sailed for the United States to enlist the sympathy of the American people and to solicit aid. They arrived January 2, 1880. They travelled speedily over the country, accompanied by Mr.

John Murdock, the Highlander who has made so thorough a study of peasant proprietary, speaking in all the large cities and being received everywhere with emphatic demonstrations of welcome. All classes of the people united in answering their appeals, and subscriptions amounting to over two hundred thousand dollars were placed in their hands. On February 2, Mr. Parnell was received by Congress while in session, and delivered an admirable address setting forth the aims and hopes of the League and the miserable condition of the Irish country. It was his intention to form a Land League in the United States, but before he could do so he was summoned back to his seat in Parliament. He sailed on February 11, 1880. Mr. Dillon remained in the United States, continuing the work which he had been commissioned to do.

After his release Mr. Davitt had been sent to France and Belgium to obtain assistance and come thence to the United States. After several preliminary meetings an American branch of the Irish National Land League was organized in New York, and branches were formed almost simultaneously throughout the country. The membership, including that of the ladies' leagues which were organized for charitable work by Miss Fanny Parnell, ably sustained by Mrs. Parnell and Miss Ellen Ford, is over three hundred thousand. The officers chosen at a national convention held in Buffalo are: president, Patrick A. Collins; vice-president, Rev. Patrick

Cronin; secretary, Thomas Flatley; treasurer, Rev. Lawrence Walsh. The objects of the League received the all but universal approbation of the clergy of the Catholic Church in the United States, and the public meetings held under the auspices of the League to raise money for those in danger of starving were addressed by the most eminent of the hierarchy, while others appealed in pastoral letters directly to their clergy and people, explaining clearly and eloquently the causes of the famine.

Said Bishop Hennessy of Dubuque: "If the government had sincere compassion on a suffering people and an honest desire to save them from the fate which was impending, would it in such an emergency, under pretext of law or any other pretext, become a party to landlord rapacity? Would it send its constabulary and military to distrain and eject, to tear down cabins and throw shivering children, their mothers and grandmothers, out on the highways in the depth of winter? Would it seize and carry off by force the crops and other chattels to which, through sheer necessity, without a thought of dishonesty, the poor farmer clung that he might have wherewith to keep the life in his little ones? Would it wrench the crust out of the hand of hunger that pampered tyranny might have the last penny of the rent? Conduct such as this betrays no pity. The aim of the British government is not to remove distress in Ireland, but rather to produce, aggravate and take advantage of it. To exterminate those whom it could not pervert was its manifest and avowed policy on the failure of the reformation. It is still the same, though not so openly. It is easy to see how it is going to work now. Famine will take some; its invariable attendant, pestilence, or sickness of some kind, will carry off still more; and emigration will follow. The three will scour the land and scourge it and multiply sheep-walks. Did not the government foresee this? Others did who are not quite so keen-sighted. If not intended, why not prevented? One per cent. of what it cost to rob and murder Afghans and Zulus in unjust wars, as worthless as they were wicked in the judgment even of Englishmen, soldiers and civilians, would have greatly improved Ireland and preserved her people. But to do this was not in the programme. The friends of Ireland, the trusted leaders of her people, will strive against emigration by argument and promises and personal influence. I fear they will not succeed to the extent of their wishes. Multitudes, especially of the young, the vigorous, the ambitious, will not be induced, cannot be persuaded, to remain in a country where famine is periodical and misery perpetual, and this not by the accidents of fortune, but by the design of their rulers."

HOW THE BOYCOTTS GOT THEIR HARVEST IN.

LAND-LEAGUERS TILLING THE FARM OF AN IMPRISONED MEMBER.

CHAPTER XII.

A LANDLORD'S AGENT GOES INTO THE DICTIONARY.

A MR. BOYCOTT, who had acquired, without getting it legitimately, the title of "Captain," was agent for Lord Erne, who had a large estate in Mayo upon which he did not reside. Captain Boycott was accustomed to rack-rent the tenants, to insult, humiliate and oppress them, and he was despised and feared. In addition to robbing them of every shilling he could extort as rent, he required the tenants to work for him at his own terms—a shilling and sixpence a day for the men, a shilling a day for the women—and to feed themselves. By a system of petty rules he contrived to reduce even this beggarly pittance: a man was fined, for instance, so much if he walked on the grass, and so much more if he wheeled his barrow out of the path. The captain was a ruffian in his manners toward the people, addressing them like dogs and compelling them to submit to galling personal affronts which poverty and dependence do not render any easier to human nature. He had repeatedly evicted the poor and repeatedly robbed those whom he did not evict, and during seventeen years' administration of Lord Erne's estate had earned the hatred and contempt of all who had tenant-relations with him. The Land League paid him some remarkable attentions.

First, it commanded the tenants to refuse to pay him rack-rents. Secondly, it required the tenants to ask of him for harvesting his crops the same wages as were paid for that kind of labor by other landlords. The League terms were two shillings sixpence for the men, and one shilling sixpence for the women. Amazed at their audacity and furious over their impudence, he swore roundly that he would do nothing of the kind. Thereupon the tenants refused to harvest his crops, and departed in a body. He proceeded into the adjoining localities, expecting to get all the help he wanted at a slight advance in wages; but he was mistaken: neither man, woman nor child would work for him upon any terms. Incredulous, he drove miles and miles, and was everywhere met with the same laconic response: "We won't." Times had indeed changed in Ireland; the people did not even take their hats off to him—those who had hats —and before the Land League every man in Ireland had to take his hat off to the landlord and keep it off while the petty tyrant drove along, even if the rain were descending. But nobody took off a hat to Captain Boycott, and neither he nor Lord Erne had money enough to buy a day's labor in Mayo or beyond its borders.

Chagrined and beside himself with rage, he determined that his crops should be harvested if he had to do the work himself. He found that it was a more difficult task than he had anticipated—much more difficult than playing slave-driver to tenantry. Then he called upon his wife and daughters and servants to help him. The delicate palms of the ladies were soon blistered, but the crops were still unharvested. Surrender stared Captain Boycott in the face, but he did not give up like a man. Instead of acknowledging the justice of the wages asked, he sent his wife down to the cabins to beg the Irish mothers to help her and her family out of their predicament, and the captain was willing to pay the terms the harvesters had asked. Then the crops were harvested.

The captain nursed his wrath for rent-day. The famine had been in that part of the country; the crops were poor for two seasons, and many of the people had been compelled to go over to England during the harvests and earn there, as laborers, money enough to keep them from starvation: they had none left. Many whose families had lived upon the generosity of the little shopkeepers had not enough to pay those debts and the arrears of rent, and they had hoped that, taking into account the failure of two seasons and their industrious efforts to repair their misfortunes, Captain Boycott would remit a portion of the arrears and reduce the rents for the next year. He would do neither one nor the other: whoever did not pay up in full must leave the estate. In that part of Ireland eviction means death, and the rumor that all who could not pay in full were to be turned into the roads and ditches flew like the news of an approaching plague.

It has been one of the privileges of the Irish landlord to use law in ways denied other creditors. A shopkeeper could not serve a writ except upon the head of a family and in person, but a landlord could serve it on a woman in the house or nail it on the door if the woman would not let him in. Captain Boycott sent by the hands of process-servers notices of eviction, and as soon as one of these approached a cottage the woman of the house sent one of the children with a red petticoat to the nearest hill-top, where it was waved to give the other women notice that the obnoxious person was coming. The women of Mayo hurried to the scene, and by gibes, taunts, jokes and still more offensive means generally drove the emissary of the law away from the cottage before he had either seen its inmates or reached the door with his hammer and nails.

Then Captain Boycott secured the services of a hundred armed constables to protect the process-server, but no man could be induced to accept the latter office. The women had found out from a Land-League lawyer that nailing the notice on the door was not statute law, but landlord law; that the notice must be served inside the house. The women determined to save the process-servers possible injury, and sent the message to the "big house" that they would leave the doors open and have plenty of boiling water on hand when the writs should arrive. No man in that part of Ireland was fond enough of boiling water to wish for it in such copious quantities, and Captain Boycott did not even propose to serve the notices himself, although he had sworn they should be served. . He determined to compel the government of the empire of Great Britain to use its army and navy, if necessary, to serve his eviction writs; and then the peasantry, under the direction of the Land League, prepared to fight the army and navy without other weapons than those of passive resistance.

It was ordered that the captain and his family be let alone. The men who fed his stock left; the house-servants left; no man, no woman, would work for him in any capacity; the village shops civilly declined to furnish the necessaries which could be no longer prepared at the house. The tenantry would not have carried these measures to such extremes had he not deliberately calumniated them in the London papers, to which he wrote the gross untruth that he was persecuted for being a Protestant. Neither he nor any of his family could buy at any price clothing, food, or any article for their use; he had to feed and water his own cattle, and his wife and daughters were compelled to do the domestic work. This condition of things became intolerable, and at last Captain Boycott voluntarily left the country.

While the passive siege was being carried on,

James Redpath visited the parish priest, Father John O'Malley, who had kept up the courage of the tenants. During a frugal dinner the American paused and became pensive.

"What is the matter?" asked the priest.

"I am bothered about a word," was the reply of the American, who was preparing to send to a journal at home an account of the novel proceedings.

"'Ostracism,'" said Father O'Malley, "will not do: the people would not understand that." After a moment's reflection he added with a smile, "How would it do to call it 'boycotting'?"

In that way a landlord's agent went out of Ireland and went into the dictionary.

CHAPTER XIII.

DRIVEN FROM HOME BY FAMINE AND LAW.

NO comment on the following figures can make them more eloquent than are their pathetic columns:

EMIGRATION FROM IRELAND FROM 1841 TO 1879, INCLUSIVE.

1841 71,392	1861 64,292
1842 89,686	1862 70,117
1843 37,509	1863 117,229
1844 54,289	1864 114,169
1845 74,969	1865 101,495
1846 105,955	1866 99,466
1847 215,444	1867 80,624
1848 178,159	1868 61,018
1849 214,425	1869 66,568
1850 209,054	1870 74,855
1851 257,572	1871 71,240
1852 190,322	1872 78,102
1853 173,148	1873 90,149
1854 140,555	1874 73,184
1855 91,914	1875 51,462
1856 90,781	1876 25,976
1857 95,081	1877 28,831
1858 64,337	1878 24,492
1859 80,599	1879 47,065
1860 84,621	

In the thirty years from 1840 to 1870 three millions of the Irish people were driven from home by the effects of foreign misgovernment.

Well might Lady Wilde write:

> "A million a decade! What does it mean?
> A nation dying of inner decay;
> A churchyard's silence where life has been,
> The base of the pyramid crumbling away;
> A drift of men gone over the sea,
> A drift of the dead where men should be."

While the Irish have thus been continually driven from home, the people of the other portions of the empire of Great Britain have increased and multiplied. The following table presents the constant contrast of diminished population in Ireland and increased population in England, Scotland and Wales:

Year.	England and Wales.	Scotland.	Ireland.
1811	10,454,529	1,881,044	6,084,996
1821	12,172,664	2,137,325	6,869,544
1831	14,051,986	2,405,610	7,828,347
1841	16,035,198	2,652,339	8,196,597
1851	18,054,170	2,922,362	6,574,278
1861	20,228,497	3,096,808	5,798,967
1871	22,712,266	3,360,018	5,412,377

The natural conditions of life are at least equally favorable in the three countries. Why should the population of two increase, and of the third so steadily diminish?

A government which produces such results is on them judged and condemned.

It is frequently asserted that the cause of Irish

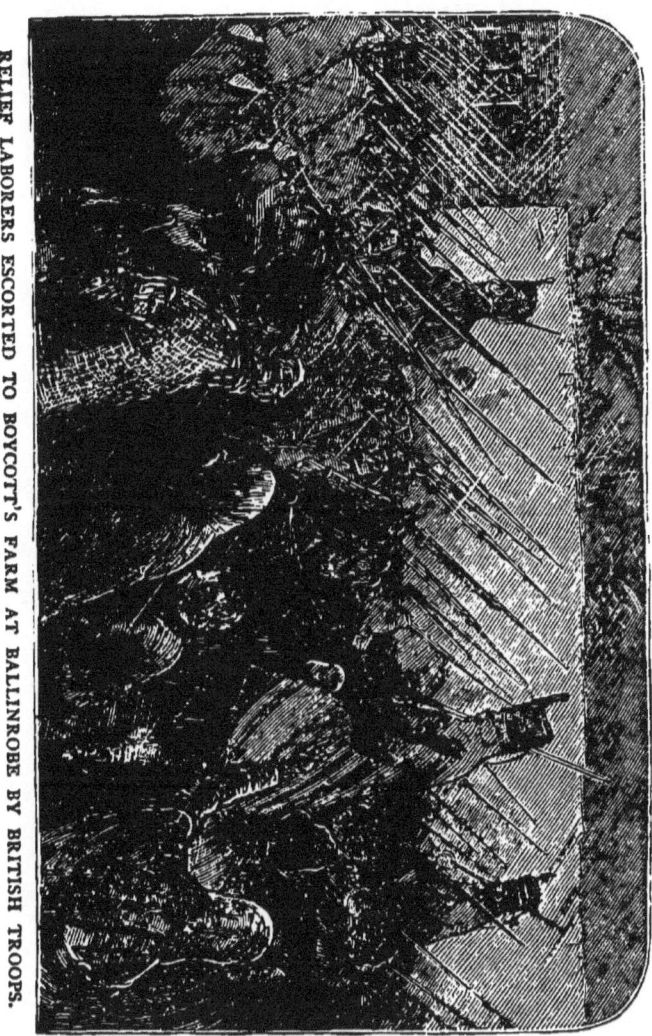

RELIEF LABORERS ESCORTED TO BOYCOTT'S FARM AT BALLINROBE BY BRITISH TROOPS.

emigration is that the country cannot feed the population. The truth is that the food which the soil produces is exported; it is the property of the landlord, to whose agents it is consigned, chiefly in English seaports. Says Thom's *Directory* (standard British statistical publication), p. 675: "The exportation of the agricultural produce of the country has always been the chief commercial business carried on in Ireland. During the Revolutionary war this country furnished a large share of the provisions for the army and navy, and it still sends supplies to the colonial markets. But Great Britain is by far the best and most extensive market for all sorts of Irish produce. By much the greater part of the export trade is carried on by the cross-Channel navigation, chiefly to Liverpool, Bristol and Glasgow, the staple articles being black cattle, sheep, swine, salted provisions, grain, flour, butter, eggs and linen.

That is, in the briefest possible terms, the complete explanation of Irish famine, Irish poverty and Irish emigration. The country produces enough food to feed many times its population—economists have even said as many as twenty times—for the soil is incomparably rich; but the food is owned, not by the people who till the soil, but by the landlords who hold the present title to it. They export the food; the people hunger, die or leave the country.

The American will not fail to notice that the entire export trade consists of products of the soil, with a single exception—linen, the one important manufacture of Ireland, whose material insignificance is shown in the chapter entitled "The Reason Ireland has no Manufactures." Here we behold the success of the policy of England in Ireland for centuries—to make her a convenient market for the English manufacturer. She has nothing to send out but the products of her soil; every manufactured article she wants must be bought in England. The money paid for the products of the soil belongs to landlords, many of whom reside abroad, all of whom spend or invest it abroad. Therefore there is no capital in Ireland for manufactures. Until the people who till the soil own it the money paid for its products will not go back to Ireland; until it goes back there will be no capital to invest in manufactures; until manufactures exist the country must remain poor, since an entire people cannot profitably live on a single occupation.

The remedy, therefore, for Irish emigration, Irish famine and Irish poverty is PEASANT PROPRIETARY—the ultimate object of the Land-League agitation.

The absurdity of saying that the rich soil of Ireland is not capable of supporting her people is completely exposed in another way. In Belgium, whose inhabitants number 5,336,185, the population to the square mile is 469; in Bavaria, with a population of 5,022,390, it is 170; in Saxony, with a population of 2,760,586, it is 407; in Switzerland, with a population of 2,669,147, it is 179; in the Netherlands, with a population of 3,579,529, it is 185. These are all small countries, peaceful, thrifty, contented and prosperous. In Ireland, also a small country, the population to the square mile is only 169, yet she is neither peaceful, contented, thrifty nor prosperous.

The population of Belgium has constantly increased. Emigration has never been suggested to her people as a remedy for poverty: they are not poor. The population of Ireland has steadily declined, yet emigration has been repeatedly suggested as a remedy for her poverty. Belgium, like Ireland, is an exporting country. She never has famine; she is able to export both food and manufactures. What is the secret of her prosperity? The people who till the land own it. There are in Belgium nearly a million and a half peasant proprietors. From 1846 to 1876 the number of these increased twenty-four per cent. The money obtained for the fruits of the soil goes back to the country, and is utilized there; one-fourth of the people are engaged in manufacturing. Although the population to the square mile is nearly three times that of Ireland, immigration there has actually exceeded emigration!

In Saxony, where the population to the square mile is 407, against 169 in Ireland, the number of inhabitants has increased; the country is contented, thrifty and prosperous; she knows nothing of famine. The people who till the land own it. She feeds them all, and is able to export food.

In the Netherlands, where the population to the

square mile is 185, famine is unknown; the people who till the soil own it. It feeds them all, and the chief exports are butter, sheep, corn, cheese and silk.

In Bavaria, where the population to the square mile is 179, against 169 in Ireland, peace, prosperity and contentment prevail. The population has increased; famine is unknown. The people who till the soil own it. It feeds them bountifully, and there is left food to export.

In Switzerland, where the population to the square mile is 175, to 169 in Ireland, the population has increased. Out of a total of more than two millions and a half, there are only half a million who do not own land. The people are among the most contented in Europe, and the thriftiest. Over a million of the citizens are supported by agriculture; the rest are engaged in textile and mechanical industries.

These are all small countries like Ireland, but the soil of none of them is equal in fertility to that of Ireland. Their population to the square mile is greater than that in Ireland, yet we are told that Ireland cannot feed her people, and that emigration is the proper remedy.

Ireland does not feed her people, because her soil is owned by foreigners, and its products are exported and sold for their benefit.

Each of the continental countries compared with her has two institutions which insure their peace, prosperity and contentment—home rule and peasant proprietary.

CHAPTER XIV.

LIBERTY AND CRIME IN IRELAND.

PROBABLY the average American believes that Ireland is a thoroughly criminal country. The cable is frequently charged with reports of alleged outrages.

The average Englishman believes that the only way to protect life and property in Ireland is to suspend the British constitution in that country, give one Englishman—called a chief secretary—power to *suspect* any number of persons of a *secret intention* to break the law, on that *suspicion* hurry them into prison, and keep them there as long as he pleases. In that benign way the blessings of the British constitution have been bestowed on Ireland.

To-day there are hundreds of persons in prison in Ireland, unaccused, untried, to be kept there, in all the horrors and sufferings of prison-life, as long as one Englishman in Ireland—a Mr. Forster—pleases. These persons are not accused of having committed any crime. A Mr. Forster, an Englishman in Ireland, having no interest in the country—a "carpet-bagger" of the most detestable pattern—is pleased to *suspect* that perhaps some of them might, under provocation, possibly break a window or throw a stone at a policeman.

Yet Ireland is not in Russia.

Yet Ireland is not at war with any enemy, domestic or foreign.

Can Americans conceive any state of affairs in which, under their Constitution, they would tolerate, in time of profound peace, the arrest of their fellow-citizens, on suspicion, by a foreigner? Is liberty no dearer to the people of Ireland than it is to the people of the United States?

By the act of legislative union, passed in 1800, England was solemnly pledged to give Ireland the benefits of the British constitution on precisely the same terms as to England and Scotland. Yet no less than fifty-nine times in the intervening period of eighty years has the constitution been withdrawn from Ireland and every vestige of personal liberty there destroyed.

Was it because Ireland exceeds in criminality England and Scotland? Here are the official returns for twenty years. Let the reader observe, first, the population of the several countries, then the number of convictions for criminal offences, not forgetting that as "justice" has been administered in Ireland judges are dependents on the Crown and juries must take their verdicts from the judges' lips:

Number of Convictions for Criminal Offences in England and Wales, Scotland and Ireland from 1860 to 1879 inclusive.

Year.	England and Wales.		Scotland.		Ireland.	
	Convicts.	Population.	Convicts.	Population.	Convicts.	Population.
1860..	12,068	19,902,713	2,414	3,054,738	2,979	5,820,960
1861..	15,879	20,119,314	2,418	3,066,633	3,271	5,788,415
1862..	15,312	20,352,140	2,693	3,097,867	3,796	5,775,028
1863..	15,799	20,590,356	2,438	3,126,587	3,285	5,716,975
1864..	14,726	20,834,496	2,359	3,155,595	3,000	5,638,487
1865..	14,740	21,085,139	2,355	3,184,873	2,661	5,591,896
1866..	14,254	21,342,864	2,292	3,214,426	2,418	5,519,522
1867..	14,207	21,608,286	2,510	3,244,254	2,733	5,482,459
1868..	15,033	21,882,059	2,490	3,274,360	2,394	5,461,299
1869..	14,340	22,164,847	2,592	3,304,747	2,452	5,443,919
1870..	12,953	22,457,366	2,400	3,335,418	3,048	5,412,660
1871..	11,946	22,760,359	2,184	3,366,375	2,257	5,386,708
1872..	10,862	23,067,535	2,259	3,399,226	2,565	5,368,696
1873..	11,089	23,356,414	2,110	3,430,923	2,542	5,337,261
1874..	11,509	23,648,609	2,231	3,462,916	2,367	5,314,844
1875..	10,954	23,944,459	2,205	3,495,214	2,484	5,309,494
1876..	12,195	24,744,010	2,051	3,527,811	2,343	5,321,618
1877..	11,942	24,547,309	2,009	3,560,715	2,300	5,338,906
1878..	12,473	24,854,397	2,273	3,593,929	2,292	5,351,060
1879..	12,525	25,165,336	2,090	3,627,453	2,207	5,362,337

Taking round numbers, when, in 1860, the population of England and Wales was four times that of Ireland, the number of convictions for crime was five times that of Ireland. In that year the population of Scotland was more than two millions less than the population of Ireland, and the criminal convictions lacked only a few hundreds of those of Ireland. Five years later, when the population of England and Wales was four times that of Ireland, crime was six times greater; while, in Scotland, whose population was only three-fifths that of Ireland, the number of criminal convictions showed but slight difference. In 1870 the ratio is more even in proportion to population.

Let us compare Irish and Scotch crime from 1875 for five years, keeping in mind that, in round numbers, the population of Scotland is three-fifths that of Ireland. It will be observed that, proportionately, Scotch crime exceeds Irish crime:

Year.	Scotland.	Ireland.
1875	2,205	2,484
1876	2,051	2,343
1877	2,009	2,300
1878	2,273	
1879	2,090	2,207

That arrests are made much more recklessly and unjustifiably in Ireland than in England, Wales or Scotland is shown by the proportion of convictions to committals. In England and Wales, for 1840 and 1879, it was, respectively, seventy-three and seventy-six per cent.; in Scotland, seventy-five and seventy-seven per cent.; in Ireland, forty-six and fifty per cent. It was not in Ireland that the *habeas corpus* should have been suspended, for, from 1840 to 1879, crime in Ireland declined eighty-two per cent., while in England the diminution was only forty-nine per cent., and in Scotland only thirty-one per cent.

It may be urged that if *habeas corpus* had not been so often suspended in Ireland, crime would be greater. An examination of the figures from 1875 to 1879—during which period there was no interference with personal liberty—is a more than sufficient answer.

KILMAINHAM JAIL.

The character of the crime in the three countries should also be considered. If, in Ireland, a too vivacious man cracks a joke at a policeman, he is reasonably certain of arrest; in England a citizen may do everything to a policeman, short of cracking his skull, before he is arrested. In Ireland the constabulary are armed with revolvers, rifles, swords, which they use mercilessly on the smallest pretence; every American who has been in London knows that a policeman cannot employ even his club upon an offender except in absolute self-defence. In Ireland one of the "crimes" which swell the aggregate of arrests is called "intimidation." If A, who is "loyal," is accidentally or wilfully jostled by B, who is a Land-Leaguer, that is a case of "intimidation;" B goes to jail, and his crime is included in the total of that month's "outrages." A very large proportion of the so-called "criminal offences" of Ireland are of so trivial a character that in any other country in the world no official notice would be taken of them.

Philadelphia is a well-behaved city: it is the "City of Brotherly Love." The tranquil inhabitant of its historic soil possibly suspects that life and property in Ireland are utterly unsafe. Yet in Philadelphia—a model city, the "City of Brotherly Love"—whose population is sixteen per cent. that of Ireland, crime of all kinds is very much greater. In Philadelphia, in 1879, there were forty-nine homicides; in Ireland there were FOUR persons found guilty of murder.

The following table[1] perfectly illustrates that, in proportion to population and to gravity of offence there is less crime in Ireland than in England and Scotland:

Classes of more serious offences.	Irish. Offences in 1878.	English. Proportionate numbers in 1877 for same population.	Scotch. Proportionate numbers in 1877 for same population.	Difference between Irish and English figures.	
				Irish, less.	English, less.
Irish numbers less than English and Scotch total of more serious offences	2886	4189	5925	1303	
Offences against property without violence	700	1774	1065	1074	
Offences against property, with violence .	458	1014	3175	556	
Suicide	93	291	163	234	
Attempts to commit suicide	69	195	108	126	
Forgery, etc.	90	157	162	67	
Offences against purity	142	200	281	58	
Perjury	15	33	27	18	

Is there any justification for the arbitrary abolition of personal liberty in Ireland?

[1] Prepared by Mr. Henry Bellingham, M. P.

CHAPTER XV.

THE LAND LAWS.

LET us consider candidly the measures which the English government has taken from time to time to remedy the misfortunes which English law in Ireland has visited upon the Irish tenant.

When the Irish Parliament was abolished, in 1800, the promise was made among many that imperial legislation for Ireland should be just and liberal. How has the promise been kept?

Said John Bright in 1866 on the floor of the House of Commons: "Sixty-five years ago this Parliament undertook to govern Ireland. I will say nothing of the manner in which that duty was brought upon us, except that it was by proceedings disgraceful and corrupt to the last degree. During these sixty-five years there are only three considerable measures which Parliament has passed in the interest of Ireland. One of them was the measure of 1829 for the emancipation of the Catholics. . . . But that measure, so just, so essential, and which, of course, is not ever to be recalled, was a measure which the chief minister of the day, a great soldier and a great judge of military matters, admitted was passed under the menace of, and only because of, the danger of, civil war. The other two measures to which I have referred are that for the relief of the poor and that for the sale of the encumbered estates; and those measures were introduced to the House and passed through the House in the emergency of a famine more severe than any that has desolated any Christian country of the world within the last four hundred years. Except on these two emergencies, I appeal to every Irish member, and to every English member who has paid any attention to the matter, whether the statement is not true that this Parliament has done nothing for the people of Ireland."

In 1866, on another occasion, John Bright said: "The great evil of Ireland is this, that the Irish people—the Irish nation—are dispossessed of the soil; and what we ought to do is provide for and aid in their restoration to it by all measures of justice. Why should we tolerate in Ireland the law of primogeniture? Why should we tolerate the system of entails? Why should the object of the law be to accumulate land in great masses in few hands, and to make it almost impossible for persons of small means and tenant-farmers to become possessors of land? If you go to other countries—for example, to Norway, to Denmark, to Holland, to Belgium, to France, to Germany, to Italy or to the United States—you will find that in all these countries those laws of which I complain have been abolished, and the land is just as free to buy and sell and hold and cultivate as any other description of property in the kingdom. . . . If my advice were taken, we should have a parliamentary commission empowered to buy up the large estates in Ireland belonging to the English nobility, for the purpose of selling them on easy terms to the occupiers of the farms and to the tenantry of Ireland. . . . What you want is to restore to Ireland a middle-class proprietary of the soil; and I venture to say that if these estates could be purchased and could be sold out, farm by farm, to the tenant-occupiers in Ireland, it would be infinitely better in a conservative sense than that they should belong to great proprietors living out of the country. . . . I have often asked myself whether patriotism is dead in Ireland. Cannot all the people of Ireland see that the calamities of their country are the creatures of the law, and, if that be so, that just laws only can remove them?"

Still later in the same year Mr. Bright defined in detail his plan for the purchase of a portion of the Irish land by the government and its sale to actual occupiers.

In 1868, in the House of Commons, Mr. Bright again spoke on peasant proprietary in Ireland. He proposed that the state lend the money to the tenant to buy, securing itself and giving him thirty-one or thirty-five years to refund it. "I would negotiate with land-owners who were willing to sell the tenants who were willing to buy, and I would make the land the great savings-bank for the future tenantry of Ireland."

The still more recent speeches of Mr. Bright have been in the same vein. I have preferred to quote from those made in former years to show that the proposition to buy a portion of the land in Ireland is not a novel one, and that it was advocated by an eminent English economist before the Irish Land League came into existence.

The Catholic Emancipation Act of 1829 removed all political disabilities (with some exceptions not worth noticing in this place) which had kept four-fifths of the people of Ireland from the civil rights enjoyed by the one-fifth. But it did not restore to the heirs of those whose civil rights had been taken away by the penal laws the land which had been confiscated by those laws. Had O'Connell been as wise as he was energetic, he would have made the restoration of the land a condition of the abolition of the statutes in accordance with which the land was confiscated. It may be objected that this would have been impracticable, on account of transfers and the difficulty of establishing heirship. The simplest way would have been perfectly satisfactory to a majority of the people. The rights of the owners in possession could have been respected, as they were in Prussia in the beginning of the century, and in Russia in the latter half of it. The state, which took the land away from the people of Ireland without compensation, could have found a way to restore it to them by compensating those who had obtained possession of it. Peasant proprietors could have been easily created in Ireland fifty years ago.

But the land was not restored. The heirs of the original owners had sunk into tenantry and poverty. The land remains in the possession of the heirs of those who obtained it first by confiscation. What has the British Parliament done to improve their condition?

Nearly half a century passed without the adoption of a single measure to that end! Then what?

Poor relief is the first lien on land in England. The like law providing for the relief of the poor of Ireland was not passed until 1846, and then only because the famine-shadow was already apparent. But the law does not operate to support the poor. If the people of Ireland had not been furnished with money to buy food from the landlords last winter, the mortality would have compared with that of 1847.

The law is so constructed that the burden is a minimum on the landlord, and when famine comes the people must die if a foreign charity does not hasten to their succor. This was abundantly proven last winter and spring.

The next legislation to modify the evils of the Irish land system was the Encumbered Estates Act. But that was an act for the relief of Irish landlords.

Until its passage in 1848 the law of primogeniture and entail, still the law of England, was the law in

Ireland. The Encumbered Estates Act set that law aside. It compelled the sale of estates encumbered to half their value. The sale was made on the petition of the owner or of any of his creditors, and the proceeds were divided among the claimants. In 1858 to that law was added the Landed Estates Act, by which the courts can deal with unencumbered as well as with encumbered estates. Under the old law of primogeniture and entail many of the Irish landlords had hopelessly bankrupted themselves. "A mountain-load of mortgages or a network of settlements rendered them powerless." The law freeing them of their bonds put the land in the market and enabled them to get rid of their debts. But at the time the law was passed there was no market for land. The famine had paralyzed the country. The immediate effect of the law, therefore, was to rob many creditors of their just dues. The law compelled creditors to submit to a sale, notwithstanding that they had an express contract that no one should ever disturb them in their claim on the land except by paying the claim in full. The new law coerced violation of contract. Says Professor Cairnes: "It proceeded according to rules unknown to our system of jurisprudence; it set aside solemn contracts; it disregarded the cherished traditions of real-property law." He admits that it would not be easy to disturb the statements of Isaac Butt that at a time of unprecedented depreciation of the value of land

SHERIFF'S SALE OF CATTLE TO PAY RENT.

it compelled a general auction of Irish estates, and that no more violent interference with vested rights can be found in English history. But, notwithstanding the justness of this criticism, does any one condemn the principle of the law? Professor Cairnes admits that according to the received maxims of English jurisprudence it was a measure of confiscation; "yet it is not less certain that of all measures passed in recent times it is that one of which the beneficial effects have been most widely and cordially recognized." If the English government for Ireland could pass, more than thirty years ago, a law for the benefit of Irish landlords, invading vested rights, need so much outcry be made about a proposition to pass a law for the benefit of Irish tenants which may apparently, but will not actually, assail vested rights?

We have seen two pieces of legislation which were intended to affect the Irish land tenure. The first was a law making the support of the poor a lien on the land; it is so constructed as to make Irish poverty a lien instead on the charity of the world.

The second was the Encumbered Estates Act. But that was for the benefit of Irish landlords.

The third was the Gladstone Land Law of 1870.

Its aim was good. On its passage through Parliament it encountered no less than three hundred amendments. When it emerged from the legislature and entered the presence of Her Majesty for signature, it had not confiscated a single valuable right of the Irish landlord, says the approved biographer of its author.

The avowed object of the Liberal minister was to make Ulster tenant-right law throughout Ireland. That was all. Ulster tenant-right is an institution which sadly recalls the pitiless efforts of former days to drive the Irish people off the land of their country for the purpose of planting it with foreign colonists. The tenant-farmers in Ulster were chiefly Protestants, Irish, Scotch and English, and to encourage them it was agreed by common consent that they should have continuous occupancy of their farms at fair rent. In other words, they were given fixity of tenure. The abstract right became a substantial property. If the tenant chose to give up his farm, he had the right to sell his fixity of tenure as a kind of good-will to his successor. The substantial value of the tenant-right was based on the improvements effected by him on the land. These improvements did not become the property of the landlord; they remained the property of the tenant, and gave him a sort of partnership in the land. This was tenant-right. The custom which fostered it never obtained in other parts of the kingdom, where the landlords were of one religion and the tenants of another. Tenant-right did not secure against eviction for non-payment of rent. But if the tenant were compelled to give up his holding because he could not meet his obligation to the landlord, he was not turned out penniless into the road. He could dispose of his tenant-right to whoever would pay him the highest price for it; the debt to the landlord was the first to be settled out of the proceeds; the balance was his own. It was, and is, in fact, compensation for improvements paid on eviction, not by the landlord, but by the incoming tenant, who thus acquires a right of ownership in them and can in his turn dispose of them. The Gladstone act of 1870 attempted to make this practice of a locality the law for the country.

But it was only a fair-weather law. It should have been accompanied by a consort statute providing for perennially good harvests. When the bad crops came there were wholesale evictions for non-payment of rent; yet the failure of the tenants to meet their obligations was not their fault; it was the "act of God." What good was Ulster tenant-right then? The tenants who had not crops enough to pay rent had no money to buy tenant-right from other tenants equally unfortunate. Besides, the value of the tenant-right was unstable, shifting, uncertain. In many cases it was simply intangible. The evicted tenant had to go out; if the condition of the market was such that there was no one to buy his tenant-right, what good did the act of 1870 do him? The premier's biographer was remarkably correct when he said that the act did not take away a single valuable right of the Irish landlord.

The act of 1870 was land reform on hypothesis. It did not touch the landlord; it did not always touch the tenant. In a season of high rents and fine crops it afforded the tenant such compensation for his improvements as he could induce some other tenant to pay him. If he could find no one to pay him anything, he must submit to his misfortune. He lost his farm, and all the labor and all the money he may have expended on it.

There was a bill with a misleading title introduced into the last session. It was called "The Compensation for Disturbance Bill." It was an attempt to compel landlords to allow to tenants evicted for non-payment of rent compensation for improvements, provided it was legally proven that their failure to meet their obligation was due to famine. The bill passed the Commons, and was thrown out by the Lords. If anything were wanting to demonstrate that the Gladstone act was hypothetical and fair-weather law, the introduction of the last measure is sufficient.

This completes the entire record which the British Parliament has made for itself in reforming the Irish land laws to 1881.

But was the English government equally neglectful of the Irish landlord? Did it merely neglect the Irish tenant, forgetting his existence, or were opportunities for helping him thrust on it and declined?

It is an error to suppose that this question of the relation of tenant and landlord in Ireland is a new one: it has been discussed throughout the entire period in which that relation has endured. There is an immense literature upon it, and there is nothing to be said of it to-day which has not been said frequently for a hundred years. This literature is not familiar in the United States, for two reasons: we have never had a land question, and we get our literature mainly from England. In the English literary market books and pamphlets on the Irish land question have not been in favor; no English publisher had any interest in circulating information which would tend to restore the publishing trade that Dublin had before the act of legislative union, abolishing the Irish Parliament and compelling Ireland to send over to London not only for all the manufactured articles she wanted, but for her laws.

The literature which is extant in Ireland, and now more abundantly than ever before in this country, is full of testimony to these facts: That the English Parliament knew very well the existence and the grievances of the Irish tenant, the existence and the oppressiveness of the Irish landlords, and that although no law was passed until '46 for the benefit of the tenant, and no land law which pretended to confer any substantial benefit upon him until 1870, laws were frequently passed for the benefit of the Irish landlord, and bills introduced for the benefit of the tenant were utterly ignored or thrown out.

The Irish landlord was given privileges and powers which were denied the English landlord. The title of many English landlords to-day is no better than that of the Irish landlords; they acquired, without paying for them, estates which the Crown confiscated, sometimes from individual owners, sometimes from the general public. But when the distress of the landless English people became so great that they were in danger of extreme suffering, the "Poor Law" was passed, making the tax for the support of the poor the first lien on the land, the first tax to be collected. No such law was passed for Ireland until the awful famine-time of '46; and, as its enforcement was in the landlords' hands, they were careful of their own interests in applying its provisions.

Soon after the act of union the English began legislating in favor of the Irish landlords. They already possessed enormous powers over the tenants; in the reign of George III. they were authorized to seize the growing crops of the tenant for rent, hold them until ripe, compel the tenant to care for and protect them, pay all expenses incurred while doing so; and then they sold the crops. As if that was not enough to drive the ruined tenant into the mad-house or the jail, they were subsequently in the same reign given new powers to evict him. Under the reign of George IV. these prerogatives were still further enlarged, even to compelling the tenant to furnish security to the landlords in ejectment suits. In the same reign the Irish landlord was given the privilege of immediate execution of judgment against a tenant. He could make up his mind at seven in the morning to drive a hundred families off his estate; he had only to apply to the nearest qualified representative of the English government, get his order, send his crowbars and muskets down among the tenantry, and in a few minutes the hundred families would be on the roadside or in the ditches, with no prospect ahead but death or imprisonment. Can any American wonder that there is crime in Ireland? But we shall see later the nature and the enormity of the crime. During the reign of William IV. the Irish landlord was accorded still larger powers, and from the passage of the first of these landlord laws until 1846 *thirty-two bills* were passed by the English Parliament for the benefit of the Irish landlord, and *not one* for the relief of his wretched victim, the Irish tenant.

The great famine of '46 and the subsequent years resulted in an effort to get the English Parliament to consider the condition of the Irish tenants, a million of whom had died. In 1852 a bill was introduced; it proposed again merely the proposition of the Gladstone bill of ten years ago—the extension of Ulster tenant-right; it was rejected. Later in the same session another bill was introduced by the government; it passed the Commons, but was rejected by the Lords. In 1855 another bill of the same tenor was introduced; nothing came of it. In 1857 another bill was introduced; it did not get even a hearing. In 1858 another bill was introduced, asking only that the tenant should be allowed compensation for the permanent improvements effected by him on the land; it was thrown out on second reading. A bill was passed in 1860 which did not alter the status of either landlord or tenant.

The inadequacy of the Gladstone law of 1870 was

so apparent from the beginning that frequent attempts were made to induce the English Parliament to examine into the atrocious wrongs still inflicted on the Irish tenant, and in nine years no less than eighteen land bills were introduced, no one of which asked aught for the tenant but the recognition of his equity in the permanent improvement of the farm by his labor. Not one of them was treated with civility.

We reach now the Land Act of 1881, of which so much has been said. In its original draft it was a wholesome measure. It reaffirmed the principles of the law of 1870, which Mr. Gladstone had fondly believed would not only transform the Irish tenant into a peaceable, loyal and successful tenant-farmer, but would enable him in time to become a peasant proprietor; for even Mr. Gladstone favored peasant proprietary in Ireland long before the organization of the Land League, and in the bill of 1870 there are what are known as the "Bright clauses," which provide for governmental purchase of the land and its sale to the tenants in the manner described by Mr. Bright.

But to make land laws in the English Parliament for the Irish landlords is one thing, and to compel the Irish landlords to comply with those laws is quite another. Instead of doing anything in harmony with the Land Act of 1870, the majority of the Irish landlords, taking advantage of its loose construction, literally cheated the tenants out of its possible benefits. They compelled the tenants to make leases by which they contracted themselves out of the scope of the

SEARCHING FOR ARMS.

law altogether. The result was soon apparent: the landlords had rendered the law inoperative. This was strikingly illustrated in the necessity which Mr. Gladstone felt in accepting from Mr. Parnell and his supporters the terms of the " Compensation for Disturbance " Bill. There was nothing in that bill which is not to be found in the Land Act of 1870; yet the House of Lords rejected it, and the minister who had carried through the same provision ten years previously submitted to the affront put upon him by the hereditary legislators, and abandoned to their fate thousands of the Irish tenantry for whom eviction was, almost in his own words, a sentence of death. He told Parliament that if the Compensation for Disturbance Bill did not pass, fifteen thousand Irish tenants would probably be turned out; and, he added, "a sentence of eviction is almost equivalent to a sentence of starvation."

The English House of Lords was sublimely indifferent to the starvation of any number of thousands of Irish tenants. That was an old story for its noble members: it did not touch their sensibilities in the least. The peers rejected the bill, although it was widely believed that if they did Mr. Gladstone would appeal to the country. They rejected the bill; but Mr. Gladstone, for reasons known to himself, accepted the affront, and was meek under it.

When the Land Act which is now the law was introduced it was affirmed, with apparently sound reason, that the House of Lords would throw out that also. It could not be expected that, having violently strained at the gnat, it would amiably swallow the camel. Perhaps we shall discover that it was not a camel it finally swallowed. It could not have been passed had not influential landlords importuned the Conservative peers to vote for it.

There has been a great deal of honest condemnation poured out in this country upon the refusal of the Land-League leaders to accept the Land Law of 1881, and upon their advice to the Irish tenants to test it before accepting it. If a State legislature in the United States should pass a real-estate law which was declared by its authors to be a practical revolution of tenure, it is probable that owners of land and tenants would alike be careful to read the new law before rushing into court to become bound by it. Now, it is equally reasonable to believe that the Irish landlords and tenants have been reading the new Land Law before rushing into court to place themselves under its terms. The expression of opinion in the United States concerning the law is based, it may be apprehended, on a considerable want of accurate knowledge concerning the contents of the law; it is within bounds to say that not one man in each hundred thousand in the United States has read the text of the law or can give an intelligent and comprehensive statement of its provisions. The impression which exists in this country concerning it has been created entirely by those agencies whose highest interest is to exaggerate the benefits of the bill.

Americans are not disposed to forget how persistently the state of affairs in this country was misrepresented abroad by English news-agents during the civil war. They do not forget, for they never can, that—so astoundingly false had been the continuous narrative sent over to London of the progress of the war—when the intelligence of the surrender of Richmond reached the clubs the loungers treated it as a good joke; that very day's papers contained the usual assertions that the Union forces were being everywhere mercilessly whipped, and that the dissolution of the Union, the destruction of our republic, was already an all but accomplished fact. They do not forget, nor shall they ever, that, so profound was the conviction in England that our free institutions were in dissolution, the eminent English historian Freeman, who wrote on the information furnished by the English news-agents on this side, actually published a volume now curiously rare in American book-stores. It was entitled *A History of Federal Government from the Foundation of the Achæan League to the Disruption of the United States.* They do not forget, nor can they ever, that even the present first minister of England, Mr. Gladstone, publicly declared that the Union was fighting for mere power, but the South for liberty. They do not forget, nor can they ever, that the great mass of the English politicians sincerely desired the success of the rebellion—not because they loved our Southern people, whom their manufacturers robbed, taking advantage of their dire necessities, but because they gloried in the prospect that democratic institutions were about to be extinguished in the world. They do not forget that, while professing neutrality, rebel privateers were built, manned, equipped and commissioned in English harbors, and that each soldier of the South who died at Antietam carried the trademark of a Manchester manufactory on every button of his uniform. It is not gracious to recall these things now; the motive is its own excuse. England hated the Southern people for being members of a free confederation democratic in essence; in their rebellion she saw a hope of the extinction of democracy; in their extreme poverty she saw a chance to sell at swindling prices everything they needed to prolong the war; and when they failed she brazenly turned around and exulted with the victors, avowing that she had always been in favor of the Union! Her perfidy is more detested to-day in the Southern States than even in the Northern, and with a good reason. She held out to them promises that were never kept; she traded in their misfortunes and abandoned them in their final extremity. Then she taunted them with their failure.

The American people, South and North, do not forget, nor can they ever, that in 1881, when the assassin struck down the chief executive of the American republic, the English court ostentatiously went into a week's mourning and in other theatrical ways sought to make us believe how deeply their queen and government shared our sorrow. But in 1881 there was no danger of the disruption of the American republic; our friendship, in the zenith of our power, is more necessary to the government of Great Britain than was its neutrality to us twenty years ago. But neither can the American people forget that when, in the gloomy days of the civil war, a blow struck at the head of the republic was a blow that touched its heart and sent a dreadful thrill through its vitality,—when Abraham Lincoln was assassinated the English court did not go into mourning. There were no theatrical displays of sorrow and sympathy then; the foul deed was supposed to presage our utter prostration and extinction; English statesmen believed that the rebellion would assume new life, and would march on to triumph; that the Union would be dissolved, democracy would shortly be extinct. So the court did not go into mourning!

Recalling these significant reminders of English misrepresentation of American history, is it not fair for Americans to apprehend that we get as much truth from Ireland through these same wilful agencies as Europe received from them concerning us twenty years ago? We know almost nothing about the Land Act of this year except what English commentators have told us. We know almost nothing about crime in Ireland except what the English news-agents tell us. They have so grossly misrepresented its quality and frequency that until the cold facts are spread out we are likely to consider all Ireland a pandemonium. The population of Philadelphia being less than a fifth that of Ireland, one would say that if five times the number of homicides that occurred last year in Philadelphia should have occurred in Ireland it would indicate that Ireland is a rather peaceful country—one, at least, in which there would not be the slightest justification for suspending *habeas corpus* or interfering with the freedom of the mass of the people. The number of homicides in Philadelphia last year was thirty-four; we may expect at least a hundred and seventy in Ireland. How many were there? Not a hundred, not fifty, not twenty-five, not ten; just FIVE persons were found guilty of murder!

If English newspapers thus grossly mislead concerning crime in Ireland, are they more truthful about law there?

What, in brief, are the main features of the Land Act of 1881, and why should the Irish people not accept it and become quiet and contented, pay their rents, attend to their own business, cease agitating?

First, because the law itself excludes a large proportion of them from its benefits. Those to whom the law denies its provisions cannot submit to them. It excludes—

1. All the agricultural laborers. They number four hundred thousand.

2. All the tenants who hold under leases. Their number is not anywhere stated, but it must be very great, for this reason: To evade the Land Law of

1870 many landlords compelled their tenants to take leases contracting themselves out of that law, and during the years 1878, 1879, 1880, when eviction stared so many thousands in the face, the landlords, fearing that the distress would result in the passage of some relief measure, as the famine of '47 resulted in the enactment of the Poor Law, seized the opportunity to compel their tenants to take leases which would exclude them from the provisions of any law which might be passed to the hurt of the landlord. The new law provides that the terms of the leases shall not be violated. The rent under these leases may be a rack-rent of the most approved fashion, but the tenant can get no relief from the new law.

3. It practically excludes all tenants who are in arrears of rent. This is the worst of the bad features of the law. The poor harvests of three years preceding the passage of the bill rendered the payment of the rents simply impossible. The chief argument in favor of the bill was that it would save these unhappy victims of the "act of God" from eviction, from death. But the House of Lords struck out the clause making the law retroactive. Mr. Parnell and his followers made a noble struggle to rescue the clause, but Mr. Gladstone accepted the Lords' amendment. There is a tortuous and cumbersome way by which, with the assistance of the landlord, one class of tenants in arrears may get some help; but as it imposes on the tenant an obligation which he cannot generally discharge—the

paying up of one year's arrears out of his own resources—the provision will doubtless be inoperative, like the Bright clauses in the law of 1870 for creating peasant proprietary.

It will be seen, therefore, that there are perhaps six or seven hundred thousand agricultural people of Ireland excluded from the law, outside its pale. It is waste of time to ask them to submit to it. They want a land law which will include them.

It has never been denied by any reflecting English economist that peasant proprietary is the only permanent solution of the land question in Ireland, as it proved the only permanent solution of the land question in every other country in which it has arisen. This law was enthusiastically lauded as a step toward peasant proprietary. But, in fact, it is the very reverse. It is a law for the diminution of small holdings; it is a law for the preservation of landlordism; it is a law for the extension of monopoly in land.

The only explicit provision for the purchase of the land from the landlord and its resale to the tenant with the aid of the government is this: If a landlord wants to sell, and three-fourths of the tenants are able and willing to buy, the government may advance a portion of the purchase-money. But on how many estates are such conditions likely to arise? The provision for extending monopoly in land is vastly simpler. It is this: If a tenancy is being sold, and nobody offers for it a sum exceeding the arrears of the rent, it falls to the landlord as the purchaser. Many instances of this kind will occur, and have already occurred. In such cases the tenant of course receives nothing for the improvements effected by his own labor and money.

But if a large number of the Irish farmers and all the farm-laborers are excluded from the benefits of the law, it contains substantial advantages for those who are entitled to them. It secures the tenant from capricious eviction for fifteen years, provided, of course, he pays his rent. Should another series of bad seasons come like those recently passed, there is nothing in the new law to save the tenant from eviction, as formerly. All the advantages he acquires under the bill are contingent on good harvests. In several of the continental countries the landlord shares with the tenant the profit or the loss of the harvests. Had this principle been incorporated in the new law for Ireland, the mass of the people would have been satisfied. They would then know that if, through no fault of their own, the crops were lost and the toil of the year thrown away, they were at least certain of having a roof under which to shelter themselves and their little ones. The new Land Law contains no such assurance. It is not, therefore, a permanent settlement of the land question in Ireland; and that question will never be settled until the man who owns the soil tills it and lives by it.

The administration of the law, with the restrictions

described, is entrusted to a commission of three, with power to appoint deputies. This commission, although at this writing in session less than a month, has completely vindicated the assertion of the Land League that the Irish landlords created famine by extorting rack-rents. More than forty thousand applications by tenants—whose aggregate is six hundred thousand—have been filed with the commissioners under the section providing that when a landlord and tenant cannot agree on the sum to be paid as rent, either may apply to the commission to have the rent fixed; and there is no appeal from the decision of the commission. The rent fixed cannot be changed for fifteen years, nor can the landlord during that period evict the tenant if the latter pays the rent. If, on the other hand, the tenant chooses to sell his holding, he has the right to do so, but the landlord may object to the incoming tenant; then appeal lies to the land court. If the tenant should sell while owing rent, the claims of the landlord must first be paid out of the proceeds of the sale. It was rational on the part of the Irish landlords to urge the enactment of such a law.

The action of the commission up to this time has been almost uniformly in favor of the tenant. Rents have been reduced materially In many cases the reduction has been twenty-five per cent.; in some, fifty; in the largest proportion, about fifteen per cent. This is the complete vindication of the Land League. The new rents are not arbitrarily fixed. The deputy commissioners visit the farm, and reach a conclusion concerning the rent according to these instructions:

" 1. Ascertain name and address of landlord and tenant.

" 2. The number of acres tenant pays rent for, and the rent per acre; when and how often increased.

" 3. Find the Poor-Law valuation on each holding.

" 4. The extent of tenant's improvement, and whether or not the landlord contributed in any way toward such improvement by way of building houses, offices, fences, drainage, walls, manures, supplying timber, slates for roofing; and if so, ascertain what amount so advanced by landlord, and when.

" 5. Deduct all improvements made by the tenant, and consider what would be the value of the land before these improvements were made. Then fix a fair rent as between landlord and tenant, putting all improvements out of the reckoning.

" 6. In settling a fair rent consider the situation and conveniences attaching to the farm, whether the farm has water on it; has it bog and meadow on it? If not, what does it cost the tenant to buy turf, hay and manure yearly for use of his farm? What is the distance from market where farmer sells the produce of his farm? All these items to be considered in fixing a fair rent. The valuators to be as conscientious as possible, without affection or favor, as it may occur that they should go before the land commission court at a future day to substantiate their award.

"7. The act of Parliament for your guidance runs as follows (section 8, sub-section 9): 'No rent shall be allowable or made payable in any proceedings under this act in respect of improvements made by the tenant or his predecessor in title, and for which, in the opinion of the court, the tenant or his predecessor in title shall not have been paid or otherwise compensated by the landlord or his predecessor in title.'

"8. Therefore it is for you, as impartial valuators, to value the land, and the land only, apart from all improvements. Keep out of your valuation the value of the houses, offices, and all other improvements made by the tenants at their own expenses, as the landlord has no claim on these improvements for rent, not having given one penny toward them."

CHAPTER XVI.

WHAT IS THE END TO BE?

THE Land League succeeded in averting famine; it succeeded in keeping down evictions. The increase of the armed constabulary and the constant pouring in of troops to aid the landlords increased the number of evictions in 1880 to ten thousand four hundred and fifty-seven persons, composing two thousand one hundred and ten families—a dreadful total, but insignificant compared with ninety thousand four hundred and forty persons in the corresponding year of the last famine. It succeeded in keeping Ireland quiet, patient and orderly in spite of starvation to incite them to commit crime against property and soldiery to exasperate them to deeds of reckless violence. The command of the League was, "Break no law;" and it was obeyed with marvellous unanimity. Numerous outrages were reported, but investigation generally revealed that they were the inventions of enterprising news-purveyors or the malicious fabrications of base persons who had a purpose to serve. The landlords, who were driven to rage by the withholding of rents and by the peaceful agitation carried on by the Land League for the establishment of peasant proprietary, implored the government to declare the League illegal and suppress it. This could not easily be done. All its operations were strictly constitutional. There was but one way to suppress it—suspend the constitution in Ireland. Abolish personal liberty. Prohibit free speech. Disperse public assemblies of the people gathered to petition for a redress of grievances. Imprison the leaders. Then the army and the constabulary could be loosed to drag the last penny from the tenantry and at the point of the bayonet turn into the highways those unable to pay.

As a prelude to this policy, which Mr. Forster proceeded to carry out, with the assistance of the greatest Liberal minister England has ever had, Mr. Gladstone, "outrage-factories" were established. One day a dreadful story of injury to cattle was reported; investigation showed that it was pure fabrication. The next a bailiff was fired at; he had hired somebody to do it. A boy's suicide in the woods was reported an agrarian crime. Informers and spies committed depredations and charged them upon the Land League.

The command of the League was, "Break no law." How faithfully that command was obeyed is demonstrated by a comparison of the crimes committed during the previous famine-period with those committed while the League controlled the people. Crime in Ireland has heretofore been largely regulated by the conduct of the landlords and the condition of the people during partial or general famine. A hungry man will strike a blow or steal a loaf. A man who sees his family dying of hunger and want and beholds the author of their misery rolling by in a splendid equipage is likely—for human nature is the same everywhere—to feel hatred and to wish for revenge. In 1847 the total number of criminal convictions in Ireland was fifteen thousand two hundred and thirty-three; in 1879, while the Land League governed Ireland, the total number of crimes reported by the police was nine hundred and seventy-seven. In 1847 the total was eighteen thousand two hundred and six; in 1880, while the Land League governed Ireland, the total was only slightly in excess of that of the preceding year. In 1848 the homicides were one hundred and seventy-one, and in the following year two hundred and three; in the corresponding years of the recent famine they were respectively five and four. It was thus that the Land League governed Ireland. Davitt had repeated the words of O'Connell: "Whoever commits a crime is the enemy of his country."

Reasonable men would assume that such an organization would have received the thanks of the government whose work it had done so much better than the same work could have been done by the government, even if it had tried in good faith to do it. But the annihilation of the League was essential to the perpetuation of the system of landlordism which still prevails in Ireland, and the government was on the landlord side. After English opinion had been sufficiently drugged, Ireland was declared to be on the verge of anarchy, and the Coercion Bill was passed early in 1881. It empowered, nominally the lord-lieutenant, really the secretary, a Mr. Forster, an irresponsible foreigner in Ireland, to arrest and detain, at least until the last day of September, 1882, any number of persons whom he might be pleased to suspect of having entertained any criminal intentions *before* the passage of the law or after it. This accomplished the complete destruction of liberty in Ireland. To-day the Irish jails are full of the best and purest of her people. Mr. Davitt was taken to Millbank prison. Among those now incarcerated are Mr. Parnell, Mr. Dillon, Mr. Brennan, and all the officers and efficient supporters of the Land League who remained in Ireland. The treasurer, Mr. Egan, reached Paris; Rev. Father Sheehy, Mr. Healy and Mr. T. P. O'Connor came to America.

Mr. Parnell was denied the privilege allowed the most infamous felons—that of having a private interview with a lawyer for the purpose of testing the legality of his arrest. When Robert Emmet was about to be tried for his life, the English government assigned him as counsel a spy in the employment of its secret-service bureau; and every fact, every paper, which he entrusted to this wretch was instantly conveyed to the attorney-general. Emmet went to the scaffold. The physician who attended the prisoners, Dr. Kenny, who had voluntarily risked his life a hundred times among the poor of Dublin during an epidemic, was not only discharged from his official position as surgeon to one of the public institutions, but was arrested, and is also in prison, his crime being that he carried a letter out of the jail. Miss Anna Parnell, who had organized the Ladies' Land Leagues in Ireland for the purpose of providing for the families of those members of the League who were imprisoned, was refused admission to her brother, although it had been publicly stated that he was ill. All the members of the League were subjected to the most rigorous regulations, and were deprived of privileges commonly allowed the meanest malefactors. Not one of them had violated any law of the country. The severity of their treatment appears to have been inspired by malice on the part of the English representatives of the foreign government on account of the issuance from Kilmainham jail of what, with their habitual and characteristic spirit of misrepresentation, the government press agents called a "no-rent manifesto." The trick of misnaming the document was so successful that some of the supporters of the League were deceived by it, and censured the prisoners on moral grounds. The "no-rent manifesto" was described as an order to the farmers who were members of the League to pay no rent at any time or under any circumstances; it was denounced as communistic. However much men may differ as to the wisdom and policy of its issuance at this time (and the fact that grave doubts on this point do honestly exist in the minds of some of the warmest friends and most active supporters of the League, both before and since, is not denied), it is simply a matter of fact—which any one who reads the text of the manifesto can ascertain for himself—that it was simply an appeal to the farmers to meet the tyranny of the government in the only way which would or could be successful—to withhold the rents due until the government restored the constitutional liberty of the country. It was not an order for the abolition of rent, it was precisely such a step as the American people took when they set up their order of "No representation, no taxation." The leaders of the League issued it only after the government had declared the League itself illegal and forbade any meetings of its members in public or private. When it is remembered that the League had saved the lives of thousands during the famine; had reduced the crime of the country to a minimum; had inculcated the doctrine of resistance only by passivity; had taught the people that disorder would only furnish the government with an excuse to set the soldiery upon unarmed masses, men, women and children, in the streets; had counselled patience, self-control, fortitude and strictly constitutional action from the day of the organization of the League until it was proclaimed,—it is difficult to understand what form of agitation for the redress of grievances which the English ministers freely admit exist would be tolerated by the English government in Ireland.

After the proclamation declaring the League an illegal body strange scenes were witnessed. Although profound order prevailed throughout the country, the constabulary had been increased and thirty-five thousand regulars were encamped at points adroitly selected. These men were frequently let loose upon the people to provoke them, and on the smallest provocation they used their swords and bayonets, as well as balls, with deadly effect, men, women, and even children, being their victims. On one occasion the soldiery, it was charged, were made drunk in order to render them the more savage, and in their maudlin condition they committed gross outrages. The civilians slain did not figure in the press reports sent over to this country, but wherever a civilian, no matter who he was or what his standing, committed the slightest breach of the peace, his conduct was charged upon the Land League, although he may have been an opponent of it.

Even the meetings of the ladies' branches, which were engaged in purely charitable work, were dispersed by armed ruffians. One day, when the women were about to assemble, the constabulary ordered them to disperse. There was no alternative; but the head of the society said to her associates, "Since we cannot work for those who are in need, at least we can pray for them," and they marched in a body to the nearest church, knelt around the altar and said the rosary while the officers, uniformed and armed, waited outside. This incident did not occur in France during the days of the Revolution; it occurred in Ireland in the month of October, 1881. On another occasion, when the ladies were ordered to disperse, and were about to do so, a Catholic priest demanded the authority of the officer. The reply being unsatisfactory, the priest told the ladies to adjourn to his house and hold their meeting there. They did so; the priest, unarmed and gentle, stood on the threshold, and the constabulary quietly disappeared, respecting, without knowing why, perhaps, the ancient right of asylum in the sanctuary.

The spirit of charity and mutual support which the League fostered is without parallel in the history of peaceful revolutions. Not only were the starving fed, not only were the evicts provided with shelter and clothing and the necessaries of life, but the temper of the people was softened; all animosities, no matter how venerable their origin, were laid away, to be for ever, let us hope, forgotten. The families of those who were arrested were daily visited; the crops belonging to the suspects were harvested by volunteers, men and women marching cheerily many miles with the necessary outfit for the task so willingly performed. The practice of "boycotting" was consistently carried on—in many cases, into the region of the quaint and ludicrous. But the first command of the League, "Break no law," was obeyed with remarkable docility. There were crimes, indeed, committed during the two years of the League's life, but they were inconsiderable in number, as already sufficiently shown, and there has been no serious attempt, even by the government, to place the direct responsibility for them on the League.

Organized for a moral, humane and righteous purpose; led by men of the highest personal character; directed by methods strictly constitutional; the promoter of peace, order, patience; the victor over famine; the harmonizer of all classes of the population and the distinct organ of the national sentiment,—the Irish National Land League was proclaimed illegal by the English government in Ireland and suppressed by force. Its foremost men are imprisoned, unaccused, untried, their persons in the custody of an irresponsible foreigner who hates them and oppresses their countrymen. All liberty in Ireland is dead. The world may well look in astonishment upon such a spectacle in a time of profound tranquillity, and in the last quarter of a century which has beheld the enlightening advance of constitutional freedom in every other part of the globe.

But, happily for the Irish people, the irresponsible foreigner who has extinguished liberty in Ireland has no jurisdiction beyond her sad sea-shore. Five millions of the Irish people in Ireland may be deprived of constitutional rights; twenty millions of the Irish people in the United States, in Australia and in Canada are free. They know that there can never be happiness or prosperity in their motherland until her laws are made by her own people on her own soil. They know that until the people of Ireland again own the land which was their fathers' there can be no thrift there. The agitation which is stilled for the moment in Ireland will be heard again; and it is not stilled in any other part of the earth where human hearts beat with sympathy for justice, freedom and the inalienable right of every nation to regulate its own affairs and shape its own destiny. England has accorded to all her other dependencies this right. She withholds it from Ireland, and her statesmen affirm that Ireland will never obtain it. But English statesmen and English monarchs have made such affirmations often before and recalled them afterward, "Never," declares the eloquent bishop of Peoria, John Lancaster Spalding, "never —and I am in my inmost soul convinced of what I say—never has England done an act of justice or of reparation to Ireland from noble or humane motives. I do not in my heart believe that the average English public opinion holds now that the Irish are worthy of justice or mercy, of leniency."

The record of English concessions to Ireland is this:

1. Independence of the Irish Parliament in 1782. But there were eighty thousand armed Irish volunteers then, and not a regiment of English troops in Ireland. They were all out in America trying to keep the king's word that he would spend his last

shilling before he would concede the smallest privilege to the American rebels. He kept his word: he did not concede the smallest privilege. But the American rebels wrested from him the right for ever to make their own privileges. In that dreadful situation, England could not pass coercion bills in Ireland, imprison Grattan, hang eighty thousand Irish volunteers, suppress free speech and deny the people the right of peaceably meeting to petition for a redress of grievances. "The wild shout of liberty was echoed across the ocean," says Bishop Spalding. England had no alternative but to concede the independence of the Irish Parliament. When her defeated troops returned from victorious America, she sent them over into Ireland and abolished the Irish Parliament.

2. Catholic emancipation was the next concession.

The king had sworn that he would die rather than sign the bill. Wellington told him that if it were not passed there would be insurrection in Ireland. He signed it.

3. The abolition of the foreign State-Church in Ireland was the next concession. But Gladstone has declared it was Fenianism which made that necessary.

The demands which are made now are two: Peasant proprietary and home rule. History will yet record the day on which both shall have been obtained.

INDEX.

A.

ABOLITION of the Irish Parliament, 70.
Absenteeism, 100.
Address of the Continental Congress to the Irish people, 65.
Administration of the new Land Law, 438, 439.
Advantages of English government in Ireland for six hundred years, 57.
Agrarian crime, 443.
All the benefits of the new Land Law for the tenant contingent on the harvests, 437.
American Congress receives Mr. Parnell, 384.
An Orangeman proposes O'Connell for Parliament, 373.
Armed constabulary, 183.
Arrears of rent exclude from the benefits of the Land Law of 1881, 435.

B.

Benefit of the American war, 70.
Benefits of the Land Act of 1881 for Irish landlords, 436; benefits for the tenant, 437.
Between six hundred thousand and seven hundred thousand agriculturists excluded from the benefits of the Land Law of 1881, 436.
Blackstone on laws against nature, 146.
"Boycotting," 389–394, 448.
Bright, John, opinion of Irish industry, 60.

C.

Can Ireland feed the population? 400.
Carew, George, civilizing the Irish, 47.
Catholic emancipation, 89.
Coercion Act, 182.
Coercion bills, nature of, 403, 444; number of, in eighty years, 404.
Command of the Land League, "Break no law," 441.
Commissioners of the Land

League to the United States, 383, 444.
Comparison of crime in Philadelphia with crime in Ireland in 1879, 409; in 1880, 434.
"Compensation for Disturbance Bill," 422, 429.
Confiscations of land, 40.
Conservative elements in favor of the Land League, 366, 444.
Contrast between England and Ireland, 27-29.
Crime in Ireland, England, Scotland and Philadelphia, 405, 406, 409, 410.
Crime in Ireland less than that of England and Scotland, 404, 410; statistical table, 405.
Criminal convictions in England, Scotland and Ireland from 1860 to 1879, inclusive, 405.
Cromwell civilizes Ireland, 47, 48.
Crops, Irish, could be seized while growing, 424.
Crowbars, muskets and evictions, 424.

D.

Davitt, Michael, 309 *et seq*; advice to the tenants, 382.
Decline of crime in Ireland, 406.
Decrease of population in Ireland, 396.
Destruction of personal liberty in Ireland, 444.
Devoy, John, letter of, 341 *et seq*.
Difference between landlordism in the United States and Ireland, 34.
Difficulties in the way of suppressing the Land League, 442.
Dillon, John Blake and John, 356 *et seq*.
Doyle on Irish landlordism fifty years ago, 197.
Drogheda women in the church-steeple, 51.
Dying in the ditches, 47.

E.

Earl of Leitrim, 238-243.
Education in Ireland, 110-135.
Effect of English society on Irishmen, 350, 351.
Efforts to revive Irish manufactures, 78.
Eighteen years of Home Rule, 71, 72.
Emancipation of the Catholics, 414.
Emigration, 195; from Ireland from 1841 to 1879, 395.
Emmet and Parnell, 444.
Encumbered Estates Act, 415, 416.
England abandoned the South after robbing it, 432.
English falsification of affairs in Ireland for effect in America, 434; landlords voluntarily reduce rents, 199.
Evictions, 196, 202, 226, 232-235, 380, 381.

Excess of crime in England and Scotland over that in Ireland, 405.
Excluded from the provisions of the Land Law of 1881, 434.
Exports and imports, 76, 399.
Extreme nationalists support Land League, 375.

F.

Factories in Ireland, 76.
Fair conduct of the land commission, 438.
Famine and crime, 443.
Famine recommended by Englishmen, 46, 191; artificial, not natural, 137, 184, 238; horrors of, 185 *et seq.*
Fed by charity in 1880, 205.
Final arrest of the Land-League leaders, 444.
First measure passed for the relief of the Irish tenant, 412, 414.
Fixity of tenure for fifteen years, 437.
Food exported during famine, 187, 399.
Foundation of landlordism, 41.
Four hundred thousand agricultural laborers excluded from the Land Law of 1881, 434.
Freeman, the English historian, writes a book not now on sale, 431.
From Essex to Shirley, 200, 201.

Froude on land-owning, 141, 146.

G.

Gladstone and peasant proprietary, 426; defines "eviction," 429; on the North and the South during the civil war, 431; Land Law of 1870, 419, 420.
Grattan, Henry, 69, 105, 106, 109.

H.

"Hold the rent," 382.
Home Rule allowed all British dependencies except Ireland, 79.
Homes of the tenantry, 138.
Homicides in Philadelphia and in Ireland in 1879, 409; in 1880, 434.

I.

Immediate execution of ejectment writs, 424.
Imports and exports, 76.
Increase of population in England and Scotland, decrease in Ireland, 396.
Instructions given to subcommissioners under the Land Act of 1881, 439.
Ireland: Area, 33; population, 33; exports food while she famishes, 399.
Irish landlords have privileges denied English landlords, 424.

Irish national Parliament, 81–190.
"Is patriotism dead in Ireland?"
John Bright, 413.

L.

Ladies' Land Leagues, 384.
Land Act of 1881 a repetition of that of 1870; not understood in the United States, 430.
Land League proclaimed to enable the landlords to collect rack-rents and evict, 441, 442.
Landlords cheat the tenants out of the benefit of the act of 1870, 426, 435.
Land-owners in Ireland, number of, 136.
Lawful to kill the "meer Irish," 45.
Laws for the relief of the Irish tenant down to 1881, 422, 425, 426; to enlarge the privileges of Irish landlords, 425.
Lease-holders excluded from the benefits of the Land Law of 1881, 434.
Liberty, personal, destroyed, 444, 449.
Life in a model British prison, 324–341.

M.

Malby to Queen Elizabeth, 44.
Management of great estates in England, 147.
"Manchester Three," the, 351.
Manufactures, adaptation of Ireland for, 58; suppression of, 60.

Misrepresentation of American news and opinion in England, 375, 431.
Misunderstanding the Land Act of 1881 in the United States, 430.
Mitchel, John, 186.
Monopoly of land perpetuated by the Land Law of 1881, 436.
Mother and son, Lady Wilde and Oscar Wilde, 351.
Mourning in England for President Lincoln and for President Garfield, 432, 433.

N.

New Land Law not a permanent settlement of the Irish question, 437.
No manufactures possible in Ireland under present system of land tenure, 152.
"No-rent manifesto," 445, 446.
Notice to quit, 382.
Number of persons employed in textile industries, 75; of Irish in other countries, 449.

O.

Oath of supremacy, 44.
Objects of the Land League, 305.
O'Connell's error, 414.
Official organization of the Land League in Dublin, 363.

Orangeism, object of, 84.
Organization of the Land League in the United States, 384.
Origin of title to the land, 51.
"Outrage-factories" established, 442.
Owners of the soil shipped as slaves, 46, 51; compelled to fight in Sweden, 46.

P.

Parliament, the Irish, 36.
Parnell, Sir John, 98, 100; Charles Stewart, 355 *et seq;* denied privileges allowed meanest malefactors, 444.
Peasant-farmer, condition of, in Holland, 154–158; in France, 159–164; in Prussia, 164–168; in Russia, 168, 169; in India, 169–181.
Peasant proprietary proposed by John Bright, 413.
Peculiarities of Irish landlordism, 183–236.
Penal code, 52–56.
Pledge given to Ireland by England in 1800, 404.
"Poor Law" in England and Ireland, 424.
Population, Great Britain and Ireland, 396; to the square mile: Belgium, 400; Bavaria, 402; Switzerland, 402.
Potato crop an index to famine, 380; value of, 380.

Powers of the land court, 437, 438.
Poynings's law, 89.
Presbyterians democratic, 84; not Protestants, 84.
"Priest in politics," 366.
Primogeniture and entail abolished in Ireland, 415, 416.
Principle of English legislation concerning Irish manufactures, 62.
Professor Cairnes on Encumbered Estates Act, 416, 419.
Proportion of convictions to arrests in England, Scotland and Ireland, 406.
Protestant Irish patriots, 69; insurrections, 371.

R.

Recent theatrical display of mourning at the English court, 433.
Record of English concessions to Ireland, 451.
Redpath, James, 202.
Religious discord fomented by the English government, 369.
Rent, definition of, by Mill and Cairnes, 141.
Representation of Ireland in British Parliament, 70.
Restoration of Irish trade by the Irish Parliament, 69.
Restrictions on Irish trade and commerce, 63, 64.
Reward of Dr. Kenny, 444, 445

S.

Scotch and Irish crime compared, 406.
Sectarianism an English policy in Ireland, 372, 373.
Seed of the Land League, 237-303.
Serious offences committed in England, Scotland and Wales, 410.
Ships, Irish, swept from the seas, 63.
Six hundred thousand agricultural tenants in Ireland, 438.
Soldiery made drunk, 447.
Specimen rack-rents, 289.
Spenser, Edmund, son of, evicted, 51.
Spy assigned as counsel for Robert Emmet, 444.
Strange scenes, 447-449.
Sullivan, A. M., 187.
Suppression of correct information about Irish land tenure, 423.
Sympathy of the Irish with the American Revolution, 65, 87.

T.

Table showing population and crime in England, Scotland and Ireland, 406.
Taxation, 217.
Tenant in Ireland required to care for crop after seizure, 424.
Tenants make all the improvements, 146.
Terms of the Land Act of 1881 concerning peasant proprietary, 436, 437.
The Land League not communistic or confiscatory, 381.
Thirty-two laws for the benefit of Irish landlords, 425.
Tithes, 370.
Titles to land no better, morally, in England than in Ireland, 423.
Trade, Irish, with foreign countries suppressed, 65.
True settlement of the Irish question, 437.
Turnips, parsnips and transportation, 190.

U.

Ulster tenant-right defined, 420, 421.
"Undertakers," English and Scotch, 41; "Articles" concerning, 43.
United States, origin of Land League in, 336.

V.

"Vagrant rays of ministerial sunshine," 66.
Volunteers of 1782, 70, 71, 88.

W.

What form of movement for redress of grievances will the English government tolerate in Ireland? 446.

"Whoever commits a crime is the enemy of his country," 443.

Why Ireland cannot feed her people, 402.

Why the Irish Parliament was abolished, 72.

Why the Conservative peers voted for the Land Act of 1881, 430.

Why we get no skilled labor from Ireland, 61.

Wilson, John, 314.

THE END.

www.ingramcontent.com/pod-product-compliance
Lightning Source LLC
Chambersburg PA
CBHW022147300426
44115CB00006B/388